About the Author

Robert Sachs moved to England from America during his late teenage years where he received his BA in comparative religion and sociology at the University of Lancaster. He began to study with Tibetan Buddhist masters, and embarked on a study of Asian healing systems, including macrobiotics, with Michio Kushi and Rex Lassalle at the Kushi Institute in London, and hatha yoga. Before returning to America in 1976, Robert completed training as a mental health counselor with the Richmond Fellowship and was certified as a hatha yoga instructor. He returned to London to complete shiatsu training with Rex Lassalle and was instrumental in starting the Community Health Foundation's "Growing Family Centre." He went on to receive a massage license from Central Ohio School of Massage and a Masters in Social Work at the University of Kentucky.

Following the death of one of his daughters, Robert was led into the study of the conscious dying practices as found in the Tibetan Buddhist tradition and has worked as a social worker, bereavement counselor, and instructor for hospices as well as assisting many friends and private clients to die more peacefully and consciously. Along with his wife, Melanie, Robert has also pursued studies in Indian and Tibetan Ayurveda and their published works in this field are considered by such teachers as Dr Deepak Chopra to be the clearest and most usable texts available.

Robert continues to work with the medical profession to integrate contemporary scientific approaches with the ancient wisdom traditions in the areas of stress management and preventive health care. He has been a guest instructor for the Chopra Center for Well Being in San Diego, a lecturer in Tibetan Medicine for the Sino-American Rehabilitation Association College in Los Angeles, as well as the instructor on Ayurvedic nutritional practices with the Academy of Healing Nutrition. He lectures at holistic health care conferences and trade shows nationally, is featured in a number of magazines along with being a guest for national and local radio and TV shows, and has hosted his own talk radio shows in New Mexico and California focusing on a unique system of astrology called 9-Star Ki and alternative health care.

Robert lives in San Luis Obispo, California, where he and Melanie co-own and direct Diamond Way Ayurveda. They have three children, Kai Ling, Harriet Christina, and Jabeth David-Francis.

By the same author

Nine Star Ki: Feng Shui Astrology for Deepening Self-Knowledge and Enhancing Relationships, Health, and Prosperity

Tibetan Ayurveda: Health Secrets From the Roof of the World

Rebirth Into Pure Land

Perfect Endings: A Conscious Approach to Dying and Death

The Passionate Buddha: Wisdom on Intimacy and Enduring Love

The Buddha At War

The Wisdom of The Buddhist Masters: Common and Uncommon Sense

becoming
BUDDHA

awakening the wisdom and compassion
to change your world

ROBERT SACHS

WATKINS PUBLISHING

LONDON

Distributed in the USA and Canada by Sterling Publishing Co., Inc.
387 Park Avenue South, New York, NY 10016-8810

This revised edition published in the US 2010 by
Watkins Publishing, Sixth Floor, Castle House,
75–76 Wells Street, London W1T 3QH

First Published as *Buddha at War* 2006
Text Copyright © Robert Sachs 2006, 2010

1 3 5 7 9 10 8 6 4 2

Designed and typeset by Jerry Goldie
Printed and bound by Imago in China

Library of Congress Cataloging-in-Publication Data Available

ISBN: 978-1-906787-53-0

www.watkinspublishing.co.uk

For information about custom editions, special sales, premium and
corporate purchases, please contact Sterling Special Sales
Department at 800-805-5489 or specialsales@sterlingpub.com

Contents

Dedication

On September 11th, 2001, while fanatics with limited and narrow fundamentalist beliefs were cutting the throats of airline crews and taking aim at the Twin Towers of New York, His Holiness the 14th Shamarpa (Kunzig Shamar Rinpoche), a high Tibetan lama and my teacher, was on a plane landing at New York's JFK airport. From the point of view of an outside, unenlightened observer, he had no particular reason to fly to New York that day. But that is how he is. He does what he does when he sees the need to do it.

As the Rinpoche's plane touched down on the airport tarmac, the first hijacked plane smashed into the first tower. As he cleared customs, the second plane smashed into the second tower. Having been picked up by his host and driving toward the city, they saw plumes of smoke rising above the towers, which were soon not to be. His car was one of the last cars allowed over the bridge into the city before police shut it down.

For three days, Shamar Rinpoche worked with the shocked and the grieving. He offered prayers for the fallen and grief-stricken and gave teachings about life, death, and the truth of impermanence. He provided comfort and showed a path that leads away from fear, hatred, and revenge toward peace, understanding, and profound compassion. Weeks later, he made a speech which, in fact, inspired me to write this book. This speech you will find in the appendices to this volume (see page 245).

In the spirit of what this great and dedicated teacher demonstrates through his Buddha-activity, I dedicate this book to the families of the September 11th bombing victims and to each and every being who has had to grieve for loved ones lost to the senseless slaughter perpetrated by humanity against itself. In the words of a Buddhist prayer:

> *"May sickness, poverty, and warfare subside*
> *wherever we may be.*
>
> *May good omens and Dharma* increase!"*

Robert Sachs,
San Luis Obispo, CA

* understanding of the way things are

Preface

by His Holiness the 14th Kunzig Shamar Rinpoche

In modern countries where materialism is strong, the concepts and practices of Buddhism can be effective in neutralizing the problems that naturally arise and create much suffering, including conflict and war. My student, Robert Sachs, has written this book to show what role Buddhism can play in creating lasting political and social change.

It is my sincere wish that *Becoming Buddha* is helpful to all who read it and that it fulfills the need to bring strength and confidence to those wanting to see a world free from sickness, poverty, and warfare.

Shamarpa,
Los Osos, CA,

Foreword

by Stephen Levine

Robert Sachs' concern for the well-being of others extends to the horizons in which we wish our children to be born, a world where mercy and awareness are its most treasured values and its rewards are from the hard-earned activation of compassion and care for other sentient beings.

Reading *Becoming Buddha*, I hear a bell ringing. It is like the bell that begins and concludes a period of meditation, and it is also the "All Clear" bell that signals it is safe to venture out, the bell that rings the end of war. The Buddha said it was less difficult to overcome ten thousand enemies on the battlefield than it was to release attachment to the hindrances to the heart. It was easier to go to war than to find peace in ourselves.

Robert Sachs recommends that we look for the flowering of peace in a close examination of the seeds of war: separation, partisanship, all the way into the seemingly inconsequential "liking and disliking" which arise from moment to moment to nonetheless form the foundation of all such confrontations and aggravated allegiances. Our identification with a particular perception singled out from a hundred possibilities, which then becomes our truth, is the most potent cause in our insistence that there is something to fight for, something to make others suffer for not sharing. From a reinforcement of the natural but unfortunate tendency to become lost in an identification with "I" and "other", we find reasons to hoard resources, to starve the hungry, to burn fields and ravage villages, to leave the homeless to fend for themselves in the refuse piles of a society which furthers the violence to themselves and to others in the insistent misuse of what is only partially consumed or recycled.

It is our fear of our unknown interior, our uninvestigated suffering, which fattens the generals and reinforces the leap of faithlessness that flattens our world and breaks it off at the edges, a piece at a time, leaving us little refuge, perhaps a momentarily uncluttered square on the game board on which to stand, one-legged and confused at having to choose between safety and the sacred.

Until we begin to roll back the battlefield one insight at a time, with each moment of self-discovery, each uncovering of the mercy and peace of our inherent nature, the continual encroachment of wars and slavery continues – of more types of wars and slavery than we notice or acknowledge. Ultimately, this book is devoted to gaining access to the battlefield – the one inside us that spawns the one we see before us – and emerging victorious.

Stephen Levine,
author of *One Year to Live* and
Turning Toward the Mystery

"All That You Can Be"

If you have watched TV in the United States over the last 40 years, you will recognize the phrase "All that you can be…" as a fragment of the US Army's ad, "Be all that you can be…" Another military ad slogan that you may be familiar with is "We're looking for a few good men (and sometimes include women)." No doubt, these or other slogans like them have been around for as many years as there have been armies in the world looking for recruits.

What is interesting about these phrases is that if we step back and out of seeing them as referring to the military and look at them with respect to our human potential, they are exactly what the Buddha promised to those who were willing to commit themselves to following his methods for awakening; that each and everyone of us can be all that we can be. Furthermore, the Buddha did not want followers. He wanted friends. He *was* looking for a few good men and women. And if they were to follow him, it was not that he was any better than any of them. Rather, he wanted to show them by his example what they, too, could be – just like him. And his name, Buddha, wasn't a title, but simply a statement of what each of us has the potential to be – AWAKE.

To be Buddha, therefore, *is* the goal of Buddhism. The Buddha taught that each of us has Buddhanature – the potential awake. If we awake from our many illusions, if we live in the vibrancy of what is rather than the phantasm of our confused emotions, what would we look like and how would we act?

All of the major and minor marks and signs of being a Buddha that are taught in the Buddhist canon and commentaries regarding a Buddha's appearance, mind, and actions are none other than what a Buddha accomplishes through the hard work of awakening. It is erroneous to think of the Buddha as some demure, passive monk sitting on a pedestal, doing nothing. The iconography that suggests such is really depicting a Buddha's inner state; free from illusion, dwelling in an unshakeable peacefulness that provides the context and resourcefulness to be and act in the most beneficial way for any being that is encountered. In truth, the Buddha is the ULTIMATE ACTIVIST, one hundred percent engaged in the world, twenty-four seven. So, once awake, what does a Buddha *do*? Just one thing – a Buddha tirelessly, endlessly teaches others how to become just like him or her, skillfully and with compassion.

In the first edition of this book, *The Buddha at War*, and in this new edition, when I write of the hard work of awakening, I do use a word associated with the military and a word that some may cringe to hear juxtaposed to the word "Buddha:" war. The Buddha saw that in order for us to awaken we need to transform the three poisons of ignorance, attachment, and aggression (which will be elaborated in all subsequent chapters) into our full resourcefulness, free from our own prejudices and tendencies towards self-preservation at all costs. It is this inner war, this inner battle with the smallness of egoistic fixations that is what the Buddha was and all Buddhas to be are victorious over. And to continuously be of benefit to others who, likewise, struggle with this smallness, the Buddha remains at war, appearing in whatever guise may be necessary to do that job. Thus the Buddha can appear peaceful, benevolent, charismatic, even wrathful depending on what is needed. In troubled times, the Buddha may be called upon in any or all of these functions.

Which also says something about you and your awakening.

This book does not promise you enlightenment. More than likely when you come to the end of its reading, you will not have become a Buddha. (If you have, however, great – and thanks for being amongst us!) But, it will provide you with a sense of path. The path described here is the classic thoughts and methods that have been taught by Buddhist masters for generations. If these thoughts and methods are taken to heart, they *will* transform your life. You will feel lighter and clearer in your being and will feel less of a burden to yourself. As a result, you will be less of a burden to others – so they will want to listen to what you have to say. As such, no matter what you choose to do with your life, you – as a budding Buddha – will have a greater, more positive impact on your world.

More to the point and to be a bit more specific, by "positive impact" I mean for it to be that one of the goals of this book is to facilitate your awakening to the effects of your personal choices and the social and political realities that you live in. Whether we want to be mountain hermits or devas downtown, we are all social beings and I firmly believe that a Buddha shies away from nothing. If you think that in your world there are some serious problems with the social and political structures and realities around you, then learning to be "in the world, but not of it" is part of the path I believe most of us must take and practice our awakening in.

In such troubled times that we are living in, we need more than a few good men or women. It is the hope of this book that many will embrace these simple teachings and enter into the world with clarity, wisdom, and joy to engage the many tasks we need to face. Whether we see fruition – the end of the sickness, poverty, warfare, and the staving off of global environmental catastrophe – in our lifetime cannot be our focus. Being a Buddha, one's vision goes beyond time and place. To do what needs to be done involves seeing what is before us and having a vision that sees down the road. We cannot let the success or failure of seeing the end or continuation of suffering sway us one way or the other from our willingness to try. In our hearts and minds, we need to become the Buddha at War. It is in this spirit that I invite you to read on.

Possibility in Troubled Times

If you have picked up this book, more than likely you feel that the world is in a dire way. With more than 40 wars brewing or under way around the globe; the growth of terrorism, both state sanctioned and from radical quarters; a global economic meltdown and the growing chasm between the rich and the poor; the dramatic climatic and environmental shifts that are bringing us more thunderous and frequent tornadoes, cyclones, and hurricanes, it all looks pretty bleak for the survival of the human race.

That all of these things are happening at once is considered by many people of a fundamentalist outlook to be signs of the end of days; a portent of an impending apocalypse. For others, in the East, these "signs" point to us being in a "Dark Age." And although that in itself sounds bad, it is not without hope. In my book, *The Wisdom of The Buddhist Masters: Common and Uncommon Sense*, I interviewed nine Buddhist world leaders beginning with the questions "What is a Dark Age?" and "Are we in a Dark Age?" Their responses were mixed. Some answered based on Buddhist canon and the predictions of the historical Buddha. Others just commented based on their astute observations. In the end, the answer I received was inconclusive, save to say that if we are not already in a Dark Age, unless we can make a course correction of significant magnitude, we are headed that way.

However, the simple truth is that little of what we are witnessing is new. Our earth has repeatedly gone through various climatic tumbles and flip flops. And, certainly, humanity has been playing the same trips on itself since the dawn of civilization. I would like to argue that whilst the rate, frequency, and lethality of these events seem to be growing in magnitude and are certainly cause for increasing concern, we have also developed the media and information technology that allow us to be more aware of these phenomena, and indeed to witness them both in our midst and in distant lands. This frequent exposure to painful and traumatic events has any number of effects on our hearts and minds. Some of us may worry and find ourselves getting more and more anxious and depressed. Others may get frustrated and angry. Still others may try to get on with their lives without noticing too much. However, the acceptance that something is happening of significance, that we are, indeed, in troubled times, seems virtually impossible to escape.

What is heartening is that, in response to the pain and suffering of those among us, we are seeing more and more acts of individual and collective kindness, compassion, and heroism that remind us that there is nobility, decency, and love at the core of our being. Increasing numbers of people see the need to somehow contribute their own efforts to social, political, economic, and environmental peace and harmony. Author Paul Hawken, in his *Blessed Unrest*, reports that there are over one million NGOs (non-government organizations) currently devoted to working on poverty, sanitation, health care, fair trade agriculture, and so on. Often against seemingly overwhelming odds and circumstances, people are reaching deep within themselves, striving to connect with "something" in order to better their lives and the lives of their neighbors.

Disaster and dire circumstances are often the teachers that wake us up to the fact that something has to change. It would be nice if this wasn't true, but it is. Most of us would like to live our lives and go about our business without too much hassle or distraction. But, as John Lennon put it, "Life is what is happening when you are making other plans." Life intervenes, things get in our way and we are forced to awaken from the hypnotic trance and slumber of our own routines. We then try our best to meet the tests and challenges that face us. But do we have the focus and fortitude to know what to do? How do we overcome our own negative emotions that can sabotage our efforts and lead us back into the same old mess or worse? How do we center ourselves and learn to become skillful in making changes for ourselves? And, looking around us and seeing that our happiness is intimately connected to the happiness of others, how do we develop the wisdom and skillfulness to create positive and lasting change in the world around us?

That is what this book is about. *Becoming Buddha* is devoted to helping you find the inner resources that will make it possible for you to not be overwhelmed with sadness, despair, frustration, anger, or inertia. It is about changing your life from within and then reaching out to change the world around you. For, as you tap into the inner resources that you already have, new possibility begins to show through the apparent solidity of the oppressive and depressing illusion of a troubled world. And in the realm of possibility, change – no matter how small – has its effects. No good thought, gesture, or act is ever wasted and will slowly but assuredly bring about the changes that each of us, as humans, wants to experience and share with those we love.

What We Want...

There probably isn't a human being on this planet who doesn't wish to have a happy life. Although happiness can mean different things to different people, some of the more commonly shared aspirations are to feel safe, have shelter and enough to eat and drink, to be with people you love and who love you, and to enjoy all of these in an atmosphere that is peaceful. And yet, so many on this planet do not feel safe, live in makeshift or inadequate shelter, have little to eat and unfit water to drink, and are always looking over their shoulder.

The ideals we all wish for, the dire conditions many on this planet find themselves in, and any number of variations between these two extremes, come about for reasons that are largely of our own making, whether we intend them or not. Some of the causes of the world's ills are glaringly obvious, and it would be comforting to think that with a few free elections, a few corporate shake-ups, and a call to higher ideals, the wrongs of the world could be righted. But such simple solutions are rarely sufficient, because the causes of human suffering are many and intricate, and form interlinked chains of events that can be traced back to the dawn of human existence. Some have ventured to scan the annals of history and look at the lives and legacies of political, religious, and military leaders, who used their charisma or force to take what some would say was more than their fair share. Such leaders often passed what they had on to their children, lineage, or clan until, over time, the original reason for them being rich and powerful was lost under a mantle of legitimacy born of privilege.

One of the many problems with such analyses is that they usually depress most and anger some – neither state of mind being particularly useful in mustering what is needed to take things in a different direction. In the end, what is going to make the greatest difference – what is going to be the spark or catalyst for creating a world where we can achieve the ideals to which we all aspire – begins with our minds. For it is the clarity or the confusion of our minds that leads us to pick up a pen, march in the street, or shoulder a gun.

Where to Start: Heart and Mind

In the East, "mind" is the connection between the head and the heart – with the master of the two being the heart. When the full power of the mind is awakened – as we gradually awaken from the slumber of our habits, and from our confining super- stitions and beliefs about the world and how it is or how it should be – anything is possible. We become wiser and our compassion deepens. Inevitably, we become conscious and engaged. Positive change, even revolution, in any field of human endeavor, be it in the social, political, scientific, or spiritual domain, has come about through the efforts of those with minds informed and fueled by wisdom and compassion, who have transformed their worlds and inspired new ways of seeing and being. Such people have shaken, and sometimes even brought down, the fortresses of the powerful.

If we want to live in a land of freedom, if we want to see conditions in which the needs of all our brothers and sisters are met, we need to develop free minds. Neither external freedom (freedom from entrenched power structures and from such conditions as sickness, poverty, and warfare) nor internal freedom (freedom from the habitual mind that narrows our vision and in turn breeds the host of problems we face both within and without) is easily won. Both require commitment, diligence, and vigilance. Both require time to change. To want change, to create the causes and conditions for change to happen and to become lasting, is no small task, and we must surely celebrate the victories that are made along the way. When we see a tyrannical regime fall, a corporation restructured in accordance with wiser and more compassionate ideals, or social services provided to the disfranchised: all of these are testimony to the hard work – both internal and external – done by individuals pursuing our basic human desire to see good in the world.

However, creating a society where a sufficient number of people are attuned to the needs of the many, and who undertake to safeguard whatever changes for the collective good are attained, requires widespread attention to and appreciation of the unlimited potential of the awakened mind. In the final analysis, it is the awakening of this potential and the freedom that we experience from within that matter to us most. And, in times like these which seem so dark and uncertain, it will be our inner strength that points us in a new direction, will provide the inspiration, ideas, and resourcefulness to create a more positive future for us all. Toward this end, and as a part of the awakening of this potential within us, we need to create a valued tradition of wisdom that in turn produces holistically minded citizens who are both spiritually attuned to their higher, ultimately good nature and able to function positively, powerfully, and with purpose amid the ambiguity and messiness of everyday life.

Based on years of my personal practice and studying the world's great wisdom traditions, the teachings of the Buddha stand out because they are extensive, well documented, and have been practiced in an unbroken fashion since the time of the Buddha himself. This does not mean that everyone needs to become Buddhist. For in truth, the methods that the Buddha taught can easily be adapted to and will amplify the benefits of whatever wisdom tradition one chooses to follow.

Cultivating Consciousness

No book could possibly examine every detail of the complex and interconnected issues in our world that need attending to. However, it is possible to focus on the inner resources that we, as individuals, can cultivate in order to meet the challenges of addressing these issues. This is the sole purpose of this book. Within the teachings of the Buddha, there are time-tested methods that anyone may easily use to become what I shall call throughout a conscious, engaged activist.

The most important word in this phrase is "conscious," for in truth, no matter how oblivious we are to our world, we *are* engaged and we *do* act. As we have a body, where we put it in space matters. Once we are born and inhabit a body, we stand on the ground and we are identified as partisan, on one side or the other of this or that. We cannot escape this. If we stand silently behind those who wave guns and perpetrate crimes against others, even if we never pick up a gun ourselves, but try to ignore, even dissociate ourselves from being "one of them," there will be those who will identify us as part of the crowd that supports the gun-toters.

Our only option, therefore, if we are no longer to feel that we are the victims of circumstance or the capriciousness of our times, is to become conscious – to make conscious choices, no matter how imperfect, and accept and live with the consequences of those choices. At least then we will have tasted freedom and will be able to stand taller in the face of the challenges that life will inevitably place before us. This foundation of becoming more awake and conscious in our engagement with the world will only grow and mature with time. It is the bedrock of our freedom.

These reflections, and what I am to present throughout these pages, are expressed in a language that comes from my training in the teachings of the Buddha. However, their essence is to be found in the words and deeds of the Founding Fathers of the country in which I live: the United States. In the last Age of Enlightenment, a group of people came together not only to secure their independence from what they perceived as a tyrannical authority, but also to create a form of government and governing that would avoid the pitfalls of emerging states throughout the course of history. Much of what they said and wrote reflects a profound appreciation of education and of the awakening of our inner resources as the most important safeguards for an emerging democracy. As such, the United States has always stood as a country founded on·higher, enlightened ideals. This, at least, is the persona of America that makes others in the world reach out to her. In recent years, there has been growing dismay at American actions, especially with respect to foreign policy and corporate meddling, and the dream of America seemed dimmer. Most recently, there is at least the appearance in an emerging administration that America is more actively reaching towards its ideals once more.

However, it is not my intention in this book to cast the United States either as an embodiment of an ideal or, conversely, as a country that has *not* lived up to an ideal. As an American, I shall simply, from time to time, draw on examples of American history, recent and more distant, in addressing issues that individuals and collectives need to be aware of in seeking to create positive social and political transformation. For it is my belief that the teachings of any philosophy or spiritual tradition can remain alive only if they can be made relevant in the context of our day-to-day lives and realities. Even my own teacher, His Holiness Kunzig Shamar Rinpoche, teaches that if we are going to make use of the wisdom and compassion that the Buddha knows is within us, we need to know our roots, our own mundane history so that in whatever land we reside, we can make a life that builds on rather than repeats history.

In reading *Becoming Buddha*, it is my wish that the reader will find in these pages the strength and resourcefulness to both deepen and awaken to their own innate potential, not only for their own personal benefit, but also to go further and use their body and mind for the benefit of each and every being that they meet. For true contentment and peace will only be attained when what brings us contentment and peace is shared.

A Bit of Personal History...

Kunzig Shamar Rinpoche's insistence that along with spiritual practice we should study and learn the lessons of our own collective history has become poignantly obvious in my own personal journey to becoming a conscious, engaged activist.

In August of 2002, my wife Melanie and I were traveling and teaching in Europe, more specifically in Germany and England. Staying with friends who have a keen interest in current affairs in Germany and having access to cable TV at our UK hotel, we were caught by images of American aircraft carriers and troops being moved to the Persian Gulf. Our friends and people we met on the street all had the same question: When was America going to invade Iraq?

Upon returning home to California, Melanie and I tuned into national radio and TV networks, and looked in the papers to try to find anything that would let us know when the war would begin. Oddly, there was no mention of troop deployment, or of aircraft carriers in the Persian Gulf. As a frequent guest on local talk radio, I went on the air and brought up this matter with the host and callers. No one knew what I was talking about. As far as the locals were concerned, sanctions against Iraq were still in place and the IAEA was still inspecting for weapons. Callers said I was paranoid, just another wacko-liberal who hated the president – which to them meant hating America.

April 2003 rolled around and America was in the air and over the ground in Iraq. And, at the time of writing, the US troops are still there: over 4,000 casualties, tens of thousands of mentally and physically debilitated, and the lowest estimates of Iraqi civilian casualties in the hundred of thousands.

After the debacle and the appointment of a faux-president by the US Supreme Court in 2000, I had finally begun to awaken from a slumber that most Americans were lulled into over the years. Because of the ideals Americans were raised to believe were the foundations of their nation, I think that most of us naively thought or hoped that our leaders would embody those ideals. Perhaps this has been the case from time to time. But, in most of the world and over the course of the longer history of many other nations, the average person on the street has enough common sense to accept that their elected officials are more or less corrupt and that money and power are behind the moral and religious justifications and other rationalizations they use for changes of policies, and expanding their might or influence in the world, peacefully or otherwise. At the end of his presidency, the late Dwight Eisenhower gave a chilling speech warning US citizens of the impending rise of a "military industrial complex." I remember in the '60s that this term was bandied about, and became the enemy of the counter-culture and peace movements of the time. Watergate, the end of the war in Vietnam and the election of a decent religious man, Jimmy Carter, seemed to be beacons of promise, a correction of course for a US government and popular hubris that seemingly gave us permission to do anything we wanted to do wherever and whenever. But in recent times, the hubris of ideologues has once again become a dominant feature of the American political and social landscape.

It's not that I was not conscious of these events going on around me. Indeed, I would say I prided myself in being conscious. I was one of the thousands of Americans and western Europeans who were opening their minds and hearts through eastern religious, philosophical, medical, and martial art traditions. I had my guru. I did my daily meditations. I was getting in touch with who I was. I was focusing on engaging in each moment with clarity; in my work and in my relationships. And I was dedicating the gathering of this insight and strength, in the words of many Buddhist prayers, "for the benefit of all sentient beings." In terms of worldly concerns, as a social worker and professional massage therapist whose interests lay outside of the conventional and would aptly be described as holistic, most of my attention to the practical realities of life on this planet had to do with food production and distribution, the availability and quality of health care, population control, and the growing burden of consumer demand on a planet whose biosphere was under assault by a species unwilling to properly regulate its thirst for more and cheaper right now.

I was aware that each of these concerns had a political dimension – and I was actively involved in supporting and promoting legislation intended to help in these matters that have been the core of the work that my wife and I have done for over a quarter of a century. But I was not so sensitive or alert to the actual political process and reality of my own country. Whilst I was aware of the pain and suffering being wreaked on the planet by tyrants, despots, and greedy corporations, I, myself, was living in a bubble – a well-protected, relatively pain-free insulated bubble of privilege; a white, upper-middle class reality. For certain there were moments of pain: the death of a daughter, of parents, accidents, difficulties in my marriage, financial woes, etc. But, on the sunny central coast of California where the weather is relatively warm all of the time and the surf is always up, I did not fear going out of my front door. I was not facing the possibility that my wife or son would be kidnapped for ransom. I did not need to develop the spiritual resolve to accept that a suicide bomber might blow me and my neighbors up at a local farmers' market. We were sending our used clothes off to those suffering from the tsunami of 2004, but I did not have to contend with the possibility of finding my house and livelihood smashed to bits. The realities of such events were far away. Unbeknownst to even myself, when it came to such matters, I had – in the words of the late '60s rock bards, Pink Floyd –

"become comfortably numb."

Following the 2000 election, watching live the falling of the Twin Towers on September 11th, 2001, and finally the US administration's manipulation of facts to justify a war that has clearly benefited the likes of Lockheed, Haliburton, and other "military-industrial" giants, I could no longer keep silent. And, having written so much in the past, it felt natural to write what I was feeling about these events. I was also inspired to read more about my country's history. Based on my own training under the guidance of various Buddhist meditation masters, I took this political awakening and this new information and wrote *The Buddha at War: Peaceful Heart, Courageous Action in Troubled Times.*

In writing *The Buddha at War*, I was at once trying to develop for myself and others a sense of path; a roadmap with practices that one could employ to develop a peacefulness that was not merely passive, but would inspire one to wholeheartedly embrace methods and actions to bring about a global community founded on sanity and mutual respect. Over the years, I have watched those who were at one time interested in peace and change fall by the wayside in despair, anger, or disgust. At one end of the spectrum are depression and suicide, whilst at the other end there is a self-justified insulation where "my peace" or "my enlightenment" or "my piece of prosperity and property" become the limits of one's vision. Somewhere in between these extremes, I foresee an ability to develop spirituality with a backbone; a willingness to truly step out into the world, to either make a difference or at least plant seeds so that in the future, such transformation has some solid roots from which to emerge.

The Buddha at War was completed before the 2004 US presidential election. At that time, my agent Bob Silverstein sent out the manuscript to those book companies in the US which he thought had an interest in either spirituality in general or Buddhism more particularly. The book was intended to have a mass appeal for those thirsty to see how they could transform their fears of terrorism, war, and growing climate instability, and the despair, anger, mistrust, and disgust for numbers of world governments and corporations devoted to power, acquisition of wealth and self-aggrandizement, by using the time-tested methods offered by the historical Buddha over 2,500 years ago. We also thought it would appeal to those more familiar with Buddhism in general.

No American publisher wanted to take the book. There were two reasons given. First, it was said that I did not have a large enough platform (i.e. popularity) to attract enough buyers for the work. Secondly, the more Buddhist publishers said that talking about political and social realities in relation to Buddhism just wouldn't sell. And, even if people were somewhat interested, after John Kerry won the 2004 election, the fire and fury in the belly of most would subside. The American Buddhist population could then – once again – go back to sleep, and read more benignly about mindfulness, whether dogs had Buddhanature, and other such pleasantries.

Of course, John Kerry did win the 2004 election. It did not matter. The US presidential race was once again stolen with little overt dissent. The war in the Middle East continued to escalate. As if they too had awakened from their slumber, every Buddhist magazine began to feature one if not several articles focusing on war, major social and political issues and how they can be looked at with respect to Buddhist practice. And responding to the Buddhist community and the world at large, now there are many teachers who have written books devoted to these thorny issues.

Fortunately for me, I decided to go outside the bubble and contacted Michael Mann, the editor-in-chief of Watkins

Publishing in London. He got what I was writing and why. And he wanted it. The title, *The Buddha at War*, which made many a fainted-hearted Buddhist shiver or express consternation, was the title we decided to go with. It was also the title my own beloved teacher, His Holiness Kunzig Shamar Rinpoche, saw as a good one; one that would grab a larger audience and speak of the issues of war and injustice that more and more around the world are trying to grapple with in order to avoid calamities of epic proportions in the future.

With the success of this book, Michael approached me with another project that he wanted me to consider. What followed was my book, *The Wisdom of The Buddhist Masters: Common and Uncommon Sense*. What *The Buddha at War* spelled out in terms of developing a personal practice for cultivating peace, sanity, and a willingness to act, was translated into words from teachers who were willing to be more specific and help us, with their wisdom eye, to look closely at the issues of the day.

The Buddha at War was immensely successful and quickly sold out its first edition. The only complaints I really received about the book were that it was not about war. People really wanted to hear about Buddhists at war. Perhaps I should have cleared up this misnomer early on it the text. But I did not.

In his wisdom, I believe that Watkins figured that as *The Buddha at War* was a prequel to *The Wisdom of The Buddhist Masters*, there could also be a sequel; that is, once people had heard what the nine masters had to say, they would need help with the next step – to become the conscious, engaged activists needed to step forward in these troubled times.

So, here it is, *Becoming Buddha: Awakening the Wisdom and Compassion to Change Your World*, the second, but expanded edition of *The Buddha at War*. Along with the Prologue and this expanded Introduction, I shall refine a few points in the original edition, bring the reader more up to speed historically, and add a new chapter devoted to the development of a conscious, engaged society along with a new Appendix. My new chapter on an enlightened society could not have been possible had it not been for the inspiring interview I did for *The Wisdom of The Buddhist Masters* with Bonpo teacher, Geshe Tenzin Wangyal Rinpoche. Thus I want to thank Rinpoche for his inspiration for this chapter.

Beyond Geshe Tenzin Wangyal Rinpoche, there are many people in my life I wish to thank for inspiring this project. Inspiration comes from both negative and positive sources. Each has the potential to draw us out and meet our world.

Thus it is that I would first like to thank President George W. Bush. Over the last thirty years, I have had periods where I would spend "dream time" with US presidents Carter and Clinton. During the debacle of the 2000 election, I met Al Gore in a dream and asked him how he could have lost what should have been such a commanding lead. Soon after that dream, I met George W. Bush in another dream. He walked by me, grabbed me by the testicles and squeezed. I vowed not to go and visit him again (I have – but that is another story). Without the illegitimacy of the 2000 and 2004 US presidential elections and the blatant corruption that led up to and ensured his assuming the office of President, I would not have been roused from and pushed past my normal "comfort zone" of being only semi-informed and partially engaged when it came to the election of my officials. Through watching the hubris of Bush's administration and the resulting debacle in Iraq I became inspired to look into the history of power and its abuse in my own country and at the wisdom of the Founding Fathers; and I was inspired also to appreciate the work of such modern presidents as John F. Kennedy, Lyndon B. Johnson, Jimmy Carter, and Bill Clinton.

I was also compelled to look more deeply into the teachings of such dear friends and beloved masters as His Holiness The

XIVth Kunzig Shamar Rinpoche, The Venerable Chogyam Trungpa Rinpoche, The Venerable Khenpo Karthar Rinpoche, and Lama Ole Nydahl, in order to see how their words and living examples could be applied to meet the current social and political climate in the US and the world in general. Without such great masters, I would not have had a compass with which to navigate the murky waters of such relative and mundane matters affecting us all. Add to this mix the polar opposites in media pundits Rush Limbaugh, Michael Moore, Ann Coulter, and Rachel Maddow. May all the living teachers, leaders, talkshow hosts, and satirists who have inspired me in this endeavor live long, healthy, and meaningful lives.

My appreciation also goes to Bob Silverstein of Quicksilver Books, who continues to inspire me to think bigger and act bolder in my writing projects. Also to Michael Mann of Watkins Publishing who had the vision to see the long-range benefit of this effort.

Most importantly, I wish to thank my Beloved, Melanie. At Christmas 2003, she gave me a pewter embossed dragon pen with a card that said she wanted to support my writing of this book. Melanie, you are forever my true muse, my inspiration, and the source of all wisdom that graces me.

May the fruition of all of the effort and inspiration that has gone into this book bear fruit in the creation of conscious, engaged activists who feel greater freedom, joy, and possibility in their hearts and minds to seek and work for the changes that all of us have the potential to enjoy.

Robert Sachs
San Luis Obispo, CA

A Call to Action in a Dark Age

"We have nothing to fear, but fear itself."

Franklin D. Roosevelt, former US President

Buddhist masters say that we are in a "Dark Age." In my twenty-five years of studying with many Tibetan lamas and Rinpoches ("Rinpoche" is a Tibetan title meaning 'Precious One' given to especially wise and revered lamas), mention has been made time and again of this fact, and what it means. When I and many other Western students born in affluent nations first heard this, it was hard to imagine what such teachers meant by "Dark Age." We had our own ideas and images spawned by history classes on medieval Europe: a land infested with disease-ridden rodents scurrying about infecting millions of our ancestors with the Black Death. In the latter part of the twentieth century, as this sort of thing wasn't happening (at least not to *our* friends and neighbors), most of us thought existentially – that the "Dark Age" must refer to being caught up in the morass of our own confusion. That seemed bad enough.

However, the world is a much bigger place than your own

back yard. To remind us of that, a good friend and Buddhist teacher, Lama Ole Nydahl, in his yearly travels around the globe, would suggest to students who came to him for personal interviews with the hope of being liberated from their personal miseries, that they should spend a week reading the *International Herald Tribune*. A week later, having acquired a new perspective on the world, fueled by the reality of the ongoing atrocities that we humans seem inclined to inflict upon each other and our environment, the students would then be told to look more closely at what they saw as "suffering" in their lives.

A Climate of Fear

Having traveled a bit myself, I have seen Lama Ole's approach as both clever and useful. However, since 9/11 and the falling of the Twin Towers in New York, a bubble protecting the Western psyche in the more privileged states of Europe and America has been forever and irreparably shattered. The illusion of safety, the illusion that the suffering in the world was not so bad or at least – if one were to be more selfish about it – not happening to "us," came crashing down. With this veil ripped from our eyes, the realities of terrorism, nuclear proliferation, political and economic injustices, AIDS, and the ongoing and escalating numbers of wars worldwide seem more vivid. No matter what spin is placed on these realities that our planet is going through at this period of history, they have become part of our daily diet of news.

According to some of the more apocalyptic traditions of the West, we are living in the end of days. Armageddon is near. We somehow slipped through the noose of the year 2000, when it was predicted that all computers would crash, and some even anticipated that a global cataclysm would ensue, and that a blessed few would ascend to the "kingdom on high." Nevertheless, a mentality encouraged by the real possibility of tragedy – a horrible end to it all – looms over us. This mentality is rooted in fear. In its least insidious expression, it makes us overly cautious, makes us shrink away from possibility and joy. As it eats away at our confidence and narrows our vision, we may experience paralysis, and some of us may become anxious or depressed.

For others, a feeling of despair may set in that in turn encourages myopic, black-and-white solutions to complex problems in our immediate lives and in the wider world. If such desperation leads us to espouse some form of fundamentalist religious persuasion – a trend that is sweeping the globe – or to take up arms, in order to wipe out the perceived sources of our discomfort, the engine driving such views and actions is always the same: fear.

Yet as dire as this all sounds, Tibetan Buddhist masters encourage us not to lose heart. Why? Because, according to them, such Dark Ages have happened before and, over the millions of years to come, will no doubt happen again. More to the point, these masters encourage us to look at what causes a Dark Age in the first place. They direct us to look at both external (in the world and cosmic) and internal (personal and psychological) causes. I shall address such matters in due course, especially as they apply to the phenomenon of war. For now, though, I wish to convey what lessons and information I have received from Tibetan masters that allow me to be cautiously optimistic even in the midst of this Dark Age. I say "cautiously" not because I have my doubts about what these masters have said but because a cautious mindfulness is very useful in helping us to move forward. Even in the current atmosphere, with biological terror and nuclear devastation as real possibilities, I have confidence in their message that we have gotten through such times before and can do so again. The risks are high, but they are not insurmountable.

The Time We Live In: Our Dark Age

Buddhist cosmology is vast in scope, embracing cycles of time that span hundreds, thousands, even millions of years. There are eras, ages, and epochs. In the 5th century BCE the Buddha Shakyamuni is said to have gazed into the future and, according to some Buddhist teachers, seen our own period as an age of decay in which mental, degenerative, and auto-immune illnesses would plague humanity. He saw it as a time of difficulty and strife.

However, many of us who were in our late teens and early twenties in the late 1960s were told that we were entering into the "Age of Aquarius," a time of love and light. Assuming we set any store by the predictive astrology of our own heritage, how can these two prognosticated realities – the "Dark Age" and the "Age of Aquarius" – exist side by side? Whatever happened to "flower power?" The answer for me came in a lecture given in 1978 by a Canadian Tibetan Buddhist teacher named Namgyal Rinpoche. In a presentation given to his students and the general public in London, Namgyal Rinpoche spoke at length about the Age of Aquarius. For many of us, being starry-eyed budding Buddhists, what he said was shocking as well as depressing. What I present in this chapter is an elaboration of what the Rinpoche said that day. My intention is to flesh it out to present a fuller vision of what, I can now see, he wanted us to look at and prepare for – and which, it seems to me, is in fact coming to pass.

An alternative Age of Aquarius

Namgyal Rinpoche said that we are, indeed, in the Age of Aquarius. That is to say, we are in an age that has the potential to see a total transformation of society toward more enlightened values and actions. Love and light can reign in such an age. It can be everything that every utopian, peacenik, beatnik, hippy, and spiritual aspirant would like it to be. However, the Rinpoche also described an alternative Age of Aquarius that looks more like the apocalyptic vision I presented earlier. This version of the Aquarian Age is what Chinese philosophers would call "interesting times," in which a high level of uncertainty and chaos is prevalent. Traditional social structures and cultural mores are shown to be obsolete or out of step with the demands of current times. One example is overpopulation, how it impacts and overwhelms current social infrastructures and support networks and challenges religious beliefs that procreation is God's will. This may seem exciting to some – a time of opportunity when the shackles of the past and parochialism can be cast off and we can then grow and express ourselves in new and unprecedented ways. But, for those with fewer material or emotional resources, such times can be tremendously challenging, if not downright frightening.

Those frightened by what they saw around them in such a period – and a good many people would be – could exhibit an extreme range of habitual, reactionary responses as they sought to survive materially and emotionally. At one extreme, with the social and cultural doors barely hanging by their hinges, some might find within themselves a rebellious, even anarchistic side that seeks to throw all caution to the wind and to live as if there were no past or future, only the present – a Generation X and a culture with a more lax view on drugs, alcohol, promiscuity, and so on. Such a reaction is not to be mistaken for a more "Zen" approach to life. In fact, in a more bohemian, hedonistic "me-first" lifestyle, consciousness, conscientiousness, and conscience are bypassed in favor of intoxication, where self-indulgence and entertainment-seeking are paramount. This starts with the mind-dulling pabulum we feed our young in the form of *Teletubbies* and other visual valium, and the behavioral morphine we ingest to buy into a more-is-always-better lifestyle, which numbs the senses and blocks out visions of poverty, starvation, war...

On the other hand, and almost at the exact opposite extreme, others might respond to the uncertainty of the times by shrinking back and seeking security, stability, and predictability, expressed in a fear of stepping outside one's front door, the need to rely on dogmatic, circumscribing faiths, or believe unswervingly in well-crafted and spun political rhetoric.

As if to answer the demands and challenges of these polar responses, social structures and institutions become super-bureaucratized and over-regulated, with more permits, laws, and restrictions in completing even the simplest of tasks to rein in the radicals and provide a sense of stability for the fearful. In this alternative vision of the Age of Aquarius, individual needs and personal expression take second place to a tendency for government bodies and mega-corporation interests to suppress and to dominate, in order to create the illusion of stability.

As fear dominates the psyche and security becomes the imperative of the majority of public and private power brokers and of the citizens they govern, there must also be belief systems that are simple and promise stability. Some may seek out the well-marketed New Age-type ideologies that make utopian promises and offer a "mother ship" to return to. Others may turn to living out their own wants and dreams vicariously through the lives of a plethora of TV and movie stars and other marketed heroes and heroines. The truth is, however, that in uncertain times the majority want beliefs that are based in a black-and-white reality so that, again, they can know where they stand. For many, such beliefs may take the form of religious fundamentalism as the religious equivalent of a secular order obsessed with bureaucracy, regulation, damage containment, and control.

Sadly as history has borne out time and again, all of these

conditions can come together to create the perfect atmosphere for the emergence of despots and tyrants. Capitalizing on fear is an old human tradition. It is, in fact, the main ingredient in leading people into armed conflict against one another. As the late Nazi commander Hermann Goering aptly put it:

> "Why of course the people don't want war. Why should some poor slob on a farm want to risk his life in a war when the best he can get out of it is to come back to his farm in one piece? Naturally, the common people don't want war...That is understood. But, after all, it is the leaders of the country who determine the policy and it is always a simple matter to drag the people along, whether it is a democracy, or a fascist dictatorship, or a parliament, or a communist dictatorship. Voice or no voice, the people can always be brought to the bidding of the leaders. That is easy. All you have to do is to tell them they are being attacked, and denounce the peacemakers for lack of patriotism and exposing the country to danger. It works the same in any country."[1]

As dire as all of this may sound, even if this is truly to be our planet's future, Namgyal Rinpoche was not wholly pessimistic. Of the two alternatives for the Age of Aquarius, the Rinpoche did not have much confidence that the utopia of love and light promised by the pop culture would be what emerged. Rather, he saw the coming of the darker version – but with pockets of light. Even in such circumstances, all joy and possibility would

---

1 Gustav Gilbert, *Nuremberg Diary*, Farrar, Strauss and Co., 1947. Recorded on April 18th, 1946.

not be absent. The opportunity for growth and transformation would still be there, though not on the scale that our early Aquarian "pioneers" envisioned. The wisdom traditions and the possibilities for enlightened ways of being would continue to exist, but would manifest as pockets or beacons of light. Such places or groups of individuals committed to enlightened possibility would be small, and would attract those who had enough space in their hearts and minds to see through or beyond the marketed and media-based visions of reality. In such communities, the growth and awakening of consciousness would be intense and rapid.

Following the ancient oriental principle of a balance of forces, what has a front also has a back. The bigger the front, the bigger the back. In the midst of darkness – in the midst of mediocrity, sickness, poverty, and warfare – there *is* possibility. And as dark as the future might look, the pockets of brightness would be of equal intensity, albeit at first sight somewhat veiled.

Looking at the evidence of what is happening in the world around us, it appears that Namgyal Rinpoche's vision is coming to pass. We have seen the consolidation and bureaucratization of a united Europe; the Patriot Act and the evident erosion of constitutional rights in the United States; the machinations of affluent nations and the IMF toward the establishment of a homogenous, well controlled global economy fine-tuned under the watchful eye of multinational corporations; the familiarity, yet confusion, we now all have for the term *jihad*; the proliferation of religious TV and radio stations juxtaposed to such grotesque and banal reality-TV offerings as *Survivor*, *Temptation Island*, and *Fear Factor*; and the media obsession with telling us all the down-and-dirty details about our superheroes. And at the same time, we have seen the gradual, organic emergence of holistic and environmentally-conscious living, against a background of growing interest in Eastern and more esoteric spiritual and healing traditions.

Around the time that Namgyal Rinpoche was conveying his vision of the Age of Aquarius, from the mid-1970s to early 1980s, other Tibetan teachers began to address global and political issues that many students wished they could forget. The rather messy end to the war in Vietnam; the escalation of the "War on Drugs" and battles with drug cartels; a succession of oil crises over the last thirty years that can not be separated from Western policy and growing unrest in the Middle East; the increase in airplane hijackings and terrorist attacks worldwide; and the climaxing of Cold War tensions that would eventually lead to the collapse of the Berlin Wall and the ensuing chaos of a Europe in transition – these were just some of the political and historical factors that Tibetan teachers saw as challenging the seeming promise of Western democracy and freedom.

Shambhala: The enlightened realm

In the early and mid-1980s, perhaps because in their great wisdom they perceived the need, His Holiness the Dalai Lama and other great Tibetan spiritual masters began to offer for the first time in the West public teachings and empowerment ceremonies of Kalachakra, the tantric Buddha. At the same time, the late Ven. Chögyam Trungpa Rinpoche introduced teachings and training in the way of Shambhala. The Kalachakra teachings are considered the pinnacle of Buddhist thought and practice. Their goal is to create powerful beings free of illusion and focused on the benefit of all. They are the basis of all Buddhist tantra and the core teachings that inspire the enlightened citizenry of Shambhala.

Tibetan Buddhist tradition teaches that Shambhala is – for lack of a better word – a "supernatural" realm, or a more spiritual/etheric plane of existence that is around us on this planet, although we cannot see it. It is a realm of nobility and honor; a society governed by enlightened principles. It is believed that emissaries from Shambhala visited the Buddha and requested that he come to their realm to teach. He consented, and seeing the advanced and gentle ways of the Shambhalians, manifested himself and taught in the tantric form of Kalachakra, the Deity of Time.

Chögyam Trungpa Rinpoche, who was also known as Lord Ösel Mukpo, an emissary of Shambhala, teaches that there have been times when the realm of Shambhala has had a direct impact on humanity. The Samurai tradition of Japan; the Magyar warrior class of Hungary; and the legacy of King Arthur and the Knights of the Round Table were considered by Lord Mukpo to be direct links to Shambhala. Chögyam Trungpa/Lord Mukpo gave direct teachings toward the establishment of what is now a non-denominational meditation organization worldwide called Shambhala Training.

Other teachers who gave teachings on the Kalachakra ceremonies also made claims about Shambhala's role in relation to planet Earth. What they said is that the Earth is a unique planet, where humanity has a suitable environment to work with its innate potential to transform itself and awaken the love, wisdom, and compassion, which are hallmarks of what Buddhism defines as enlightenment. As such, the Shambhalians consider Earth to be too precious to allow it to annihilate itself. According to this tradition, the Shambhalians are in a sense our local, invisible guardians, watching what we do, periodically interceding in earthly events when the stakes are too high. Although no teacher I have met has ever been specific about these interventions in modern times, I often have wondered about the abrupt end to the first Gulf War in the early nineties and whether there was some Shambhalian influence in the matter. Furthermore, although we may view our current world situation as dire, it is predicted that the trend toward fundamentalism in both its Eastern and Western forms will continue for another two centuries. The Ven. Khenpo Karthar Rinpoche, a contemporary Tibetan Buddhist master of incomparable insight, once commented that the times we are currently in will seem peaceful compared to the times we shall face over the next two hundred and fifty years as societies deteriorate, fundamentalist factions vie for superiority, and unrest grows. Then, at some time in the twenty-third century, it is predicted that the Shambhalians will once again intervene in earthly affairs to avert an all-out war between the fundamentalist factions.

We in the West have our own tradition of guardian angels and are used to hearing promises made from pulpits that all will be well. Some may think that such words are spoken primarily to keep attendance high and church coffers full. But perhaps there is more to these promises than we know. Similarly, it may just be that the words of Tibetan masters on the realm of Shambhala are there to let us know that we are not alone in the struggles that we go through, both within and among ourselves, and will not be abandoned to our baser and more negative impulses. Both visions, Christian and Buddhist, tell us that we are being watched and looked after. Hatred and war will not win, will not end us. Hatred is not at the heart of humanity. Buddhists take this even further by saying that the planet upon which we assume dominion is, by virtue of that dominion, centered around the force of love and our basic loving nature – what in Buddhism is termed *bodhichitta*, or "awakened heart."

The teachings of the Buddha do not agree with those Christian sects that foresee Armageddon or an "end of days" scenario. No matter how dire, desperate, or dangerous the times might appear, the Buddha foresaw that we will not annihilate ourselves. But in order for the full potential of our loving nature to emerge victorious over our confusion and despair, we need to be willing and committed to do the work that needs to be done. The degree to which we ignore or put off that work is the degree to which sickness, poverty, and warfare will continue to manifest in the course of human history. In other words, even though at the most basic level all is well and the survival of humanity is assured by those who stand witness to our struggle, our future is up to us.

The inner struggle

This book has a lot to say about war. For those concerned about the current political climate, I will go on to discuss how to live with, work against, and, better still, transform the self-interested and government, corporate, or otherwise partisan-sanctioned aggression that seems so apparent in these times. But, more importantly, these pages will look at the deeper causes of conflict and war. In fact, this book is about the greatest of all wars, the war against the cause of all the worldly conflicts that we have had to endure since the dawn of humanity. It is the war that the Buddha himself fought: the war with the forces of darkness that are in each and every one of us. These forces – what in Buddhism are known as the "Three Poisons" of ignorance, attachment, and aggression – are reflected in our individual and collective thoughts, attitudes, emotions, and reactions, and are the root cause of our current Dark Age. They are the source of all our misery and mischief, whether it be in the form of personal suffering or excessive bureaucracy, the homogenization of culture to the point of global marketed mediocrity, religious fundamentalism, and the host of ways in which we torment our brothers, sisters, and fellow species on this planet we call home.

The Ven. Khenpo Karthar Rinpoche taught many years ago that the cosmic and external forces that appear as a Dark Age, and manifest as sickness, poverty, and warfare, are the result of the Three Poisons gathering as a cloud in each of our minds, and then gathering as one great stormcloud that covers us all in darkness. Whether the seemingly insurmountable external causes and conditions that we face are the result of a cosmic, divine, or human hand, it is the inner causes that need to be addressed. Once we are truly on a path of resolving and transforming these internal causes, the environmental and geopolitical chaos that we witness today will, in turn, begin to be resolved and transformed for the benefit of all. What is important to understand, however, is that working on the inner causes is always linked to working with the outer manifestations. They cannot be separated. We need to address the Three Poisons within ourselves and also simultaneously address them as they manifest in the world around us.

Conscious, Engaged Activism

Knowing that the Three Poisons are not who we really are and that at our core is a loving nature and "enlightenment-potential," the Buddha offers his teachings – the Dharma – as the medicine to transform the "poisons" and our self-created attitudes and circumstances that stifle and nearly destroy the possibility of our awakening. The goal is to encourage and support us to wake up – to become conscious of our true nature and our intimate relationship with, and role in, the world around us – and to focus our thoughts and actions on behavior that contributes to a peaceful future and the wellbeing of others as well as ourselves. This is what I mean by *conscious, engaged activism*. It is altruism with teeth. The Buddha wants us truly to "be all that we can be" – spiritual warriors in whatever form or capacity we can fulfill. Until we have won the inner war against darkness and the Three Poisons within us, until each and every one of us has actualized our potential for enlightened living and our lives are wholly conscious and engaged, the Buddha's gaze will not swerve: he and all those who serve as our guides and friends in this world, supporting our awakening, will remain at war.

For those who want to break free from the duality, inner turmoil, and partisanship that will only continue to polarize us and separate us from the common good that we seek, what follows are insights and tools from the Buddha's teachings, which can help the reader to become a conscious, engaged activist – a spiritual warrior. For in times of strife and warfare, if we are to awaken, we have no choice but to become warriors. To strive for a lasting peace, to put an end to war and all else that haunts us, requires the courage to embark on the sublime and arduous spiritual path in order to end the warfare of confusion and conflicting emotions within us. If we can base our actions on a mind and heart transformed, the global transformation we seek will be set upon a lasting foundation. That is the purpose of this book.

We cannot escape the times that we live in. We cannot escape the truth that to be alive and acting in whatever way we do has consequences, whether we like it or not. If the saying is true that a butterfly flapping its wings in one place can cause a hurricane thousands of miles away, there are global consequences whenever we step outside our front door. This is not meant as a flippant ploy to swell the reader's head with delusions of grandeur, or a means to goad us to do something against our will. It is just a simple, sobering reminder of our connection with each and every being. We are responsible to one another. It is not that we *can* make a difference, but that we *do* make a difference. The difference we make manifests in accordance with the choices we make.

In these dark times, we are being called to action. Our loving nature – the enlightened potential that the Buddha recognized as lying at our core of being – is calling us. For those willing to answer this call, there will be trying times. There will be tests along the way. These tests will often be very difficult. We may not pass some of them and have to try again and again. But in the end we shall not fail. For failure is not at the core of who we are.

War and Buddhism

"*In traditional societies such as the Tibetan society I came from, you ride your horse, you pitch your tent, you make a fire. Whatever you do, it is done simply and directly. If you have to kill your enemy, you do so in the same spirit of simplicity and directness. Your enemy should die in your lap rather than being slaughtered from a distance. And having killed your enemy, you're supposed to kiss the enemy. I don't know if you can understand this. In America, the white man just wiped out the Indians.*

There was no sense of sacred warfare. What I'm talking about is quite the opposite of that approach."

Chögyam Trungpa Rinpoche[2]

For many Westerners, Buddhism is synonymous with pacifism. The Buddha himself is pictured as still, demure, and detached; and the most common image of a Buddhist is either a monk with a shaved head, wearing orange robes and sandals, or one of the peaceful and benign media shots of His Holiness the Dalai Lama.

If we were to look for examples of Buddhist leaders running imperialist, aggressive Buddhist nations, we would not find any. Nor has Buddhist doctrine ever been the sole justification for dominating one group or another economically, politically, or militarily. I say "sole" because in the case of Tibet, for example, aristocratic families with allegiance to particular Buddhist lineages have vied for power. No doubt, as in other nations of the world, one may find examples where leaders and politicians in Buddhist countries in Asia have used religion as the rationale for political, economic, or military action. But because Buddhism tends to cultivate independent thinking, its followers are generally less susceptible to being drawn into mass movements or mass hysteria, or to taking propaganda seriously.

When countries which have a large Buddhist population or are governed by Buddhist leaders have experienced political, economic, or military struggles, the actions of Buddhists at such times have not always been peaceful or passive. Contrary to the images of demure, passive monks, consider those Vietnamese monks and nuns who burned themselves to death in protest against American involvement in their country's civil strife. In my own life, I have had the privilege to meet one of the former kings of the Tibetan region of Kham, who told me how some of his people responded to the Chinese invasion of the late 1950s. Under his guidance, the locals sold drugs to Chinese soldiers by day so that they could more easily scare them off or

---

[2]   Chögyam Trungpa Rinpoche, *Great Eastern Sun: The Wisdom of Shambhala.* Shambhala Books, Boston and New York, 1999, p.196.

– if there was no other option – kill them at night. More recently, there is the example given by one Western lama of his Russian Dharma students who run raids into Chechen strongholds to rescue those who have been taken hostage. Knowing the bad karma it is to kill, the lama advises them to shoot at the captors' kneecaps rather than kill them, to leave them crippled and unable to fight in the future.

Even more dramatically, I am reminded of stories passed on by His Holiness the 16th Gyalwa Karmapa. In his book *Dzalendara and Sakarchupa* he tells of his previous incarnation as an assassin whose purpose it was to murder a tyrant, who would otherwise have caused the death of countless others.[3] The tyrant's assassination not only prevented the suffering of others, but also prevented the tyrant himself from accumulating more and more negative karma in the future. The action of this "enlightened" assassin was an example of what in Buddhism is called "wrathful compassion" – a term which we shall address later in the book. The point is that from an enlightened perspective, pre-emption and pre-emptive strikes are permissible.

Is War Truly Evil?

Buddhism, therefore, does not shy away from conflict or war. In 2001, in his speech accepting the Nobel Peace Prize, former US President Jimmy Carter said: "War may be a necessary evil. But it is always evil." But while there is probably no person on this planet who truly prefers conflict and war over peace and harmony, does it stand to reason that war must always be defined as evil? The most profound of the Buddha's teachings speaks of what is called "emptiness," the notion that everything is "empty"

[3]   H.H. the 16th Gyalwa Karmapa, *Dzalendara and Sakarchupa*. Karma Drubgyud Darjay Ling, Eskdalemuir, Scotland, 1981.

of intrinsic, independent existence. All things are interconnected. Hence, nothing can be judged as wholly and ultimately "good" or "bad." The degree to which they are either is determined by the mind of the perceiver. Thus, whether conflict, even war, is – in the long or short term – good or bad depends on what side of the fence you are standing on. Another holder of the Nobel Peace Prize, His Holiness the Dalai Lama, expressed this in his own acceptance speech for the award in 1989:

> "War or peace; the destruction or the protection of nature; the violation or promotion of human rights and democratic freedoms; poverty or material well-being; the lack of moral and spiritual values or their existence and development; and the breakdown or development of human understanding, are not isolated phenomena that can be analyzed and tackled independently of one another. In fact, they are very much interrelated at all levels and need to be approached with that understanding. Peace, in the sense of the absence of war, is of little value to someone who is dying of hunger or cold. It will not remove the pain of torture inflicted on a prisoner of conscience. It does not comfort those who have lost their loved ones in floods caused by senseless deforestation in a neighboring country. Peace can only last where human rights are respected, where people are fed, and where individuals and nations are free." [4]

If peace is merely the absence of war – if injustice, poverty, and strife are brewing underneath a seeming calm – then of what value is it? The forces that seek to maintain such a peace may

---

[4] H.H. the 14th Dalai Lama, *A Policy of Kindness*. Snow Lion Publications, Ithaca, NY, 1990, pp17–18.

succeed in preventing the chaos that could exacerbate conditions, but they may also suppress the free expression of frustration at the status quo which at times may also necessitate conflict beyond a level of verbal disapproval. The introduction of something new, the awareness of other options or possibilities, always brings with it discomfort, conflict, breakthrough, and reintegration. This is as true for our own hearts and minds as it is for the macro-structures of society around us. That is why civil protest is an essential ingredient in democracy and probably why Thomas Jefferson spoke of the importance of suspicion of government control as an important feature of an active, dynamic democracy truly focused on personal freedom.

There is an old Buddhist saying that it is far more difficult to cover the world in leather than it is to put on shoes. What this means is that it is very difficult when our own minds are not transformed to work on transforming the world around us. Hence, if we want to see qualitative change in the world around us, we must begin with ourselves. In his Nobel Prize acceptance speech in Oslo, the Dalai Lama went on to speak about the importance of developing inner peace as the prerequisite for external peace. This is a critical point and one that is central to what this book offers. At the same time, it would be overly idealistic to suggest that anyone with a conscience should suspend their actions against poverty, destruction of the environment, or violations of human rights because they have not reached a totally enlightened state – the state of inner peace. I do not believe that the Dalai Lama was suggesting this. However, his words are a warning of the risks of acting to resolve what we see as the world's difficulties without equally being committed to looking within ourselves. Until we do so, it will remain difficult for us to know whether our actions are skillful or wise; and our unskilled, unfocused actions will give rise, at best, to unskilled, unfocused consequences.

At the same time, despite the fact that most of us are gripped by the "Three Poisons" of ignorance, attachment, and aggression, because I hold to the fundamental Buddhist tenet of basic goodness or a loving nature being the core of who we are, I truly believe that unenlightened as most of us are, we always go into life's situations with the intention of doing our best based on what we currently know. Our knowledge may be flawed and incomplete and our actions imperfect, but in our desire to make and see a difference, we act nevertheless; and because our minds are not cleared of confusion, inner conflict, and unresolved feelings, we shall see these mirrored in the consequences of our actions in the world around us.

Thus the confusion within ourselves, and the uncertainty of knowing what is the most skillful path to take in order to change the world around us, can lead us to make hasty judgments that lead us down the road to what may seem to us to be justifiable conflict. And if a sufficient number of people around us also have less than adequate information and harbor a host of similarly unresolved inner conflicts, it is more than likely that, like clouds gathering to cause a storm, tensions may accumulate that may lead to actual physical conflict or war.

It is said that "The road to hell is paved with good intentions." In any given situation, we may sincerely believe that what we are doing is the right thing, and the only thing we can do. War that results from mental confusion may not necessarily be "evil." But the Tibetan Bön master Tenzin Wangyal Rinpoche describes such an outcome as "failure" – a failure to resolve matters in ways that most of us would prefer.

However, this is not necessarily to deny that there are times when conflict or war, however undesirable, may be the only way to shake up what may appear to be, as we are currently able to see it, an intractable situation. There may seem to be no alternative way of allowing otherwise suppressed feelings, needs, and forces to free themselves and be expressed. Is this messy? Absolutely. But reality is by nature relative, ambiguous, and messy. Until we are enlightened and have acquired the capacity to see the past, present, and future clearly, and our actions are pure and have only the consequences we intend, there will always be unintentional effects, or "collateral damage."

Hopefully, we learn and grow from our mistakes. Hiroshima and Nagasaki made us realize that the unchecked proliferation and use of nuclear weapons was a short cut to the total annihilation of the human race and most other forms of life on the planet. Thus we closely monitor the development of nuclear technology throughout the world. Having witnessed the effects of nuclear weapons only twice, we are more enlightened about the truth of a nuclear disaster. Hindsight, looking back upon what we have done in the light of the consequences of our actions, is definitely one way to learn what to do and not to do in the future. Unfortunately, it seems to be the teacher we end up relying on most.

The Four Aspects: Intention, thought, action, and reaction

His Holiness the Ven. Shamar Rinpoche made some poignant comments about conflict and war in the wake of 9/11. In an attempt to take the dialogue beyond the sentimental to a place where people could truly reflect and learn, he spoke of the Buddhist teaching of the Four Aspects that characterize each of our actions. To explain this briefly for now, every action consists of the following four stages: intention; contemplation and thought; action; then our reaction to the action we have committed. In other words, we want some action to happen and set our determination to perform it; we consider *how* we are going to perform the action; we perform the action; and then we look back and assess what we have accomplished. All actions proceed in this way.

If our actions are directed by positive intention and clear thinking, and we have the skill to perform what we intend to do, then more than likely the outcome will also be positive and clear. This is one end of the spectrum. At the other end is where we have negative, harmful intentions, focus all of our thoughts on accomplishing that intention, successfully commit an act that brings great harm, and take delight in our success. Such actions are the most "evil." While even these actions are, in Buddhist terms, intrinsically "empty" in themselves, we can call them "evil" from a relative point of view, in the sense that they are almost entirely negative, harmful, or destructive in effect.

Most of our actions fall into the wide range of possibilities that lie somewhere between these two extremes. Perhaps we have a positive intention, but don't think things out all that well, commit actions that do some harm, and then feel confused or ambivalent about the result. Equally, if we have negative intentions but lack the clarity of mind and the skill to pull them off, we may end up angered at our lack of success. Again, there is a mixed result and how we react afterward will more than likely reflect that. The action and what follows will generally provide us feedback on our lack of skill. In an appendix at the end of this book, Shamar Rinpoche reflects and gives advice on how to view the events of 9/11 based on this perspective (see pages 245–6).

If we look back on the long history of warfare, we shall always find the motives of the participants occupying a similar gray territory. A side that goes to war usually does so for mixed reasons – to end a tyranny and free the people, say, but also to increase business opportunities and open new trade markets. If those who decide on war are not entirely focused or have a number of altruistic and self-serving aims in mind, similarly –

and more than likely – they may think even less clearly about the means they will use to achieve their ends. Consequently there are generally mixed results: a campaign may be well planned and the military well trained, but perhaps some of the necessary information about strategic and civilian sites is incomplete, resulting in "collateral damage" affecting noncombatants. In all wars, after the dead are buried and the wounded tended to and sent home, a legacy is spawned on both sides. The "victors" may think that the end justified the means. Those on the other side, the so-called "losers," however, may be embittered and disfranchised. The legacy of resentment often, down the line, leads to further conflict and war.

Of course, each side in a conflict will generally view the outcome differently. We should also remember that history tends to get rewritten by those who have control of the pens, so that a war seen as negative in outcome at the time, may be seen by later generations to have had a more positive impact, and vice versa. Probably the only reliable indicator that any given conflict has had a more positive than negative impact is whether or not it has been the spawning ground for further mayhem and pain. A Buddhist perspective and the tools which it offers may be helpful in guiding our assessments and seeking more skillful alternatives if and when conflicts arise in the future.

In the end, we learn from war, as from many other areas of human experience, that we are victims of our own frailties and need to view the past as no more than a foundation upon which we can build better ways to be, and act, in the future. And so, if we want a more positive, loving, and viable future, all we can really do is take ourselves in hand, commit ourselves to not reacting to our situation in a negative way, learn methods to transform our negative mental and emotional states, and perform all our actions with the best possible aims in mind.

Our Challenge And Our Potential

Is it possible to hone our emotional and perceptive skills, to develop deeper wisdom from the start? Can we learn right away to act appropriately and effectively in the predicaments we encounter – when to be peaceful, when to enter into conflict, when to let things mature in their own way, or prompt them along? The Buddha says in no uncertain terms, yes. The fact that we as humans prefer peace and happiness is a testament to what he saw as our inherent loving nature: the fact that we are basically "good." At the same time, because we are confused, in that we don't see the real correlation between our happiness and the happiness of others, our view of how to gain peace and happiness will more than likely disagree with someone else's view. When we do not see common ground, but only difference, conflict – perhaps, on a large scale, even war – is inevitable. In a 2004 campaign speech while running for the US presidency, retired General Wesley Clark spoke of entering into conflict only "reluctantly." If our basic nature is a loving one, it makes sense that to engage in conflict at all should only be a last resort, unless we are so wise as to be able to foresee the future accurately. But there are few of us who have that capacity.

Transforming the Three Poisons

To summarize this discussion so far, we have seen that all actions have consequences. If our actions are skillful and based on wisdom, we will more than likely achieve our objectives with few, if any, unintended side effects or "collateral damage." The degree to which there is "collateral damage" is the degree to which our actions were not as skillful as we thought or the knowledge we had was not as thorough as we supposed. Regardless, we do the best we can based on what we know. If we blow it, hopefully we shall be wiser and our actions more skillful in the future.

Knowing that this is how it is for us as humans, and seeing the suffering caused by disasters that we are often so slow to learn from, the Buddha discovered methods that would skillfully guide us through the pride, jealousy, lustfulness, torpor, greed, and anger that distort our actions and lead to future calamities. Because he had first and foremost in his mind that we are all basically good and that at our core is a loving nature, he saw these negative mental states – what his teachings, the Dharma, call *kleshas* – not as permanent flaws, but rather the result of habit patterns.

Such habit patterns are formed as a result of the so-called Three Poisons that we are all inflicted with. These Three Poisons, which I already touched upon in Chapter 1 (see page 12) are **ignorance** (not understanding what the world is about or who we really are in relation to it), **attachment** (blind adherence, rooted in ignorance, to our own point of view), and **aggression** (toward anyone who disagrees with our point of view). The Buddha also came to know in his heart of hearts that if we transform our ignorance we can experience a wide array – "a rainbow" – of amazing capabilities, opening our minds to unlimited possibility and in turn transforming our attachment and our aggressive tendencies. In doing so we can release the heat and passion within us that create great joy and a spontaneous and effortless way of being and acting in the world. We can become who we are meant to be – ultimately, we can become just like him: an awakened or enlightened being.

The Buddha developed many methods to transform the Three Poisons. All of them encourage us to apply ourselves to developing what are classically called the "Six Paramitas" (Perfections) of patience, openness (or generosity), discipline, perseverance, meditation, and the deepening of wisdom, until these states of mind are the guiding forces in all our actions. **Wisdom** (the guiding light, which the Buddha saw as a female principle) conjoined with "**skillful means**" (the resourcefulness to bring that light to all our actions, which he saw as a male principle) result in actions that are inherently compassionate. Through training, our loving nature – our desire to be happy and to see happiness all around us – manifests as a compassion built on a foundation of wisdom and skill. Having fought the war within, and armed with the resourcefulness of an awakened being, the conscious, engaged activist is ready to meet the world.

The path one needs to tread to accomplish this noble task is what the reader will find systematically laid out in the following chapters. Each chapter will provide information, contemplations, and practical methods that will, in turn, become a foundation upon which the subsequent chapters are built. This organizational method was used by the Buddha himself to foster progressive understanding and growth for individuals wanting to connect with their loving nature and realize their inherent enlightened potential. The information, contemplations, and methods that are to follow, while Buddhist in origin, are universally applicable and will be of tremendous value in helping all those who wish to transform themselves and the world around them to remain focused, relaxed, and energized, when they work with the personal and global dimensions of the Dark Age as they inevitably arise in our lives. It is my fervent wish that what follows becomes an antidote to cynicism, apathy, and despair.

The Venerable Chögyam Trungpa Rinpoche used to say that it is always possible to cheer up. Ultimately, it is only from a mind that is transformed, free, and cheerful that actions to create lasting peace and happiness are possible. Let us enter on that path, starting now.

Why Bother? Revolutionizing the Mind

"You can explore the universe looking for somebody who is more deserving of your love and affection than you are yourself, and you will not find that person anywhere."

Anonymous

Human experience and the circumstances that humans find themselves in vary dramatically. Some live in a Beverly Hills reality with servants who lay out their clothes each morning and make sure that their Mercedes is fueled, warmed up, and ready to go for a light lunch in Malibu or a day of shopping. Others wake up in the garbage dumps of Calcutta, scrounge for restaurant morsels or spoiled fruit, then spend the remainder of their day sorting mounds of rubbish to find anything that might have a street value they can haggle for. Most of us live our lives somewhere in between these extremes.

Yet, no matter how apparently idyllic or deprived our circumstances are, our experience of those circumstances can be surprisingly varied. Someone in the lap of luxury may be bored with life and take no delight whatsoever in their "good" fortune. At the same time, a poor person in Calcutta may cherish every moment of their "dire" life. And then there are the rest of us who at times feel good and motivated in our circumstances and at other times close to despair.

So, while the Buddha's teachings say that our circumstances are the direct result of our previous actions, which have led to the consequences we now encounter as a palace, a dump, or somewhere in between, it does not mean that our experience of these circumstances is cast in stone. The laws of karma, which I address in greater length later on (see page 121), teach that what you have done in the past – your actions and your attitudes when taking those actions – have led to your present. In the same way, your response to your current situation will lead you to act in a certain way, setting a course for you into the future. However, while where you are now is in a sense linked to your destiny, your future is neither predetermined nor inevitable. There is only possibility. The question, then, is how free and flexible is your mind when it comes to recognizing this possibility, when it comes to choosing options and attitudes that will create better rather than worse outcomes for you in the future?

Recognizing possibility is crucial in the life of a conscious, engaged activist. It is what allows someone in poverty not to give in to despair and hopelessness. It is also what prevents someone of wealth and privilege from hardening their heart, becoming selfish and self-absorbed, or becoming too complacent to think that there may be something else, something better that can be done with their opportunities. In fact, it is important to learn to traverse a path that avoids the extremes of "I've got mine. I have worked so hard to get mine. Other people can do the same. Why should I bother with them?" and "My life is horrible. I can't change anything. I'm so worthless and small. What could I possibly do? Why should I bother?"

Between the numbing intoxication of self-absorption and self-aggrandizement and the depressing blackness of self-denigration is where most of us live our lives. And if we use enough gray matter we at least see how fickle life is and how the winds of fortune can blow this way or that. If we believe that all is capricious and that these changes are whimsically out of our control – if we don't understand the role of karma and our own authorship of the causes and conditions of our lives – then a "why bother?" attitude would make sense. But it doesn't. Our loving nature, the enlightened potential within us, is whispering to us. This is why somewhere inside us, to a greater or lesser degree, we know better. And that knowledge is what the Buddha appeals to.

The Four Thoughts that Revolutionize the Mind

To help us understand our situation better and to inspire us to seize possibility by learning methods to free our hearts and minds, the Buddha asks us to consider "Four Thoughts." These contemplations are seen as a preliminary to embarking on a more spirit-oriented life. For our purposes, they are the starting point for becoming a conscious, engaged activist. These four notions are called by different names: The Four Thoughts that Turn the Mind to Dharma; The Four Thoughts that Turn the Mind to Spirituality; and the one I like the most – The Four Thoughts that Revolutionize the Mind. These thoughts are presented in a set sequence. Yet, like interdependent building blocks, each thought reinforces and supports its predecessor and becomes the foundation upon which the logic of the next thought arises. Their goal is to cultivate a deep sense of appreciation for life and what it has to offer us. They are the perfect foundation upon which a revolution of the mind can occur.

Thought 1: Loving our lives

The first of the revolutionizing thoughts deals with what the Buddha called "precious human birth." He distinguishes between this and ordinary or regular human birth and life as being human. This distinction is significant and what is meant by a "precious human birth" exactly will be explained shortly. However, the Buddha saw that, in general *all* human birth is special. The reason for it being special is because of the "Six Realms of Existence" that the buddha identified. The human realm is, reatively speaking, the only one not governed by any particular overwhelming emotional experience. The "higher" realms of gods and demigods are governed by an intoxication with pride and competitive jealousy respectively. The "lower" realms of animals, hungry ghosts, and hell-bound beings are caught in the grasp of reflexive survival-based stupidity, insatiability, and hatred respectively. No doubt humans experience these emotions, and we may even argue with the Buddha's observations and conclusion that we do not experience such emotions as intensely as those in the non-human realms. Looking at all realms with an enlightened eye, what the Buddha saw was that human life is neither "too good" (like the life of a god) nor "too bad" (like the life of a lower being). What does dominate human consciousness with respect to emotional experience is desire and passion. Although this can be experienced intensely in such forms as ordinary lust or overwhelming longing, it also, when we desire something seemingly beyond our reach, gives us the impetus to change. Desire and passion, what the Buddha called "craving" will be discussed more fully in the next chapter. What is of importance here, however, is the Buddha's recognition of this craving as being central to our experience, hence central to our process of awakening and transformation. The highest expression of desire comes in the urge to awaken – to become enlightened, and ultimately free of all selfish desire – while passion can be transformed into compassion for all beings. It is these qualities that led the Buddha to assert that we are basically good and that there is in humans the unique quality of wanting, *and* actually having the capacity, to truly benefit others.

Returning to our distinction between precious and ordinary human birth, precious human birth is a life that has specific internal and external factors which the Buddha classifies with respect to what we possess as individuals and what the environment provides for us. From the point of view of achieving enlightenment, the most advantageous human birth is one where all of the sensory organs are intact and operating, the limbs and organs do what they are designed to do, and the mind is functioning within a "normal" range of intelligence. Ideal external factors include living in a peaceful and nurturing social and natural environment that provides access to education and training, which in turn lead us to becoming a resourceful and – ultimately – an enlightened being.

Classically, if all of these circumstances come together, the one who possesses them can take full advantage of the opportunity of human birth. This is both precious and rare. At the same time, this does not mean that enlightenment is not possible in other, less idyllic conditions, but that it is more difficult and consequently rarer. However, it is unfortunately also rare that individuals whose lives possess all the ideal factors do take advantage of them. Too often, like a pampered cat, we just lie there, basking in our fortune, falling asleep when we can. That is why Buddhist teachers say that to have the motivation to do something, to take full advantage of these circumstances, is as rare as when a tortoise comes up from the bottom of the ocean every thousand years and manages to slip its neck through a yoke that just happens to be floating along.

Motivating a person to take full advantage of the circumstance of precious human birth is what the three remaining revolutionizing thoughts are about. Many Buddhist teachers, seeing the opportunities that our Western, democratic culture provides us with, try to encourage us along this path.

Looking at the realities that so many face on this planet, the precious opportunity of a human birth may not bring these ideal internal or external advantages and may, in fact, come with an array of internal and external challenges. We are perhaps blind or deaf, or we may have a disease or some other physical limitation; we may live in a land and society where there is warfare or strife that allows little opportunity for much beyond basic survival; and our educators may focus on selfish or myopic goals reinforced by beliefs and superstitions that make us fearful to trust, love, or grow.

Yet the difficulties of such conditions may exist more in our perception of them than in how things really are. This point has been mentioned again and again by Buddhist teachers, who talk about the fortunate circumstances we are *all*, in fact, living in. For the most part, we live in a world that is a mixed bag, where as one Tibetan friend put it, "anything is possible." Thus, even though our internal or personal (physiological and psychological) causes are not optimal, a positive external environment can be supportive of tremendous growth and opportunity. Conversely, with a fully functioning mind and body we can find possibility even in the most hostile of environments. In the midst of warfare, someone can create something of exquisite beauty or demonstrate a heroic and inspiring compassion. Where such disabilities as blindness would once have been the cause of a limited quality of life, there are now technologies and schools, at least in some societies, that make education and the opportunity to live a full and fulfilling life possible. So it is that we see a heroic businessman like Oskar Schindler, a deaf and blind writer of inspiring words like Helen Keller, and a crippled world leader like Franklin D. Roosevelt. In the midst of conditions that seem less than ideal for growth, individuals *do* excel and societies *do* change.

Whether our own resources are plentiful or inadequate or our environment is supportive or challenging, what seems to be crucial to us as humans is that we recognize and appreciate what we have. **You cannot hate your life and despise what resources you have been gifted with.** If you can only feel poverty and lack in your life, your mind is caught in the extremes of either self-absorbed self-aggrandizement, where you think you deserve better, or self-denigration, where you convince yourself that nothing is possible anyway. With such a mindset, there is little room for, or consideration of, real change. In such cases the experience of love is based on someone or something distracting us from our basic sense of lack. Our sense of self-worth depends on our worth to others. The spiritual life or a life focused on spiritual revolution cannot begin with such a hollow, negative state of mind. It can only lead to change based on the whim of sentimentality and a co-dependency that robs life of its vitality.

Buddhist teachers coming from the East have noted that Westerners tend to be self-effacing and prone to self-denigration; that our bravado is often a cover for a weakness of ego structure. Although the ego is eventually to be dissolved in the process of aligning ourselves to our true spiritual potential, a certain degree of confidence in ourselves at a core level is something each of us needs. There is value in being familiar with our flaws in order for us to grow as individuals. But we also must cherish those existing strengths and qualities we have that make us more effective in certain areas of our lives. Spiritual teachers Stephen and Ondrea Levine speak of "treasuring" oneself. This means "warts and all." Many of us just get into accepting the warts; it seems that it is harder for us to cherish our qualities and strengths or accept compliments for them. Without a full embracing of both dimensions, our sense of lack will sooner or later spawn a desperation that will infect our minds, corrupt our intentions, and yield ineffective, even harmful actions.

Only if you appreciate and love your life, and can embrace what tools you have to help with transformation, will you be able to live and act in a manner that is open to possibility and free from constant second guessing. **To change the world, you first have to be friends with what you have. Only then are you able to use what resources you have effectively.** Consequently, it is important to take serious stock of your life and situation. Each of us is rich and resourceful in our own way. If we are materially rich in funds, then we have a capacity to reach out to many that others may not have. Or we may not have money, but we may have time to devote to others: to help the elderly, the dying, the homeless. Some may be rich in skills or the intellectual capacities to write, teach, and research. I shall discuss this further in Chapter 9, when I examine what a fully conscious, engaged activist looks like.

With this frame of mind there arises a wholehearted and genuine gratitude. When you love your life, you are not apologizing for being. Your resourcefulness, the richness that you discover you have, gives you an opportunity to do something useful with your life. However, this gratitude is not about being meek, groveling in thankfulness, or about being benignly content just with what you have. To help us to overcome such tendencies and to further inspire a gratitude that we feel, as Tibetans would say, "in the marrow of our bones," the Buddha offers the second revolutionizing thought, which focuses on impermanence.

Thought 2: Ashes to ashes

The Buddha said, "Life is as fragile as a bubble." Here today, gone tomorrow. All is impermanent. All that is created, all that I manifest, will eventually dissolve back into the elements from which they were created. When we are conceived, within the seed of our being that is to grow and live are also contained the processes and mechanisms by which we shall surely die. Life and death come as twins, never alone, each showing its face when it is its time. Wealth comes and goes, as does poverty. Wars come and go. Peace comes and goes. How slowly or quickly these all occur is generally beyond our reckoning.

If we look at our own life, there is no point in being smug about what we have, for all of us have seen others whose fortunes have come and gone. Can we be so certain that, at some point, it will not be our turn? Similarly, we may have seen friends in dire straits rise to fame and riches. Everything is possible and everything is transient. Nothing is set in stone and even stone will one day crumble and wear away. We change within ourselves, too. If we look at our own attitudes, we see that what once gave us pleasure may no longer do so. Our source of joy at one time can be our source of misery at another. Our joy, our love of life is not dependent upon what is "out there." Our attitudes, like the seemingly solid objects or situations to which they are tied, are also impermanent.

Impermanence teaches us not to take our life for granted, nor to expect that our current resources, either internal or external, will always be there for us. As we can lose our house, we can also lose our minds. However, as frightening as this may seem on the surface, the unrelenting truth of impermanence is actually quite liberating. It can transform the way we see the world in a variety of ways. For example, if we have not fully appreciated the First Thought and view our lives as a problem, impermanence teaches us that "this too shall pass." It can help us to "lighten up" or be the cause for us to develop courage. If we appreciate our lives in general, yet recognize difficulties we are facing at this particular moment, an understanding of impermanence can give us the strength to endure. On the other hand, even if we have everything we could ever want today, but know that there is no guarantee for tomorrow, we are prompted to action. We embrace the preciousness of our lives, what is available to us, and learn to maximize what they can yield. Impermanence teaches us to be focused and resourceful. If we were to put that in political terms, say, we would see that peace is both dynamic *and* fragile. Without constant appreciation and vigilance, it can soon easily degrade into discontent and conflict.

Impermanence, therefore, can give us a sense of urgency, but it need not be tainted with panic or desperation. However, if we should happen to lapse into thinking that we must desperately hold onto what we have, the third revolutionizing thought offers the antidote.

Thought 3: Responsibility

Once we appreciate our life and its impermanence, it is a logical step to consider what we need to do if we want to maintain or improve our conditions in the future. The third of the Four Thoughts asks us to look at time and causation. The Dharma uses examples from nature to help us get a clearer picture.

Consider any plant that we wish to grow and harvest. We take the seed and put it in the ground. This sounds simple enough. But the process involves a number of steps. First, we have to be sure that we know what seed we are planting. Next, if we are to be successful with our planting, we need to know what season is best, what kind of soil is best, what depth to place the seed, when to water it, how to protect it while it germinates, sprouts, and grows. If we have inadequate information or are inattentive to any one of these details, our yield will be affected. If we cannot identify clearly what seed we are planting, why should we be so surprised if what we thought would be an apple tree turns out to be a fig? If we know we have planted an apple seed, but do not provide the right nurturing environment for the seed, why should we be surprised if the young sapling dies or the fruit is sour and infested with bugs?

The logic that applies to this example applies to everything. Everything in nature has a previous cause that is intimately and directly related to its outcome. From this we must come to understand that what we have in our life does not come to us by mere chance. The fruits of our lives, whether they are sweet or sour, are the direct result of the seeds we planted in the past, whether we see the link or not. Right from the start, we need to recognize and accept that where we are at, the resources we currently have, are the result of what we have done and how we react to what has been done to us in the past. So if we want to keep what we have, or change things for the better, it matters what we do next.

If it was positive previous actions that brought us to where we are now, then reinforcing and building on those positive actions, learning to be even more skillful, is the path we must pursue in order to improve things even further. The third of the revolutionizing thoughts is, therefore, about our own role in our own past, present, and future. In Buddhist terms this is expressed in terms of **karma** or the laws of cause and effect. In contemporary Western terms, the laws of karma are the laws of personal responsibility.

"Take personal responsibility" is almost a mantra in modern psychology. The Dharma takes this concept even further by helping us to appreciate the inevitable truth of responsibility. As we learn to love our lives and understand that rigidly holding on to what we have – or obsessively desiring what we view ourselves as not having – assures us of nothing, we learn to "let go." We release ourselves from the role of victim in our own lives, from judging ourselves in relation to others and what they have, and from seeing ourselves as being created in someone else's image. We lift our minds above a sea of self-absorption. We see "the bigger picture" – the world becomes larger and our place in it, and our hand in how things are, become more obvious. No matter how spectacular or disastrous our current lives may seem, consciously or unconsciously we have written the script in which we are acting. Knowledge of this helps us to keep our focus and to appreciate what potential our resources have. It teaches us to look down the road a bit, with a clearer sense of where we want to go next and how to get there. And, if we want positive results in the future, we must start off with a positive attitude, which is reinforced by loving our life and cherishing the possibilities we have in the moment.

Thought 4: No time to waste and nowhere to run

The fourth thought that the Buddha asks us to consider is both a summation and reinforcement of the previous three. If we love our life, know that it is impermanent, and understand that we need to accentuate what is positive in order to build something even more wonderful for the future, we have to feel a sense of commitment. We must develop the resolve to become conscious and engaged in whatever we do.

Ultimately, nothing we do is a "waste" of time, because even the time we use to distract ourselves, shirk responsibilities, or ignore what we don't want to pay attention to, become building blocks in what is to come next. The author and Buddhist nun Pema Chödrön expresses this concept in the very title of her book, *The Wisdom of No Escape*: You cannot escape your own life; all that you do, all that you have done *will* haunt you, *will* be with you to the end of your days, and – if we accept the Buddhist notion of reincarnation – beyond.

Having awakened to the truth of the first three thoughts, we are set upon a course and it is up to us whether we want to embark upon it consciously and joyfully or fight it every step of the way. Our habitual tendencies will lead us at times to resist the course. This is normal, and we can always hope that we may learn from our mistakes. But can we be more proactive, more prevention-oriented? Can we inoculate ourselves against the Three Poisons of ignorance, attachment, and aggression and their resulting negative emotional patterns, so that we can avoid habitually diving into blind alleys? When we fully appreciate how precious our life is and that it can be lost more easily than it was gained, and understand also that we cannot escape the life that is our own handiwork, it dawns on us that there is nowhere else to escape to, and no time to waste. To think or act as if this were not true is merely an exercise in futility.

Moving Forward with Heart and Mind

Living in the truth of the Four Thoughts that Revolutionize the Mind brings us to a remarkable point where we cherish every asset we have and move forward more resolutely to do what life calls upon us to do. We embark on a life that is more conscious and engaged. And that usually means that our hearts and minds have expanded sufficiently to be able to see the absolute necessity of embracing others and working for their benefit in whatever capacity we can. **When we show up in our own lives, we find that we are actually showing up for everyone.**

Knowing that experience alone may not teach us this over the course of our lives, the Buddha set out these Four Thoughts right upfront for those who would be receptive to their message. Like a sun that burns away the fog, these thoughts bring with them warmth and possibility. They cut to the chase – bring us to our senses. There is no better way to embark on any action than by allowing the Four Thoughts to be a foundation. With the Four Thoughts in mind, let us now look at the steps we need to take next in order to develop the wisdom and skill to further awaken our potential and set ourselves upon a more conscious path.

A Fine Mess: Handling the Truth

"First we make our habits. Then our habits make us."

John Dryden

The Four Thoughts that Revolutionize the Mind (see pages 30–40) go a long way toward awakening our potentiality. At least, they build a sufficient foundation to allow us to appreciate what life has to offer – they are the beginning of embracing life in a positive way and an excellent antidote to pessimism and cynicism. Life is rich. Life always holds potential. But if this is so, if all people are equal in possessing a loving nature and a "Buddha-potential," why do some see it and others not? And why do we find ourselves slipping in and out of the awareness of these possibilities?

The Four Noble Truths

These are all fair and very human questions. They are questions that bespeak the truth that we are, indeed, endowed with a loving nature at our core. These questions, set upon a foundation of appreciation inspired by the Four Thoughts, prepare us to handle what the Buddha wants us to contemplate and understand next. We are ready to deal with what he called the "Four Noble Truths."

Truth 1: Suffering is a part of human life

We suffer. For some, the first of the Buddha's "Four Noble Truths" may seem more obviously true than for others. Physical or mental sickness, poverty, warfare, and so on and on. We see all kinds of suffering around us. Yet, we also see that some people, in the midst of what we ourselves could not put up with, not only endure, but excel. Remember Helen Keller, Mother Teresa, and FDR?

On the other hand, what if we are oblivious to all of these problems? We're fit, we have our Mercedes, life is good. If there is suffering in the world, it must have to do with someone else. *We* don't suffer. *They* suffer. People can be so insulated as to think this way – and yet at the same time feel little or no motivation to care about other people's suffering. Sadly, this is one image that many in the world have of the very affluent, among whom the Americans usually feature highly.

However, this does not mean that such people do *not* suffer. The word the Buddha used for suffering was *duhkha*, which can mean anything from extreme physical pain and death to a general sense of unease or dissatisfaction with yourself and what you've got. This is the kind of underlying suffering we are talking about. This suffering is not inherent in any particular situation, but it is a part of our experience so long as we are not awakened to the strength and power of our loving nature and potential for enlightenment. **Because we are not enlightened, we are not free.** If we are not free, we suffer. Therefore, **suffering is about not being free.**

We are not free: each of us is trapped in some particular perception of how the world is and who we are in it. Of course, for the time being, everything may feel just grand. But the truth of impermanence teaches us that everything will change. Nothing is guaranteed. There can be no sanctuary, no refuge, in any knowledge that our world will stay this way. And if nothing else, even if things stay just the way we want them to, we are going to grow old and die. So we will continue to suffer until our minds are free and we can "embrace change," "go with the flow" or, as Werner Erhard, the founder of EST, used to say, "Ride the horse in the direction it is going."

As a person wanting to be an agent of social or political change, you need to understand suffering at this level. The extremes of physical and mental suffering – the suffering of personal or geopolitical adversity and disaster – is easy to see and understand. But the level of suffering we speak of here goes much deeper and is far more insidious. It can cause you to make grave errors of judgment. You have to understand that you suffer from your biases: your biases and preconceptions lock you into seeing only certain possibilities and not others. If you are not free to see the whole picture, the greater is the likelihood that your actions will be shortsighted and partisan, and have unexpected and unintended effects. If we want to be more accurately focused – if we want our hearts and minds to be free and thus have access to deeper wisdom and greater skill to accomplish what we set out to accomplish – we need to understand the underlying cause of this deeper suffering, this "unsatisfactoriness." The Buddha wants us to focus on what part we ourselves play in our not being free. To answer this question, he gives us the Second Noble Truth.

Truth 2: We suffer because we crave

According to Buddhist cosmology, there are Six Realms of Existence (see page 31). Beings are born into various "realms," or types of existence, each of which is dominated by a particular strong negative emotional or psychological pattern. In the realm of the gods (*devas*), the dominant emotion is said to be pride. Beings in the realm of the "jealous gods" (*ashuras*) – the wannabe *devas* – are bound up in issues of envy and power. The inhabitants of the realm of "hungry ghosts," or restless spirits (*pretas*), are driven by insatiable greed that leaves these beings wandering and dissatisfied. Beings in the realm of *hells* – places of fire and ice – are caught so tightly in a mindset of anger and rage that they cannot but see the world as either too "hot" or too "cold" to endure. In the realm of animals, beings live instinctually, hard-wired to their senses, preying on others and in fear of being preyed upon. Then there is the human realm, in which the beings are governed by desire, or **craving**, which the Buddha called *trishna* (literally, "thirst").

The Six Realms are understood both literally, as a description of the beings that inhabit the universe, and also metaphorically, as a description of human emotional and psychological states. While we will all attest to having experienced most of these states at one time or another, craving – wanting, desiring – is the strongest force in the human psyche.

Each of these six negative emotional states are, in various forms, manifestations of the "Three Poisons" of ignorance, attachment, and aggression (see page 12). Simply put, and in human terms, we don't fully understand what is going on around us; we have our own beliefs about what we think is happening around us based on our desire to see things a certain way; and we actively resist anyone who tries to get us to see things differently. If we look at any aspect of our lives, we shall see these Three Poisons at work. For example, say we have a pain in our lower back but do not realize it is because our kidneys are not working all that well. Not understanding how various foods in our diet affect us, we carry on drinking ten cups of coffee a day. We may observe, even acknowledge, that our pain gets worse when we drink coffee. But, *we* just love coffee. What would life be without our Starbucks? But then our doctor diagnoses a kidney problem and suggests to us that we might want to cut back or eliminate coffee as it might be contributing to our kidney pain. Because we want to believe in a world where this is not true, we refuse to acknowledge the facts and carry on drinking coffee.

Or take another example, in relationships. We see a good friend talking to someone we despise. We have no idea what they are talking about. But, in the emotional turmoil of wanting not to believe what we are seeing, we draw erroneous conclusions about their interaction. "Maybe they were talking negatively about me? How can I ever trust my friend again?" And so the drama of a personal soap opera begins.

One final example from political reality. Most of us don't understand all of the ins and outs of the US government's Middle East policies. Nevertheless, in spite of our ignorance, some of us want to believe so badly that our officials know what they are doing that we become vehemently defensive in favor of the government. On the other side of the political fence, some of us – equally ignorant of the full picture – want not to believe what the government says and become equally emphatic about what we believe to be the administration's lack of credibility and even legitimacy.

Because everyday reality is so infinitely complex, relative, ambiguous, and multilayered, ignorance will remain a part of our consciousness until we are fully enlightened and can see all the interrelated factors and how they dynamically come together to create what they do. Ignorance causes us erroneously to see things in simple, seemingly solid terms, and informs our decisions and actions. What holds ignorance in place, what makes how we see things seem solid, is *not* their solidity, but our *wanting* to have things solid, so that we can feel more secure. But this is like trying to hold onto a handful of sand – it slips through our fingers. The solid and secure position that we crave in the universe is an illusion.

This wanting or craving arises from our illusory belief that we can know ourselves by fixing our relationship to what is outside of ourselves. But because that which is outside of ourselves is constantly changing, the belief is false and, in fact, our clinging to it only creates more insecurity. Thus, while the other two poisons of ignorance and aggression wreak their own havoc in our lives, the Buddha focuses on the linchpin of our humanity, which is our craving – our attachment to things, sensations, beliefs, and emotional patterns.

Truth 3: There can be an end to craving

To reassure us that not all is hopeless, and to motivate us to change our point of view, overcome the Three Poisons that drive our lives, and activate our potential, the third of the Noble Truths tells us that **there is a way out of this mess**. The way out is to free our minds of craving. For until we stop wanting the world to be a certain way, we shall have no option but to limit our possibilities and drive away – even, on a larger scale, wage war with – those who see the world differently from us. Our actions will become reinforced into reactive, habitual patterns that seem intractable and irreversible. And the cycle of suffering, unease, dissatisfaction, will continue.

Because we are beings of desire, to eliminate craving altogether seems a bit rash. It sounds inhuman. After all, what about the desire for something good, something better? Then again, how can we really know what is good or better if we are still wallowing in ignorance? Understanding this dilemma and knowing that our humanity and how we express it will always be marked by desire, the Buddha is not asking for some immediate or radical shift that renders us passionless automatons. Rather, he offers a well-developed plan to dismantle this craving and transform it into a wellspring from which to benefit others. This is what he presents to us as the Fourth Noble Truth.

Truth 4: To be free of craving, follow the Eightfold Path

The Fourth Noble Truth is to help us free the unlimited potentiality of our minds and bodies. It is about helping us "to be in the world, but not of it." We can learn to be detached, but engaged; passionate, but not obsessed. This is the purpose of what the Buddha spelled out as the **Noble Eightfold Path**, which he described as: "right view, right thought, right speech, right action, right livelihood, right effort, right mindfulness, right concentration." They are traditionally divided into three categories: morality (right speech, right action, right livelihood); meditation (right effort, right mindfulness, right concentration); and the development of wisdom and insight (right view, right thought).

The Eightfold Path or *Middle Way* is a blueprint for a life lived as a conscious, engaged activist. The eight aspects of this path are essentially an educational process that embraces all the ways in which we become a well-rounded, intelligent, civilized, and useful member of humanity. The Buddha's teaching, the Dharma, outlines ways of focusing and deepening our minds, and provides guidelines for how we behave in the world. Through meditation, the application of morality, and the cultivation of insight, our thoughts become clearer; our view of the world becomes more based in reality, our speech becomes more precise, our actions become more skillful and focused; our livelihood becomes more productive and beneficial to all those around us; our efforts focused and constant, our memory unlimited; and our meditation practice unending – and the constant source that underpins and fosters all the other seven aspects of the Path.

The word "right" as an adjective before each aspect suggests that what is offered supports an unfolding of the true Buddha-nature, our loving nature, that the Buddha knows is our birthright. As we build each of these dimensions in our lives we grow as individuals until, in the end, we manifest and contribute to a positive vision of the future for all those around us. It is a model for enlightened citizenship.

For someone "wanting" to tap into and grow through the wisdom that informs all aspects of this conscious, engaged lifestyle, meditation is a key ingredient. It is one thing merely to understand intellectually the workings of the Three Poisons and the incessant allure of craving in our lives. However, because as humans we have the in-built capacity to change, the main emphasis of the Dharma is on us actively taking greater responsibility for our lives by learning methods that allow us to see the strands of the web that holds together our habitual patterns. As we work with these meditative methods, freedom begins to emerge and inform our choices. We access our inner resources more easily and effortlessly and can discern how to use them and when.

This may seem a long, lonely road to walk. But with workable methods and the support of friends along the way, it will not be long before we begin to develop a lightness of being. When that happens, the fresh air of freedom will be exhilarating.

Intention: Planting the Seed of Action

"If you always think what you've always thought,

You will always do what you've always done.

If you always do what you've always done,

You will always get what you've always got.

If you always get what you've always got,

You will always think what you've always thought."

Anonymous

As a therapist, I periodically work with relaxation techniques. Many years ago, I learned of a method that ended a period of deep rest with the thought of "intending to move." I would say to my blissfully resting client, "Now, I want you to think about moving. Just think about it. Focus all of your intention on moving, but don't yet move a muscle." The effect of this preparation for coming out of relaxation was dramatic. The client would come out of the exercise both deeply relaxed and totally charged and alert to get on with the day.

So powerful are our intentions that the Vajrayana, or Tantric, Buddhist tradition goes so far as to say that intention is the key: it is even more important than the act that follows from it. As the inspiration of what arises from emptiness to become manifest, one cannot speak of action without first speaking of intention. The power of intention is the beginning of a gathering of a force: a focusing that is possibly more dynamic in terms of what it mobilizes inside us than the resulting act itself. It is intention that informs our thoughts and emotions about the action we plan to carry out. It moves us to the threshold of action, and the degree to which we are certain or uncertain, committed or reluctant in our intention will determine the energy and force that go into making our action deliver the impact that we intend – regardless of its positive or negative virtues. But before we get too carried away, let's look at action in general first.

The Force of Karma

The biblical adage "As you sow, so shall you reap," is a Western way of expressing what in the East is called **karma**. The word karma itself means literally "action." Such "action" is a part of a continuum of events – which we conventionally distinguish from one another although in reality they are all interlinked –

which leads from the past, through the present, into the future. This can lead some to assume that there is a kind of "predestined" quality to things that happen, as when we hear people saying "It's your karma," or that such-and-such an incident was "karmic." The result can be a fatalistic view which certainly is neither Buddhist, nor, to my understanding, what the biblical adage was driving at. Rather, all events or actions are "precursors," which predispose what follows to have one outcome rather than another.

However, in a universe where anything is possible, the unexpected can occur. In the realm of human action – in the karma that we as humans create – it would seem that this possibility often arises because of our capacity to choose. The degree to which *we follow* the path along which the precursors seem to point determines the predictability of the outcome. This is neither good nor bad. It just is.

Karma, as we speak of it here, is a process. Circumstances that arise in our life in the present are the result of the past. How we interpreted situations in the past and acted on them, and our mental/emotional state following those past actions, determine how we act and feel now. How we act and feel now, how we interpret our current experience, is the basis of what we are to experience in the future. Thus in our lives, we have a habit of returning to "the scene of the crime." The "crimes" are ours, rooted in the Three Poisons (see page 12), reinforced into well-trodden, seemingly intractable habitual patterns. These patterns can create the illusion of predestination – the tangled web we weave, the vicious cycle – and cast us into a despair that seeks salvation at the hands of something or someone outside of ourselves.

The possibility of change

However, the Buddha taught that the reins for steering a new course are always in our hands. We always get a chance to make something new from our past. If we re-enact our old pattern, more than likely the pattern will go on into the future. As the quote at the beginning of the chapter says, "If you always do what you have always done, you will always get what you have always got." On the other hand, if we learn to step back, learn ways of being able to create space mentally and to see openness and opportunity – rather than another scene of a soap opera or tragic drama – then we can take a new course. History need not repeat itself if we sincerely make the effort to wake up from what would otherwise be habitual, reflexive reactions that have been reinforced time after time "since beginningless time."

To stop the repetition of history – what the Buddha called cyclic existence as depicted in traditional Tibetan paintings of "The Wheel of Life" – requires work. This work is, in fact, the purpose of the Dharma, the Buddha's teachings. These teachings are rooted in what he himself experienced in the process of his own enlightenment. As a fellow human going through the full array of thoughts, emotions, and experiences that we all go through, he saw that the work he had done in himself was a useful path for others to consider putting into practice in their own lives. Just some well thought out suggestions based on his experience. And for generations it seems that these suggestions have been useful.

The path that the Buddha suggests is not based on something so radically different from how we might try to resolve and work with matters in our own lives. However, he offers a systematic way of looking at and using our own resources wisely and with skill. If ever there was a "roadmap for peace," the Dharma – which literally means "the way things are" – is the Buddha's recommended route.

In Chapter Six, you will be presented with various meditative exercises and practices to help you to focus your mind more clearly. They can be done alone or in a group. Their purpose is to help the mind to disrupt the habitual patterns that send us blindly following courses of action that afterward leave us with varying degrees of regret. These universal mind tools can be applied to whatever course of action you will choose, providing you with greater discernment through each stage of every action.

In Chapter Two, I mentioned the idea that every action has four distinct aspects, or components (see page 22). Therefore, the action of stepping onto the path of the Buddha – or any other path for that matter – has the same four aspects. These elements and how they come together determine whether an action yields positive, negative, or mixed results for the future. To recapitulate and elaborate on what I said earlier, the four aspects of every action are **intention, contemplation, the act committed as a result of these,** and lastly, **one's attitude or demeanor both while doing the act and in response to its result.** As intention is the beginning of the process, it is now time to give it our attention.

Intention: The Road to Hell...

History offers us countless stories of individuals and nations whose intentions were good – at least from their own vantage point. Looking back, we can now say with some degree of certainty that these intentions and what followed from them were not particularly beneficial. The siege of Canaan in the name of God; the Babylonian conquests in the name of many gods; Hellenic and Roman imperialism; the Crusades; the Spanish Inquisition; the Mogul invasions; the American Civil War; the Russian Revolution; the rise of the Nazis; Hiroshima and Nagasaki; the Chinese Cultural Revolution; the Korean

War; Vietnam; "ethnic cleansing" in former Yugoslavia and Rwanda; and now the conflicts in the Persian Gulf: conquests, empires, and wars perpetrated by people convinced of the supremacy of their own spiritual or secular ideology, believing that the world would be a much better place if only everyone was like them, agreed with them or, if necessary, was controlled by them – for their own good.

But to focus only on extraordinary individuals and events, misses in many respects the ordinary workings of intention in the everyday lives of each and every one of us. Our own conquests, empires, and wars may be on a smaller scale but they happen for very much the same reasons. Achieving mastery over our delusions at the most personal level is the essential antidote for preventing disasters of greater magnitude.

Chain reactions

Buddhist philosophy speaks of what is called **dependent origination** (the term is also rendered as "dependent arising" or "interdependent origination"). The Buddha explained it as follows: "Because this is present, that will arise, and because that was born, this is being born." Simply put, it means that nothing arises independently – everything has causes and consequences. This is also described as a "chain of becoming" called the Twelve Links, or *Nidanas*. These twelve steps, each leading to the next, flesh out the process by which the Three Poisons of ignorance, attachment, and aggression are linked together. These links, which our minds naturally go through in forming our likes, dislikes, or sense of indifference, may be distilled as follows: Not knowing who we are (out of ignorance), we fall prey to a cascade of mental, emotional, and physical events that we classify according to one of three categories: attachment, aversion, indifference. In other words: what we like, what we don't like, and what we don't notice or care about one way or the other.

We habitually set our intention to have more experiences that we like (things to which we are attached), and eliminate or minimize those experiences that we don't like (things to which we feel aversion). Perhaps we like chocolate ice cream, but gag at the taste of strawberry or butterscotch. Most likely we'll arrange our lives in order to have more chocolate and less strawberry or butterscotch. Or say we like cold weather and skiing; this may plant in our minds the intention of moving to Colorado in the future. And when people talk about vacationing in Florida, we scratch our heads and don't understand why anyone would want to hang out on a humid beach on the edge of a swamp.

And so it goes on. Maybe these choices aren't the best for us. Maybe we don't have the full picture and are missing out on something. But our intentions are driven – for better or worse – by craving, as the Second Noble Truth tells us (see page 45). The choices we make are subjective, for obviously others might choose the opposite with just as much zeal and intent. Let's look at a more interpersonal example. We may intensely dislike someone who is deeply loved by another. We may even see someone as a demon or a tyrant, while to another they are a saint and savior. And consider how even our own view of someone may change radically, depending on time and circumstances.

An extraordinary example of this is the case of Osama Bin Laden. For years he helped in the resistance against the Soviet Union in Afghanistan, for which the US government paid and praised him. Then, following his various attacks on American interests where Bin Laden demonstrated that he was no longer happy with his relationship with the US, he became a demon in the West. Yet he is viewed as a saint and savior by those who believe that what he is doing is upholding their traditions.

This process of dependent origination, which takes us through our likes, dislikes, and indifferences, happens in an instant and over time. It is the commonplace path we have trodden since birth and (in the Buddhist view) before. Because it is commonplace, it seems "natural." But, because it is rooted in the Three Poisons, we can easily mistake what is *habitual* for what is natural. That is why, when it comes to breaking habits, everything seems so topsy-turvy and unnatural. We get caught up in the belief that what we think and the meanings we give to things, how we act and how the world appears to us, are all solid realities. We fail to look behind the scenes to see that it is our cravings and intentions based on those cravings that lead us along our habitual well-trodden way. Possibility is limited as we follow the path of predictable outcomes. This pattern is neither good nor bad, but if we want to change it and go in a new direction, we need to be a bit bolder.

The truth is, as the Dharma teaches, that all phenomena are characterized by "**emptiness**." What this term means in a Buddhist context is that nothing has a permanent, constant, unambiguous identity, because everything is dependent on something else. Nothing exists purely in and of itself. So there can be no clear distinction between good-bad and like-dislike. The so-called reality that we perceive is merely an intellectual convenience, a way of ordering the world so that we can try to understand it. But we do not see this. How we measure and define the world and our reaction to it is based on misinformation and a craving for things to be a certain way. As long as this remains true, it is completely out of the question that our intention can lead to whatever perfect consequence we are pursuing. Our course of action will inevitably have pitfalls and unintended effects, no matter how "perfect" it seems for the moment.

The Ultimate Intention: The Four Limitless Meditations

His Holiness the Dalai Lama and other Buddhist teachers say that in the final analysis, all any of us ever wants is to be happy. And because, as the Buddha himself believed, we have an inherently loving nature, we also want the people around us to be happy too. As we focus on becoming conscious, engaged activists, happiness – for ourselves and others – is what we would like to see as the consequence of whatever we do, be it a small personal act or one that has geopolitical implications. The Buddha suggests that we hold this intention as the general, ultimate basis that informs and shapes every other intention we have to change the world for the better in some way. In Buddhist terminology, we are speaking about ultimate and relative bodhichitta. Bodhichitta means "awakened heart." Ultimate bodhichitta is the clear, unbridled, profound, altruistic intention of wanting all to be truly happy. Relative, or actively manifested, bodhichitta is how we set out to accomplish turning that intention into an everyday reality.

Bodhichitta underlies a wonderful meditative prayer of aspiration in the Buddhist tradition called the Four Limitless Meditations. In one translation, it reads as follows:

> "May all beings have happiness and the causes of happiness.
>
> May all beings be free from suffering and the causes of suffering.
>
> May they never be separated from the great happiness that is beyond suffering.
>
> May they dwell in great equanimity which is beyond passion, aggression, and prejudice."

Each line of this prayer has multiple layers of meanings, from the most mundane, everyday way of understanding the words to more profound levels of Buddhist philosophy. The prayer can in itself be a foundation for focused meditation practice and study. My comments will stick to the more general meanings, as they apply to setting one's intention for actions that create the most beneficial outcomes. To accomplish this, let us briefly examine each line of this prayer separately.

"May all beings have happiness and the causes of happiness."

We all want to be happy, and this line expresses the intention that happiness will come about in our lives. This happiness is not the feeling most of us have from time to time: a pleasant experience but an all too transient one. What the prayer is aspiring to is a *true and lasting* happiness, which is another matter. Rather than being tossed about on an ocean of highs and lows by the Three Poisons, we are seeking a happiness rooted in the enlightened freedom achieved by transforming these poisons. We wish to see ignorance transformed into an experience of our unlimited potential and capacities; attachment transformed into a mental and emotional state that is light, spacious, and capable of knowing anything and everything; and the heat of our aggressive tendencies transformed into the fire of joy and spontaneity.

But even before our happiness becomes rooted in such enlightenment, any experience of happiness, however fleeting, itself creates space and possibility. When we are happy, "in a good mood," we tend to act in ways that are more benevolent and beneficial. At such times we may be happy for reasons growing from the shaky ground of selfish desires, and the benevolence or kindness we show may be limited to those who in turn will bring about more happiness for us. Still, there is virtue in it and it demonstrates that at our core, there is a loving nature.

Of course, we may not agree with what another person does or find the reasons for their happiness acceptable. We may even challenge them directly about their actions, and this challenging may express itself in the form of conflict at every imaginable level. We may, in fact, be their active adversaries. But if we understand that the greatest good comes out of a happy mind, we shall retain at all times the ultimate compassionate wish that how they think and what they do now will become transformed into a better way of being – a way of being that guarantees a lasting happiness.

What often makes this difficult for us is when we see someone being happy at our or other people's misery or misfortune. Because a positive emotion is associated with what we find disagreeable, we want to lash out, to make them suffer like we have suffered. We want to "wipe the smile off their faces." To curb a mind inclined towards retaliation is no small thing. But it is the high road, the noble road that this particular line of the meditation encourages. I can recall seeing on television the jubilant Palestinians celebrating the fall of New York's Twin Towers. For certain, such jubilation more than likely arose from a general dislike for American policies or values. It may, therefore be understandable. But, happiness at someone else's expense is always problematic and sows seeds for further enmity. It is born out of attachments to mental and emotional patterns – rooted in the Three Poisons – that have given rise to a skewed view of the world. We don't want anyone to stop being happy. But we sincerely want them to be happy for the right reasons. That is compassion in action.

Along the same lines, in a conversation about the current US political situation, Lama Surya Das commented that he was dismayed to see Western Buddhists entering into the political fray for negative reasons: being depressed with the current situation, disliking the current administration, the president, the military, and so on. Although we may have perfectly valid reasons for not being pleased with what is happening around us, to succumb to negativism, name-calling, belittlement, and the deriding of character just poisons the situation further, making people defensive and weakening our own character in the long run. Former President Bill Clinton believed in trying to operate on higher moral ground by avoiding such negative tactics. While he may not always have succeeded, I believe that this generally positive approach may, in the long run, lead to more people and historians remembering his presidency in a favorable light.

More to the point, if we really want people to be happy, then does it matter who is creating the conditions for them to become happy? If it were possible for our political opponents to create better circumstances in the long run, should we be so partisan as not to be supportive and wish them good luck? If winning comes about only through attacking and destroying everything the other side wants and does and not valuing it for whatever it has contributed, then we do not move on. We are always in the position of starting over again – and more than likely having to fend off the enemies we have created with our negative attitude.

This doesn't mean that we let up on our vigilance. It does not mean we don't vote for change. What it does mean is that we value everyone and appreciate that they are doing their best based on what they know. And, if their actions are rooted in the Three Poisons, then we hope that the causes and conditions that will allow them to see things differently will arise for them.

Toward this end, we look at the last portion of the first line of the prayer: may all beings have "the causes of happiness." The causes of happiness can be all of the conditions we looked at in the discussion of the "precious human birth" (see page 31). We would like people to be strong in body and mind, to have good mental and emotional capacities, and to find themselves in an environment that is conducive to supporting their experience of a lasting happiness. The Buddha's idea of the precious human birth reminds us of both the internal and external conditions needed to bring happiness about. It provides us with the general guidelines for what needs to happen. It is then for us to see where we are and set our minds and hearts on whatever aspect of these conditions we can improve.

At a deeper level, there is one single cause of happiness: the transformation of the Three Poisons. As we can see that all of our suffering and despair are the result of the Three Poisons, creating the conditions for us to learn how to uproot and transform the Poisons is, in the long run, the only guarantee that "happiness follows us to the end of our days." Depending on our capacities, we may have a greater or lesser ability to transform our living conditions and situations, or those of others. Having few material resources, we may nevertheless possess the ability to influence others by uplifting their experience and providing them with ways to transform. If nothing else, we can at least start with ourselves.

The attitude behind this meditation is **unconditional love**. Understanding that every single being looks for happiness, we realize the power that lies in first and always looking for the best in ourselves and others. For as we do this, and as the space this creates in our hearts and minds becomes a more ever-present reality, it encourages us to work in the world in even stronger, more dynamic, and more powerful ways. This leads us to the remaining three of the Four Limitless Meditations, each of which must be built upon a foundation of love.

"May all beings be free from suffering and the causes of suffering."

None of us wants to suffer. None of us wants to endure conditions that cause us to suffer. We try our best to eliminate those things in our lives that make us suffer. However, because we often fail to understand fully how we got into our predicament in the first place, we are usually at best only partially successful in our efforts. We may be able to get out of a particular abusive relationship or become free from some other oppressive force in our lives and our suffering, as we currently understand it, may be diminished dramatically. However, unless we understand that the reason this suffering *arose* is the result of the work of the Three Poisons in our lives, it is likely that we shall fall into a similar pattern in the future.

If we meditate on this we see how difficult it is to make real, lasting changes in our lives. Certainly our worldly, material conditions may change for the better. But how hard it is to overcome our own impatience, anger, frustration, pride, greed, or torpor. Real, lasting change – to be "away from suffering" – requires us to cultivate the Six *Paramitas*, or Perfections, of a compassionate, awakened being: diligence, patience, generosity, wisdom, exertion, and meditative insight. Developing these attributes within ourselves ultimately transforms us and they become the basis upon which we work with and transform the lives and conditions of others.

Understanding this meditation fully, we do not get discouraged when we work at changing something in someone else's life, only to watch as they re-enact the whole scenario over again. Nor do we disregard or disparage those whose lives it seems are devoted to creating suffering in the lives of others. Of course, it is much easier to show care and compassion for a victim than for a perpetrator. But here, we must understand that even the most heinous villain, torturer, or despot is living their lives in the midst of the Three Poisons. They may be hopelessly misguided, but we must always remember that they *are* misguided. Hopefully, in creating positive conditions around someone, we support them in accessing their own resources to make the necessary internal changes.

But, as we know from the chemistry lab of our own experience, making these internal transformations can be an incremental, painstakingly slow process. While the transformation of the Three Poisons within ourselves yields the greatest, lasting results in ensuring that our old habits do not prevail, we should not abandon trying to improve the external conditions that hold back the process of internal change. Changing the world takes time. Changing the mind can, in the Buddhist view, take lifetimes. We need to do both, and accept that the time frame for the transformation of each is radically different. Our world can look so different from one election to the next. But, until our minds are truly transformed, the change we so desperately wanted and celebrate upon its arrival will, once again, fade from view and the cycle of suffering will continue.

We may look around our world and see that we are not doing a very good job at eradicating or preventing suffering. But I think it is important to remember that we *are* capable of overcoming sickness, poverty, and warfare. Indeed, we have done it, time and again. There are parts of the world where most people live in peace, free from many dangerous illnesses and from extreme poverty. That we desire to see an end to these things *at all* is a testimony to the compassionate heart of humanity. This is what this line of the meditation appeals to. If we can reinforce this tendency through overcoming what is base in our habitual personal and collective lives, then we can create a society whose foundation for change, growth, and transformation is assured.

According to the Buddha, this is not just some Utopian dream. It is said that in all of the universes that can be seen with the eye of enlightened wisdom, suffering-free societies and worlds do exist. That we even imagine a world without such suffering lets us know that it is conceptually in the realm of the possible. At times we may seem closer, at times further away from this as a reality in our own lives. This is natural while we have not yet cleared our own lives of the effects of the Three Poisons. Nor can we ever really give up, for to give up would be to disregard fully our loving nature – our humanity. Ultimately, we cannot do that. Our loving nature will not stand for it.

In committing ourselves to developing the love and compassion expressed in these first two of the Four Limitless Meditations, we are undertaking to cease contributing to the perpetuation of suffering. And that is no small thing.

"May they never be separated from the great happiness that is beyond suffering."

The "great happiness" that is referred to in the third of the Four Limitless Meditations is the lasting happiness of enlightenment; that is, being free from the fetters of the Three Poisons. Our craving no longer exists so nor does the suffering that it generates. This releases all of our potentiality and makes it available to benefit everyone around us.

No effort, however small, that we make toward attaining this end is ever wasted or lost, if that effort is made with love and compassion. We understand that if we seek to become a conscious, engaged activist committed to seeing good happen in the world, love and compassion are not options. They are prerequisites. By developing a loving attitude and acting in the world compassionately, we create healthy positive conditions in which the true cause of suffering, the Three Poisons, can become transformed. Knowing that this is how true change for the good takes place, we embrace whatever we do wholeheartedly, with joy.

"Joy" in Tibetan is *tsultrim*, a word that also means "discipline." This does not mean pushing yourself or placing some kind of external constraint on yourself in order to force compliance. "Discipline" in this sense is what naturally arises when you know that what you are doing makes sense and guarantees a positive result. You can put all of your energy into what it is that you are doing and, if it is truly a worthwhile effort, a natural warmth or joy will arise.

Knowing that what we do is worth doing bolsters our commitment and resolve. This in turn can inspire the actual willingness to stand up for what we are doing and protect those who need to be protected. Hence this line of the Four Limitless Meditations not only contains the grandest of all wishes – that all may be uplifted and transformed – but it also inspires courage and a willingness to go the distance. It is a line of unshakeable conviction.

"May they dwell in great equanimity, which is beyond passion, aggression, and prejudice."

This last line of the Four Limitless Meditations is about our altruistic intention to benefit all *impartially*. With the gathering up of our love, compassion, and conviction, we are asked to meditate on the importance of using these assets for the benefit of all. Many Buddhist texts talk about altruistic intention and doing whatever you do "for the benefit of all sentient beings." If one fully understands that we are inextricably interlinked with everyone and everything around us, then to be preoccupied only with one's own wishes and interests is a horrible miscalculation. Holding to an illusion of separation from those around us ensures that cooperation in our efforts will always be limited, partisan, and eventually attract attention from other parts of reality denied. For usually what is denied must, in effect, speak louder to get its fair share of attention. Thus it is that those who feel disfranchised or disregarded in society must often resort to tactics that draw attention, whether they be brash, outlandish, or antisocial. Protests, civil disobedience, even terrorist attacks basically aim to get their perpetrators acknowledged as part of the equation, worthy of consideration.

In essence, then, this line is about overcoming self-interest or partisan behavior. There may be some short-term benefits to such behavior, but in the long run a strategy of exclusion will eventually leave us out in the cold. The truth of this is evident and can be witnessed at almost every level of human interaction. Putting our earlier examples in more theoretical or philosophical terms in the public arena is the way partisan interests have spawned (and have always spawned) political polarization; where the gray, ambiguous realities of relative reality are forced into the starkness of simplistic black-and-white, good-versus-evil debate. In such an atmosphere, even if "your" side prevails, the tactics deployed to counter the "opposition" often simply serve to generate further partisan behavior that in turn reinforces and perpetuates the polarization – and so on and on.

If we embark on the process of transforming the Three Poisons – in this meditation referred to as "passion [craving/ attachment], aggression, and prejudice [ignorance]" – we logically begin to enter the state of equanimity, treating all impartially. This state progresses as the Poisons weaken and our being and actions take on more enlightened qualities. At the same time we should not understand equanimity or impartiality as meaning that we treat everyone and everything equally, in exactly the same way. Impartiality has more to do with an attitude than an action. It involves greater discrimination.

For example, let us look at the saying, "One man's meat is another man's poison." Supposing we make a meal for two visitors, and for dessert we offer one visitor ice cream and the other just a plain apple. From an outsider's point of view, this seems unfair. And certainly, if we are basing this selection on liking one person more than the other, then we are acting from bias based on the poison of ignorance and the judgment against us is true. However, if our decision is based on the simple fact that we have taken the trouble to find out that one visitor prefers ice cream and the other prefers fruit, we are displaying a concern to be impartial based on discernment. In doing so we have taken a step away from ignorance toward true knowledge and compassion. And compassion, as we shall learn in a later chapter, is best applied with knowledge born of discernment.

Nor does impartiality necessarily mean that you have to *like* everyone equally. The great Tibetan teacher Gampopa once said "It is the sign of a superior person that he treats all with equanimity, yet still has a few good friends." We each have our preferences, and tend to befriend those with whom we feel an affinity. Buddhist teachers say that much of this is karmic, based on bonds created in previous lives. Regardless of whether or not you believe in reincarnation, we still feel a kinship toward some more than others. This is only a problem if your view of others is skewed by prejudices rooted in ignorance. In political terms, this is the basis of "good old boy" or "school-tie" politics and "cronyism." Preferential treatment and favoritism is always divisive.

What this line of the meditation helps guard against, therefore, is elitism. Meditating on the meaning of this line, and thus committing oneself to opening up to others and to making the effort to live and act in a more enlightened way, a natural charisma emerges. This charisma, together with all the other positive attributes we are now committed to developing, leads to a widening of our sphere of influence. The four meditations are considered "limitless," or immeasurable, because the more one lives in their truth, the greater the effect one has in the world – an effect that potentially knows no bounds.

Reflecting upon, and attempting to embrace, the Four Limitless Meditations is a tremendous antidote to corruption. Truly contemplating its meaning in relation to the acts one is intending to embark upon in the coming day, and then reflecting upon those acts in the evening, is a way of keeping us honest and disciplined. Until we are completely enlightened and can see beyond the illusions of time and space, the outcome of any of our actions will always remain a mystery unfolding. No doubt there will often be times when we blow it. If we have a small influence on what happens in the world around us, more than likely we shall see small mistakes. If we have more power and influence in the world, we shall more than likely see larger mistakes. At the end of each day, consider asking yourself the following questions:

> Am I happy tonight? Are the people around me happy tonight?
>
> Am I upset by what I have done today? Has anyone been harmed by what I have done today?
>
> Are there ways I can improve what I do to ensure that any harm caused is reversed, that those around me are protected from harm, and that those who are happy can continue to be happy?
>
> Did I act in a way today that is impartial? Did I treat all around me with the same degree of fairness and loving concern?

If we ask ourselves these questions daily, then recommit ourselves to fulfilling the Four Limitless Meditations in the days to come, we anchor our lives and actions in a way that helps us to grow into the potentiality that we are now beginning to awaken.

The Power of Confession and Dedication

When we begin our day with the altruistic intention to be of use and service, and end it with a reflection on the fruits of our actions and attitudes, what we are creating is a spiritualized life. This way of being is reflected in the Vajrayana Buddhist practice of *sadhana*, a highly structured meditation form that follows the ways in which we psychologically prepare for action in the world, then carry it out. A sadhana starts with focusing on creating the inner resources to act in accordance with our altruistic intention, our "awakened heart," or bodhichitta (see above, page 58). We seek to access, then expand, the energy of particular positive qualities (wisdom, compassion, power, protection, and so on). Following such a template, we can focus our intention, assess what positive resources we have or need to have to carry out the action that is the manifest expression of that intention, and then act with clarity and good heart. What rounds out this process is our ability accurately and honestly to reflect upon what has happened as a result. In most of our activities the longer term results of our actions may barely be known, camouflaged in the clouds of the future. So, while we cannot necessarily judge the outcome of our action, we can certainly reflect on our efforts. We can assess our efforts honestly.

Throughout our day, did our mind stray? Were we always thinking altruistically or did some self-centered wishes and thoughts invite themselves in? Did these wishes and thoughts make our efforts sloppy and less effective, and if so, how? We examine these shortcomings with an eye to making our actions even more precisely focused and effective in the day to come.

To clarify this process and to demarcate it more succinctly and powerfully in our minds, the formal practice of sadhana ends with confession and dedication. In the ordinary course of carrying on our business, these words may sound a bit too religious or sanctimonious. However, the psychological discipline and willingness to go through these processes as part of our actions makes their effects even more potent.

Confession embraces all of the daily questions we can ask

ourselves in order to evaluate how well we have carried out our intentions through our actions. To make this process more dramatic and effective as a cause for change in the future, confession is about fully acknowledging where our actions were done with less than pure motive, where they were ineffective, and where they created unintended outcomes. We accept our responsibility for this and take it on board, not in order to punish ourselves, but rather to acknowledge *with compassion* our human frailties. We show compassion toward ourselves and do not lapse into negative self-denigration, and so create a positive springboard upon which to recommit our efforts to act with clear intent, more skillfully, and free of self-interest or partisanship.

Confession reintroduces us to our purity. It brings us back to our loving nature in a very simple and direct manner. And then we can go one step further. We can dedicate our efforts.

As I have said at other times, nothing is ever lost. No positive thought or action, however small or seemingly insignificant, is a wasted effort. Just as it is possible to compound misery, it is also possible to compound virtue and goodness. For this, we need to celebrate. We celebrate in order to connect with the joy and warmth that is an expression of our loving nature. We do this not because we want some warm, fuzzy, feel-good pleasure from what we've done. We do it for others.

Focusing again on the altruistic intention that we started our day with, we use our warmth and joy as a force to spread out the fruits of our actions to each and every being. Initially, we may think of seeing these good feelings spreading to those whose lives and hearts we wished to touch today. But, in improving the lives and conditions of these people, we create a ripple effect that touches those to whom these people are in turn connected. And so on and so on… Therefore, in dedicating the fruits of our efforts today, we don't hold back. We see them as limitless, touching more and more beings.

In the Vajrayana tradition of Buddhism, altruistic intention and dedication are the crown jewels. Altruistic intention immediately makes the application of our actions more effective. But dedication is even more powerful, as it takes the wish that you started your day with and sends it out into the world, riding on the energy of our tangible efforts. In a very powerful way, we turn our intention into a reality. It becomes a building block upon which tomorrow's renewed efforts can be constructed, inviting and generating more virtue and goodness.

Dedicating our efforts is more than simply *wishing* to make a difference. In dedicating, we celebrate that we *are making* a difference. And we invite everyone to join the celebration.

It would be interesting to speculate whether world leaders, present and past, have ever begun or ended their day with their intentions focused in the way outlined in this chapter. If so, particularly in the case of those known as tyrants or the perpetrators of great crimes and wars, would they have stopped before they went as far as they did? Was there any degree of self-awareness that would have allowed them to choose another course? Or were they, like most of us, so blinded by the Three Poisons that they could see no option, and just did the best they knew how based on the information they had at the time?

In the midst of difficult times, if we are to strike out on a more promising course, we need to learn and affirm ways that demonstrate love, compassion, conviction, and impartiality – even to the point of embracing those we deem as "evil" or "enemies" and acknowledging them compassionately as part of our human family. And if we do not yet possess in our hearts and minds the wisdom and skill to embrace others whom we view as dangerous or misguided, we can at least begin and end our days with the Four Limitless Meditations that set our intention for cultivating and affirming the possibility of doing so.

Meditations and Mantras for the Conscious, Engaged Activist

"May I be a guard for those who are protectorless,
A guide for those who journey on the road.
For those who wish to go across the water,
May I be a boat, a raft, a bridge.

May I be an isle for those who yearn for landfall,
And a lamp for those who long for light;
For those who need a resting place, a bed;
For all who need a servant, may I be their slave.

May I be the wishing jewel, the vase of plenty,
A word of power, and the supreme healing;
May I be the tree of miracles,
And for every being, the abundant cow.

Like the great earth and the pervading elements,
Enduring as the sky itself endures,
For boundless multitudes of living beings,
May I be their ground and sustenance.

Thus, for every single thing that lives,
In number like the boundless reaches of the sky,
May I be their sustenance and nourishment
Until they pass beyond the bounds of suffering"

Shantideva.[5]

Through his own personal examination of the human predicament, the Buddha saw meditation as an essential method of uprooting and transforming the Three Poisons in a truly lasting way. As the son of a king, he also saw the practicality of meditation for slowing and averting the course of conflict in the world.

For the Buddha was quite aware of partisanship, intrigue, and the ways in which belief could be used to create harm. Not unlike the medieval European crusaders, inquisitors, and witch-hunters, the kings and empires of ancient India went to war believing in, and motivated by, their own special relationship to God. Seeing this, the Buddha posed a simple question: If God is

[5] Shantideva, *The Way of the Bodhisattva*
(*Bodhisattvacharyavatara*). Translated from the Tibetan by the
Padmakara Translation Group. Shambhala Books, Boston, 1997.
The passage is from Chapter 3.

an objective truth, how can both sides in a war claim to be on God's side or to hold the right view, the right beliefs? It is not possible. Such claims and beliefs must, therefore, be subjective and based on preconceptions – in other words, based on the Three Poisons. The Buddha therefore concluded that if we are ever going to get to the objective truth about God, we need to begin by taking God out of the equation and examining our own minds. Peace does not come from believing in God. Peace comes from creating peacefulness in our own minds. Wisdom and skillfulness in action are not *bestowed* upon us. We need to work to obtain them. Again, we come back to our own minds.

If we sit quiet and relaxed, free from being too tight or too loose, our loving nature will become more and more evident. As we become accustomed to just *being* – here and now – our identification with the turmoil and confusion in our life is disrupted. We can then access whatever resources we need to face whatever life puts before us. We also come to understand how easy it is to get sidetracked, lured by one emotion or another. Thus, our compassion for others grows naturally as we come to understand how easy it is for others, too, to be trapped in realities that they may not want but don't know how to get out of. In the laboratory of our own experience, we come to an inner recognition of the value of altruism – being with and helping others.

Buddhist Meditation Practice

The Buddha taught a number of meditative methods. Some rely on nothing but an awareness of the breath. Others involve visualization or gazing upon an object. Most of the visualization practices also involve the use of archetypal sounds, such as mantras, to invoke specific qualities in our being. There are also meditations that have a particular philosophical or moral focus, such as to generate compassion, healing, or protection, or to dispel negativity between people or in the world in general.

The meditative practices offered in this chapter are either traditional Buddhist meditations or meditative exercises based on Buddhist tradition. All of them are suitable for everyone, regardless of your faith or orientation. At the same time, the format that they follow can be used as a framework upon which you can build other meditations or visualizations that you think will help you in your activist work.

The benefits of meditation

If I were to summarize what benefits you should get from meditation practice, it is that you should become more open, flexible, spontaneous, joyful. You won't "burn out" from the exertion that is demanded of you in the face of those habitual forces within and around us, which reinforce and make the scourges of sickness, poverty, and warfare almost seem permanent. The resistances that make your work difficult dissolve as the wisdom and skillful means inherent in your loving nature more easily manifest. No matter what task we face, the furrowed brow of zealousness, stress, and desperation is no hallmark that you are being any more effective in doing what you are called to do. And, more than likely, if such stress to your mind and body is not released – not transformed into naturalness – it will eventually undermine your efforts.

A good friend, Lama Ole Nydahl, speaks of meditation "teflon coating" your neurons. From the perspective of the Ayurvedic medical tradition, this metaphor is not far from what are claimed to be the physical benefits of meditation on our body and mind. With greater peace, joy, and equanimity you develop a natural immunity to getting too attached to irritations and challenges as they arise in your life and activities. You are able to let go of what is petty and inessential and get on with what matters.

Spiritual conviction born of the open-mindedness created by meditation – regardless of the tradition from which it comes – is an important asset for world leaders as they confront the turmoil of the twenty-first century. A number of leaders in the world are known to have a deep spiritual life and practice: His Holiness the Dalai Lama, Kofi Annan, Nelson Mandela, Aung San Su Kyi. Each demonstrates how their convictions need not create a close-minded exclusivism of the sort exhibited by those of fundamentalist persuasions, who see themselves as so unswervingly and exclusively right as to be prepared to line up against each other in preparation for Armageddon. Each of the above mentioned leaders has borne an immense burden of responsibility. And yet, in their measured continence, one has seen how peacefulness has informed their decisions.

How To Begin and Stick With a Meditation Practice

When we add something new to our schedule, such as the regular discipline of practicing meditation, other parts of our life get shoved around. For most of us, time is one of the things we perceive ourselves to be short of. Our schedules are, more than likely, too full to begin with. Therefore if we are thinking of scheduling a time to meditate, we might define it as one more thing to get done in the day and as such turn it into a burden. But this is no way to approach meditation. In his *Instructions on Meditation*, the great Tibetan master Dudjom Rinpoche wrote:

"Allow yourself to relax and feel some spaciousness, letting your mind settle naturally. Your body should be still, speech silent and breathing as it is, freely flowing. Here there is a sense of letting go, unfolding, letting be. What does this state of relaxation feel like? You should be like someone after a really hard day's work, exhausted and peacefully satisfied, mind content to rest. Something settles at the gut level, and feeling it resting in your gut, you begin to experience a lightness. It is as if you're melting." [6]

You settle down to meditation in this way. It is a time to feel nourished, to feel replenished. Enjoy it! This doesn't mean that you shouldn't take your meditation seriously, but if it becomes stiff, habitual, and an enforced discipline, meditation will provide you little benefit. More than likely, in the beginning, you will feel a certain amount of awkwardness. That is natural when you are rearranging your life a bit and also starting to practice something new. To get over these bumps, a little serious push is necessary. But, be cautious of getting too uptight, self-righteous, or judgmental with yourself.

Start with meditating for a short period and gradually build up your sessions in small increments of time. Work up to a time frame that feels comfortable and doesn't make you feel like you are being squeezed in other aspects of your life. At the same time, if there is a weekend or other period that you can devote to more meditation, go for it. Over time, as you allow the discipline of meditation to infiltrate your daily life, it will feel more and more natural and your sense of joy and commitment to the process will grow.

Clarifying intentions

As we have said previously, Buddhist practice is based on altruism. This altruism comes from a profound understanding

---

[6]   H.H. Dudjom Rinpoche, *Instructions on Meditation*, a small pamphlet published by the Vajrayana Foundation, Hawaii.

of our interconnectedness. Our happiness, our healing, our enlightenment itself is dependent upon this recognition and on placing everyone else in our thoughts as we meditate. To help develop and hold this perspective, in preparation for a meditation session or a meditative exercise, it is useful to contemplate the Four Thoughts that Revolutionize the Mind (see pages 30–40) and the Four Limitless Meditations (see pages 58–69). Many traditional Buddhist practices begin in this way. Spend a few moments reflecting on both.

A Preliminary Breathing Exercise to Transform the Three Poisons

The following exercise was taught to me by Dr. Lobsang Rapgay, a Tibetan doctor and former monk who is now a well established clinical psychologist in California. It can be done on its own or as a preliminary to other forms of meditation. Energetically, it can be like a more advanced version of counting to ten when emotions are running high. The exercise aims to help us loosen the grip of the Three Poisons on our consciousness by focusing on the movement of breath and also on working with the "subtle energy body." Before I describe the exercise itself, let me explain a few things about what this means.

The subtle energy body

Classical yoga as well as the most advanced Tantric Buddhist practices make reference to a subtle energy body, a system of *chakras* and spiritual energy channels in the body. Many in the West are familiar with the term chakras, or energy vortices. These are envisioned as whirling centers of energy at various points in the body, from the base of the spine to the crown of the head. Hindu tradition relies on theories and practices based upon there being seven chakras. However, in Buddhist Tantra, the root chakra (*muladhara*) and crown chakra (*sahasrara*) are considered points of entry and exit respectively, with the five chakras in between being the ones that we need to work with. Thus, following the instructions given to me in the context of Buddhist Tantra, these chakras are linked to spiritual energy channels: two that run from about three finger-widths below the navel and finish at the edge of each nostril, and a central or main spiritual channel (*shushumna*) that begins in the same area below the navel, rises to the crown of the head, then drops down to around the middle of the forehead, finally turning inward toward the center of the brain. The two side channels twist and criss-cross around shushumna and it is at the constricted points where they cross one another and around the central channel that the chakras are said to be located.

Meditations are done to focus on the various chakras, loosen the constriction of the two side channels and allow for the movement of spiritual energy to ascend more freely through the central channel. According to Tibetan tradition, the chakras can only be "opened" either through the strong blessing of a master, or through the individual performing intense and effective meditation practice. No one else, like a massage therapist or a healer placing special stones or toning over your chakras, can open them for you. If they say they can, thank them and run in the opposite direction.

Some may ask, does this subtle energy body actually exist? It is true that if one were to try to find the exact anatomical location and physical presence of the chakras, you would be hard pressed. There is "something" there – for instance, the third (abdominal) chakra is regarded as the "survival" chakra, the seat of ego and personal power – and this area is indeed where we physically feel a "gut reaction" in the face of a physical or verbal threat to our person. And the chakras and channels may, like Chinese acupuncture meridians, be related to the modern understanding of the nervous system in some way (like Chinese meridians). But exactly *what* the subtle body is proves elusive because it is essentially an intangible, non-physical notion. Yet Tibetan masters and yogis of the East learn meditations where they focus on the chakras and the channels in very specific ways and venture to access and utilize the energy that arises. In their practices, the chakras will be visualized mentally as lotuses of different colors and numbers of petals that are sat, stood, or danced upon by small gods and goddesses. There are some of a more materialistic persuasion who get caught up in these details and try to make such descriptions into solid realities. His Holiness the Dalai Lama calls these "useful fictions," not necessarily to be taken literally. If we can relate to these chakras and channels as such, something of value does happen.

So in doing the following exercise, please relax. Try to imagine that these energies and their channels are as ephemeral as a rainbow. In the visualization for this particular exercise, the two side channels do not wrap around the main channel. The right channel should be viewed as a transparent RED tube, hollow and about as thick as your little finger. It is representative of the female energy (wisdom). It starts three finger-widths below the navel and moves deep within the body at a distance of one *tsun* (about half an inch) from the right side of the spine. It passes through the neck, over the brain but underneath the skull, drops down from the right side of the central fontanel, ending at the outside tip of the right nostril. The left channel is a transparent WHITE color, also hollow and of a similar thickness. It is representative of male energy (skillful means) and its path mirrors that of the RED channel but on the left side of the body.

Shushumna, the central (or spiritual) channel is visualized as a straight tube that is two little-finger-widths in diameter. It is often visualized as having a yellow tint, but in this exercise we see it as a transparent BLUE tube that starts four finger-widths below the navel and goes up through the body just in front of the spine. It goes through the neck and head to the central fontanel point, where it makes a tight downward turn to the area of the "Third Eye" (behind the center of the forehead) and hooks inward toward the pineal gland. It is understood as neither male nor female.

The exercise:

1. Begin the exercise by assuming a sitting position, either cross-legged on the floor or on a chair. You want to be comfortable, without your lungs or diaphragm feeling constricted in any way. If it feels comfortable and natural to sit cross-legged on the floor, sit so that you maintain the natural curve of your lower back. You may need to sit on a few cushions to achieve this. Generally, it is best for your behind to be somewhere between four to six inches off the ground, with your knees below the level of your navel. If you know other yogic or meditative sitting poses, feel free to choose one of those. If you need to sit on a chair, sit with your spine away from the back of the chair so that your chest can expand fully. Place your feet squarely and firmly on the ground, about shoulder width apart.

2. Visualize that the beginning of the WHITE channel or tube is slightly smaller and inserts into the beginning of the RED channel, below the navel.

3. With your right thumb resting at the base of the right little finger, wrap all the fingers of your right hand around the thumb, with the exception of your index finger. Keep this finger extended. Block your right nostril with your right index finger and inhale through your left nostril. Imagine

that the air you are breathing in through your left nostril is pure and fresh, and that this pure and fresh air is being drawn through the WHITE channel to where the WHITE channel is inserted into the RED channel, just below the navel.

4. At the point where you visualize the pure, fresh air reaching the opening of the RED channel, let go of the right nostril and, with your left hand in a similar arrangement as your right one, block the left nostril with your left index finger. As you exhale through the right nostril, visualize that the pure, fresh air that entered through the WHITE channel is pushing whatever is unclean, contaminated, and polluted out of the RED channel, like wind that blows away dust. As you breathe out, see especially that you are releasing the defilement, or poison, of **attachment** or clinging. Visualize these negativities as smoke leaving the right nostril.

5. Repeat this process two more times. After this, allow yourself to breathe through both nostrils and visualize the right, RED, channel as being luminous and purified of all negativities. Breathe in and out naturally three times, and as you do so visualize the right channel as radiant as a ruby.

6. Now repeat stages 1 through 4 for the cleansing of the WHITE channel. This time, visualize the end of the RED channel inserted into the end of the WHITE tube. Start by blocking the left nostril. As the fresh, pure air goes from the RED channel into the WHITE channel, you breathe out the impurities and the defilement of **aggression**. Do this three times and then breathe in and out normally three times, seeing the WHITE channel now as luminous and pure, like a diamond.

7. Now visualize shushumna, the central, spiritual channel. It is a BLUE tube the thickness of two little fingers. Visualize that the ends of both the WHITE and RED channels are inserted into the end of the BLUE channel. Once you have this in your mind's eye, place your hands in your lap. Allow the back of the right hand to rest in the palm of the upturned left hand. The thumbs then touch to form a triangle. With your hands in this configuration, raise them enough to place them around your navel so that it is in the center of the triangle.

8. Breathe in through both nostrils and visualize the pure, fresh air going up from the nostrils, through the RED and WHITE channels, and down to where they join the entrance to shushumna, the central BLUE channel.

9. As you exhale, feel this pure air moving up and cleansing the BLUE channel and with it the defilement of **ignorance**. You visualize that ignorance and all other impurities are pouring like smoke out of your forehead in the region of your Third Eye.

10. Repeat this two more times. Finally, lower your hands to your lap and breathe normally three times, experiencing the central channel as luminously blue, supple, and purified. It is radiant like a deep blue sapphire.

Peacefulness Meditation

Peacefulness or "Calm Abiding" (Sanskrit *shamatha*, Tibetan *shinay*) Meditation is intended to encourage the development of a calm and clear mind. It is an excellent method for developing equanimity – toward others as well as ourselves. As agitation in our mind settles, a sense of wholesome aliveness arises naturally. And rather than feeling trapped in the predictable patterns of our ignorance, attachment, and aggression, there is a spaciousness that allows us to "think out of the box," as it were. New solutions and new possibilities emerge out of the "clear blue."

In Peacefulness Meditation, we focus on the breath. We do not do this as in the previous exercise, or as in the yogic *pranayama* practice, where we actively regulate the flow of our breath. Here, all we do is *observe* the natural rhythm of the breath, in and out. The exercise has six steps. As usual with any meditation or visualization practice, we begin with our sitting posture.

1. Sit in a comfortable manner, either cross-legged on the floor or in a chair, as described in the previous exercise (see page 82). Allow your hands to rest, palms down, on or just above your knees. Alternatively, you can place your thumbs at the base of your little fingers and wrap the other fingers over the thumbs. This is the sealing *mudra* (hand posture) of a Bodhisattva, or Buddha-to-be. It connects you more with your compassionate heart. If doing this mudra, rest your hands so that your knuckles face up and your folded fingers are tucked and resting downward on your knees.

2. Allow your neck to relax with your chin slightly tucked in and your throat soft. The head should not be craned back or tilted forward. Wet your lips with your tongue and then rest your tongue on the palate, just behind your top teeth. If you are sitting on the floor, your eyes should have a slight downward gaze, resting approximately eighteen inches to two feet in front of you. If you are on a chair, aim your gaze between your knees, letting it go a bit further. In either case, it is generally considered best to have your eyes slightly open. This helps to keep you grounded, oriented in

the space that you are in, and relaxed. If you find the room or space too distracting, then you may close your eyes. However, if what you get when you close your eyes is a great movie, it is best to keep your eyes partially open.

3. Take a deep breath in, draw up your pelvic muscles, tense your buttocks and abdomen, straighten your arms so that your palms or hands are pushing down on your knees, and lift your spine. Hold the tension for a moment; then slowly breathe out, and as you do so, let all the tension leave with the exhalation, giving you the sense of feeling more settled on your cushion or chair. Allow your diaphragm to become soft, your breath natural as it rises and sinks from deep within.

4. Now concentrate on the cycle of your breathing. Bring your attention to the natural breath as it passes in and out past the tip of your nostrils. Breathing in, feel the air passing in through the nostrils and moving down into your abdomen to a point about three finger-widths (about one and a half inches) below your navel. As you breathe out, the abdomen contracts slightly as the air moves upward and passes out of the nostrils. Its invisible stream travels along the pathway of your gaze. As your eyes softly remain fixed on a given point, imagine that this stream dissolves about an inch above the ground.

5. To further this initial concentration, we count the cycle of the breath, especially focusing on the out-breath. As you inhale, be aware of the breath passing in through your nostrils, but pay particular attention as the out-breath leaves the nostrils. As the breath goes out, count to yourself "One." The next breath comes in, and as it passes out at the

nostrils, you count "Two." Continue to count like this for twenty-one cycles of breath. There are two ways of counting: either count up to twenty-one, or count up to seven three times. In either case, if you find your mind drifting from the counting, start at one again until you complete the counting without distraction. This is easier than it sounds, so be patient with yourself. There are times when I have found myself spending a whole meditation session just getting through the counting!

6. Once you successfully complete the counting, allow your concentration to relax, focusing only on the passage of air as it leaves your nostrils and dissolves into space. If you get distracted by thoughts, just tell yourself, "Thinking," and then come back to the breath. It doesn't matter what you are thinking. What you are trying to do here is break your habit of being hooked on one thought after another. If the thought is truly important or some amazing inspiration, rest assured it will come back to you later on, after your meditation session. For now, let it pass.

Begin your practice of this meditation slowly. Five or ten minutes to start with is a good beginning. Gradually increase the meditation to twenty minutes. When you have time, you can do it for longer. Some people will spend weekends or entire months meditating like this for hours a day. What matters most is consistency. A daily practice is best. If you can periodically get time to do it for longer, great.

Taking peacefulness one step further

The Peacefulness Meditation is a wonderful practice to do with a group of people. Like the principle of the "hundredth monkey," where the consciousness of a collective becomes synchronized, the turmoil within each person can be affected by the peacefulness generated by the group. At the same time, it can be an excellent meditation to create peacefulness between people who are in conflict or have communication difficulties. In this regard, it does not even matter whether the person you are having problems with is there or not. Just visualizing them in your presence, meditating with you, can yield a powerful, healing result. The person that you imagine sitting with you doesn't even need to be someone you know personally – it could be, let's say, a world leader toward whom you have difficulty feeling any compassion.

To make this visualization more powerful, Tantric tradition suggests imagining that if the person you want to be at peace with, or communicate with more effectively, is female, imagine that they are sitting beside you on your left. If they are male, imagine them on your right. The positioning of males and females has to do with the subtle energy theories and practices of Tantra. As we are each a blend of male and female energies, it is possible to utilize these energies for better results.

This can be a simple, unobtrusive way of breaking the ice or beginning the process or transforming our perceptions of others. See whether or not it helps when you actually do come face to face with them.

Tong Len Meditation: The Practice of Taking and Sending

Through observation, contemplation, and meditation, we come to the realization that nothing lives in isolation. We are inseparable from everyone and everything around us and this at-oneness is also quite intangible and ever changing. Furthermore, in our inter-connectedness, we see that we are always as much a part of the problem as we are part of the solution.

So, even if we cannot solicit the participation of others in the resolving of tensions, conflicts, and problems, we can begin by working on ourselves and our relationship to others and to these difficulties. One practice that can be useful toward this end is *Tong Len*, or "Taking and Sending," Meditation.

In the context of our relationship to the world and our attempt to dissolve the imaginary boundaries created by the Three Poisons, which in turn lead to confusion-laden judgments and projections, Tong Len can be an effective meditation. It can be practiced on its own or with other meditations, and can even be done on the spot when we face a crisis. One of its foundational benefits is that it helps us to own and acknowledge our projections.

According to the great Indian Buddhist master, Atisha, the first person we need to do Taking and Sending for is ourselves. There are many levels of meaning in what he is saying. At the simplest level, we realize that all of our suffering arises from our own unmitigated Three Poisons; it is therefore useful for us to breathe in and *take back* from the world around us the thoughts, words, and actions that we have committed based on ignorance, attachment, and aggression. Breathing in with this thought in mind, we place in action an intention and commitment no longer to pollute our world and the people we love. As we breathe out, we send a breath of freshness, vibrancy, and good intentions out into the world.

As we come to own our projections and create more space for others, we become sensitive to their projections, the effects of the Three Poisons on them. We become more sensitive to why they are the way they are. As we breathe in, we then feel more compassion to take in and transform *their* pain and confusion and send waves of understanding and love out to *them*. If, in the context of a seemingly intractable situation, we breathe in whatever pain, confusion, or horror we see before us along with our own projections about the situation, we create a space within us that allows us to come to a problem afresh, less burdened by the weight of history.

What is offered below is a basic Tong Len meditation that can be done both formally, as when sitting in meditation, and informally, when dealing with difficult or painful circumstances on the spot.

1. If you are doing this as a formal meditation, begin by sitting and adjusting your posture and breathing in a similar fashion to how you worked with the Peacefulness Meditation. Come to the point where all you are doing is observing the passage of air at the tip of your nose.

2. Begin the Taking and Sending process with yourself. As you breathe in, put your intention and commitment into absorbing all of your tendencies to project ignorance, attachment, and aggression out into the world. If you are stuck at this time with any particular negative emotion, breathe it in, knowing that this emotion colors and distorts your actions. The negativity that you breathe in goes to your heart, in which there rests a deep blue syllable, HUNG, pronounced hoong. You can visualize the letters H-U-N-G in the center of your heart, or just a deep BLUE light. This light is considered in Tantric tradition to be the nature of your mind. It is also a powerful healing color. Thus you are allowing the Three Poisons and their projections to be dissolved and healed in the deep blue light.

As you breathe out, imagine that pure, radiant love pours from your heart center, floods your entire being, then expands into and fills the space around you. Feel this radiant love as clear and WHITE, extending out as far as you can imagine.

3: Having done several breath cycles like this with yourself in mind, it is now time to bring your attention to others. Imagine that behind you are people in general, people you have no particular thought or emotion about one way or the other. Some teachers say that you should think of these people first, as you have few strong emotions or biases about them. For them, you start by focusing on their general pain and confusion. As you breathe in and out, repeat for them what you did for yourself. In your mind's eye, see their negativity come out of their bodies and minds and enter into that BLUE light in your heart where such negativity, the Three Poisons and their residues, are dissolved and healed. Imagine this negativity as being like black tar or smoke. As you breathe out, see the radiant clear WHITE light spread into their bodies and minds, filling them with clarity, joy, and love. You are forging a closer connection to them – to humanity and all beings in general – as a result.

4. Now, focus on those with whom you have a close or personal relationship. See these people on either side of you. As in the variation on the Peacefulness Meditation (see page 84), place the women on your left and the men on your right to make the meditation more energetically effective. Breathe in and out on behalf of these people in the same manner. Do this for several cycles of breath as well. Of course, you may even focus on a particular individual whom you are concerned about.

5. You are now ready to go to the next step of focusing your attention on people you have difficulty with. These can be those with whom you have a personal relationship, or a world leader, and so on. Imagine that they are sitting

directly in front of you. Repeat the process for them as you did for all of the others in steps 3 and 4.

Take your time building up your strength and resolve to do this practice. Start with yourself. Gradually include others in a way that does not push you past a general sense of equanimity. There is not much value in finding yourself obsessing in the meditation about someone you love or someone you totally despise. Certainly, you want to work past these emotions to get to a place where you see a more workable relationship or situation. But it is more useful to acknowledge first where you are within yourself and build Tong Len slowly as an effective tool.

As mentioned earlier, besides being a formal meditation practice, Tong Len can be done on the spot in situations with others where there is pain or difficulty. In such circumstances, you can always breathe in and breathe out in accordance with this practice without others needing to know what you are doing. As you hold the intention of wanting to absorb rather than react to the pain, suffering, bad feelings, or confusion of the moment, this will have an effect on how you relate to the situation. In hostile situations, Tong Len can even dispel the tension or bring it to a resolution more quickly. In any event, you have stopped yourself, through your intention and breathing, from contributing to the problem. This can go a long way in moving relationships and situations forward.

Visualizing world peace

The bumper sticker with this slogan is found everywhere. Perhaps it is even translated into a variety of languages. The sentiment is obviously something many share. But is it possible to make this wish more potent? In this regard, Tong Len can be a useful practice. With respect to the visualization, you can imagine that you are out in space looking down on the planet.

Alternatively, you can have the sense of sitting on the planet, feeling its presence underneath and all around you. Whatever way makes you feel most connected to the Earth is probably the best.

Imagine that as you breathe in, you are taking in all of the negativity, the harsh and negative forces that you feel contribute to the pain and suffering on the planet. Dissolve these in the HUNG syllable or BLUE light in your heart. As you breathe out, see WHITE light radiating out from you and enveloping the entire planet. See the power of goodness in this light changing people's attitudes, ending wars, ceasing pollution, or whatever you want to focus on. Expanding your vision to be so inclusive is very powerful and liberating in its own way. It can help to dispel hopelessness and give you a greater sense of connection, love, and compassion.

In this visualization, as with all the variants on Tong Len Meditation, remember that nothing is ever lost, and that the power of a well focused thought and intention is never wasted.

The cloak of light: A self-protection exercise

The deep blue light that is used in the Tong Len practice can also be used like a "cloaking" device; a way of not being noticed or detected when one does not wish to be. This was explained by Lama Ole Nydahl, who has found it useful while driving or in difficult or dangerous circumstances. It is not a Buddhist practice per se, but is in keeping with the energetic logic of these practices. All you need to do is to imagine that a layer of deep blue light surrounds your entire body in these situations. If you are traveling, you can even imagine that this light envelops your entire vehicle, plane, and so on. What this does is to make you seemingly less detectable by malevolent or other forces that may interfere with what you want to do. Like any energetic exercise, intent and concentration strengthen the affect. See how it works for you.

Helpful Mantras from the Tibetan Buddhist Tradition

The reciting of mantras is an important aspect of meditation in the advanced methods of the Tibetan Buddhist tradition. They are archetypal sounds, either single syllables or a combination of syllables, that help us to focus our energy and access our inner resources for specific purposes. For example, there are mantras that help us to access compassion, power, or protection, and others for developing deeper wisdom. They are connected with visualization meditations that are about seeing the world for what it is, based on a certain enlightened angle or viewpoint. Combined with a positive intention and the recitation of a mantra, these visualizations can dramatically enhance our personal transformation and our ability to access our inner resources to benefit others.

Intention, visualization, and mantra recitation are a powerful threesome when combined, but positive intention and the use of the sacred sounds of mantra on their own can be a potent means for mustering the compassion, power, wisdom or other quality you need to meet a given challenge. Lama Ole Nydahl cleverly describes mantras as syllables that "put a virus in our neuroses programs." While these syllables are often words or parts of words in Sanskrit or Tibetan, their actual meaning is of little consequence and it can even be an impediment to using them effectively as we might then focus on the meaning rather than the vibration. What is more important is their vibrational quality. Reciting mantras over and over again, we bypass our discursive mind, cutting through the mental obstacles to compassion, intelligence, power, protection, healing, or whatever quality the mantra aims to enhance. This allows that quality to shine forth more clearly in our being and action.

Before using the following mantras, which are all given in a simple phonetic transcription, begin by thinking about the quality you especially wish to access, then choose the mantra that helps you to access that quality and the energy within you directly. Include the altruistic wish that not only will *you* access and manifest that quality, but that each and every being will also access that quality. As you recite the mantra, feel as though the energy of the mantra is vibrating in all of your cells and imagine that its sound vibration reaches out and touches everyone around you in all directions in the same manner. This is an important step in becoming less self-centered and partisan, and more equanimous.

At a later stage you may wish to investigate the use of visualizations to enhance the power and energy of these mantras. If you do, I encourage you to seek out the advice of a qualified lama or meditation master. In the meantime, I have provided a bit of background regarding the mantras that you can use for visualization purposes. You can also find pictures of all these visualized aspects of enlightenment online and in many reference books on Tibetan Buddhism.

The Medicine Buddha mantra for dissolving the Three Poisons

TAY-YAH-TAH OM BEH-KAHN-DZEH BEH-KAHN-DZEH MA-HA BEH-KAHN-DZEH RAH-DZAH SAH-MOOD-GAH-TAY SO-HAH

Using the power of the Medicine Buddha mantra is excellent for uprooting and transforming the Three Poisons. It is for this reason specifically that it is included as the first of the mantras that is helpful to the conscious, engaged activist. Although the historical figure named Siddhartha Gautama is commonly know as *the* Buddha, the term Buddha ("Enlightened One") itself does not refer to any single individual. All the various Buddhist traditions claim that other Buddhas existed before Siddhartha, and that more will appear in the future. One of these earlier Buddhas is the Medicine Buddha, who according to Tibetan Buddhist tradition is the source of all healing. As a Buddha, he too awoke to the awareness of what caused us to suffer and what we need to overcome suffering. Specifically, he identified the Three Poisons and various means to cut through them. Although Medicine Buddha meditations are used by Tibetan healers and by those wishing to be healed of specific physical or mental illnesses, as we all suffer from the effects of the Three Poisons, it does not matter whether we are physically sick or not.

The mantra of Chenrezig for developing compassion

OM MAH-NEE PEH-MEH HOONG

The mantra of Chenrezig, *Om Mani Padme Hum* (given above in its usual Tibetan pronunciation) is probably the most famous of all Buddhist mantras. Carved on stone tablets found across Tibet, it is for generating and developing the qualities of compassion. Alongside the various Buddhas, the Buddhist traditions recognize many enlightened beings called *bodhisattvas*, "Buddhas-to-be" who work actively to help all beings to become enlightened. The bodhisattva of compassion is called Avalokiteshvara in Sanskrit and Chenrezig in Tibetan, and his name may be translated as "Loving Eyes." In the Chinese tradition, he became female, in the form of the goddess Guanyin. Loving Eyes is the functional aspect of the great Buddha Amitabha's discriminating wisdom in the world, manifesting as compassion in all of its forms.

The mantra of Green Tara for Accessing Fearlessness and Generosity

OM TAH-REH TOO-TAH-REH TOO-REH SO-HAH

According to legend, the female bodhisattva Tara was once an ordinary human being who was very devoted to spiritual practice. So impressive were her diligence and the results of her meditation that great masters told her that in the future, she would have good enough karma to be reborn as a man and thus have the best opportunity for reaching enlightenment. Hearing their words, she vowed that if she attained enlightenment, it would be in the form of a female, not a male. Tara's fearlessness to fly in the face of convention, and her dedication to giving to and helping óthers are the qualities one helps to access when reciting the mantra of Green Tara, a popular form of the bodhisattva. This is true whether one is a man or woman. Tara generously shares with all. Generosity is also, therefore, one of the qualities gained when accessing the energetic qualities of Green Tara.

The mantra of Guru Rinpoche: A mantra for our time

OM AH HOONG BEN-ZAH GURU PEH-MAH SID-DHEE HOONG

Padmasambhava was an Indian Buddhist Tantrika who came to Tibet in the eighth century and successfully introduced Vajrayana, or Tantric, Buddhism to Tibet. Others had tried before, but Padmasambhava had the wisdom and skill not only to speak clearly to the Tibetan people and their rulers, but also to subdue many of the adversarial forces that did not want him to succeed. So successful was he in his transmission of Buddhism to Tibet that he became known simply as *Guru Rinpoche* – Precious Teacher.

Guru Rinpoche was also renowned as an alchemist and wizard who had clairvoyant abilities and could see far into the future. It is said that he hid many teachings throughout Tibet that he knew would be useful to people of future times. Although many tried to find these hidden teachings, or *terma*, searching in caves, under rocks, and so on, only those who were destined to do so, and had the proper karmic connection to Guru Rinpoche, discovered them. One of these *terma* is the renowned *Tibetan Book of The Dead*.

It is said that Guru Rinpoche himself never died but simply disappeared, and his activity and power are still considered a potent force to this day. Sincere supplication to him, and using his mantra with the intention of benefiting others, are said to help clear away obstacles, eliminate disease, remove famine, and overcome unrest, to name a few. I have met Tibetan teachers who say that of all the mantras that are useful in a Dark Age, this is one of the most special.

"Be All That You Can Be…"

The purpose of sharing all of the meditations, meditative exercises, and mantras in this chapter is to give the conscious, engaged activist a daily focus or practice that will help to elicit the qualities he or she needs to meet the challenges of this Dark Age. These practices take the thoughtfulness and intention discussed in earlier chapters and give them greater focus, clarity, and power.

Depending on what you are called upon to do, you will, no doubt find that different qualities are demanded. The mindfulness of the Peacefulness Meditation and Tong Len are always indispensable. The mantra practices will help you to summon and access those qualities we all know that we possess, but have never had the tools to awaken. Regardless of whether you use the meditations as they are presented here or take them to deeper, more profound levels, in the end, the goal is the same – to awaken and make fully manifest that loving nature which we already embody in full measure.

Our resourcefulness is limitless. As we learn to access those resources in ourselves, we will also learn to evoke them in others. In this alone we shall begin the process of dissolving the causes for our Dark Age.

CHAPTER 7:

The Power of Compassion

"If you plan revenge, dig two graves."

Old Welsh saying

Compassion is action informed by wisdom. When we understand what needs to be done, and choose the most appropriate
means to carry it out, based on an altruistic intention to help
others, our action *is*, in itself, compassion. It is a demonstration
of *caring enough*. Compassion, therefore, is not neutral and
dis-passion-ate, but rather *with-passion*-ate. It is intimate and
involved. It is conscious and engaged. Compassion may seem an
obvious quality to have in dealing with others and the world, but
true compassion only comes about through all of the steps we
have discussed so far. We need to understand the Four Thoughts
that Revolutionize the Mind (see pages 30–40), the Four Noble
Truths (see pages 42–49), and the altruism of the Four Limitless
Meditations (see pages 58–69), and develop meditation and
contemplation as a regular part of our lives. With these as a
foundation, only then does compassion become truly integral
– the basis on which we initiate any action.

Discriminating Wisdom

According to the Buddhist understanding, compassion is the active, functional aspect of what is called "Discriminating Wisdom." This means understanding situations for what they are. When we have trained our minds to understand the transitory, yet precious nature of every moment and cultivated the strong altruistic intention to step forward in our lives so that our world is made better along the way, compassionate action becomes both logical and inevitable. It is not an easy journey. For as we turn from the path of self-interest or prejudice, we walk into a minefield – or maybe we should say a *mind*-field – of progressive tests that arise from the resistance of our habitual minds, which are still ruled by the Three Poisons. We encounter deeper levels of avarice, covert intention, and tendencies of self-preservation. As these arise, the journey that started out so peacefully takes a wrathful turn as we face the tough psychological and emotional issues in our lives. The Tibetan doctor, monk, and clinical psychologist Dr. Lobsang Rapgay explained that this is why in the Tibetan Buddhist tradition new Dharma students are introduced to peaceful meditations and visualizations of such beatific deities as Chenrezig, or "Loving Eyes" (see page 96).

As progress is made and stability is developed, the teacher then begins to introduce the student to forms of compassion that have less appeal until in the deepest, most profound dimensions of practice – the meditation student meets the "protectors": wrathful deities that represent the most difficult forms of compassion. These forms confront us to see if we really have the resolve to go farther, to really get the job done. In many respects, knowing how starry-eyed and idealistic we tend to be when embarking on something new, such as starting upon a quest or joining a group, be it a meditation or political action group, the Buddha was well aware that familiarity and time would eventually lead us to the "underbelly" of the situation. The more we get involved, the more we have to deal with the "dirt," so to speak. Rather than allowing us to lapse into cynicism, depression, and apathy, the Buddha engages us with teachings about the wrathful side of compassion. For if one cannot embrace and develop a compassionate attitude when facing the negative emotional states that every group or situation offers us over time, then bitterness and backbiting are inevitable.

This is an important lesson for the conscious, engaged activist: if you are really doing your job, if you are really creating something that is going to make a difference, you should expect confrontations and disagreements, both internal and external. Thus, while we may dismiss a saying such as "No guts, no glory" as bravado or macho nonsense, the Tibetan images of gore-spattered wrathful deities sporting garlands of human skulls while chomping on entrails with bloody fangs, are reminders of the truth that the path of compassionate engagement is not always a pleasant or comfortable one. A fellow Buddhist practitioner who was responsible for a military coup against a corrupt government and spent eighteen months of his life on death row, used to say that committing oneself to a route devoted to any significant change, be it at the personal or geopolitical level, is "not for tiny tots."

The four forms of compassion

In keeping with what arises as we develop along a spiritual path, there are four types of compassion that arise from discriminating wisdom. They are usually presented in the following naturally arising sequence: **pacifying** or peaceful compassion; **enriching** or empowering compassion; **magnetizing** or what could be described as seductive or charismatic compassion; and **wrathful** or destroying compassion.

This order is in keeping with a logical progression that is found in every action we initiate as humans. Initially, we hope that what we do will meet with no resistance, and can be accomplished peacefully. When this is all that a situation presents us, then our actions will be peaceful in nature. But more than likely, we will encounter some resistance and think of how we can win support for our cause. We attempt to convince those who are resisting us of our way of seeing. We attempt to overcome their hesitancy by trying to convince them that to join or support our efforts is in their interest as well. If such promises and guarantees do not *work,* we try to draw them to our side, through a charismatic display of some sort, something that is overwhelmingly impressive, or makes what we offer almost irresistible. If we still meet resistance, we may need to use stronger means to overcome it so we can get on with what we want to do. We render them powerless, irrelevant, brush them out of the way, or vanquish them in some way if necessary.

A similar progression occurs whether our intent is compassionate or malicious. How compassionate it is will reflect the degree to which we have transformed our actions with altruistic intent, skillful means, and wisdom. Such is the way of things between us in playgrounds, corporate boardrooms, halls of power, and on battlefields.

As I mentioned above, the four forms of compassion also reflect what happens to us internally on the spiritual path. Each stage of the sequence presents its own challenges as we move from a self-centered to an all-serving perspective. For an example of this sequence we can look to the Buddha's own progress to enlightenment. Each stage – as in most stories of great heroes in all world cultures – represented an initiation on his road to becoming, and manifesting for others, compassion in all of its dimensions

The Buddha's private war

The Buddha's spiritual development culminated in the final hours that he sat in meditation beneath a *bodhi* tree as his enlightenment fully manifested. At this point, the climax of a process which, according to Buddhist tradition, had taken many lifetimes, he faced his final tests. Siddhartha, the Buddha-to-be, was engaged in a private war; a final struggle against all of the inner and outer forces that keep us engaged, mesmerized, and locked into a matrix that thrives on predictable outcomes and shrinks in the face of true freedom. And, in his enlightenment story, what leads to war and how to be ultimately victorious is revealed.

Like each of us, Siddhartha started off confused and suffering. He was a wealthy prince, and did not suffer in a physical or material way, but he had no satisfaction in what he had, or in his experience of it. He sought for something else, and in his seeking he saw how distraction, and the craving that brought riches to some and disaster to others, needed to be dissolved. Being rich and privileged, he first thought that if he gave everything away and led a more simple life, this would bring him the peace of mind he was seeking. But, he soon learned that simplicity is a state of being that is determined by the mind, not by whether or not one lived in great material comfort or total austerity. So he sat quietly in simplicity, neither indulging nor starving his human senses; neither mentally engaging in the world around him nor retreating from it. Agitation and sloth were both overcome, and became a relaxed alertness. His attachments and fixations to things around him, even states of mind within him, began to loosen, and his mind became more and more aware of its vast potential. Siddhartha became wholly peaceful, and his peacefulness expressed itself in his ability to empower others to experience the same.

As his peacefulness deepened and his mind expanded into

its natural, undistorted state, the illusions that he had been living under began to leave. But more subtle aspects of these illusions and other unseen illusions remained and came into Siddartha's awareness. Each of these illusions has a hook, a way of saying to us, "Do you really want to get rid of me? After all, haven't I served you well so far? I'll stay around if you really want me to." Images arose in Siddhartha's mind: images of wealth, power, and lustful delight. Why should he bother himself with overcoming what so many desire? Surely he, more than most, knew what was out there for him if he were only to give up on this silly quest. After all, he was a royal prince, a king-to-be, one who could possess many lands and riches, and plenty of opportunities to do whatever he wanted to with them.

But Siddhartha persisted against these disempowering thoughts and images. We can *never* know what really went through the Buddha's mind, but at this stage in the process of self-development, we can all fall prey to various ploys of disempowerment from voices within ourselves or from those around us. Such voices might tell us: "What you are doing is a waste of time and worthless. There is nothing virtuous in what you are doing. What's the point? You're missing out on so much!" Equally, pride and self-aggrandizement can arise: "Wow, I'm really great. I'm so serene. I'm the serenest of them all!" Such thoughts only keep you hooked to an egocentric, non-altruistic way of being. Alternatively, you can fall prey to the premature congratulations of others who want to identify with you. Whatever the Buddha thought or saw during his own process, he sat still. With peacefulness as a foundation and altruistic intention extended even to himself, he gave in neither to self-denigration nor to self-aggrandizement. He transformed both into the compassionate activity and state of being that could grace others with a sense of their own inner richness. And Siddhartha's enlightening deepened and his personal power grew.

As his power grew, what manifested in his mind was the discovery that anything he wanted he could have. He did not need to go out and seek what he wanted. Things would just come his way. It is said that on this part of the final spiritual journey, temptation arose, and Siddhartha saw before him beautiful, seductive women, offering him anything he could possibly want. He no longer needed to ask. He would just be given. All he needed to say was "yes" and allow himself to be indulged.

But with an eye steadfast on what he felt was his true destiny, Siddhartha continued to sit still. With his peacefulness and his enriching power growing, he cut through another web of self-deceit. His attraction to such physical desires withered, and with it the possibility of being seduced into reconsidering his choice. Transforming his in-built, animalistic desires and the power of seduction, Siddhartha was empowered with the charisma to divert others caught in the web of seduction with visions of freedom and the possibility of being able to relate to something far greater and of lasting beauty: their own awakening potential.

Yet Siddhartha's transformation was not complete. In the deepest recesses of his mind, the forces of attraction and seduction were replaced by one last challenge: fear. This test was not so much rooted in residual self-centeredness, as in self-preservation: the threat of not-being – of no longer being identified by all that is familiar. To shake us up, to "bring us to our senses," all that seemed beautiful becomes hideous and threatening, to entice us to recoil into the familiar, the pre-dictable, the seemingly safe. In his mind, Siddhartha saw demon warriors hurling spears and shooting arrows, and vicious beasts set loose to attack and devour him – before it was too late.

But with his compassion toward himself and others growing indestructible, Siddhartha saw these fears, too, as just a phantasm of his own creation. Siddhartha still persisted in his commitment to awaken. With his inner foundation of peace and the powers to repel any forces – within or without – that distracted him from his task, he summoned his courage and mentally met his foe, disarmed him, and made him a powerful ally. As all vestiges of an ego rooted in selfish desire died away, Siddhartha absorbed these demons, harnessing them with a "wrathful compassion" that could protect others from harming themselves and, at the same time, scare them to action when he saw them to be braver than they saw themselves.

As the energy inherent in his enlightenment potential was no longer trapped and focused on preserving one fixed reality over another, what had been used for self-centered pleasures and self-preservation were now the limitless resources the Buddha had at his command. He had opened up to, and become, the conduit for endless possibilities in a universe focused on the wellbeing of all its inhabitants.

The four forms of compassion embody all the potential of what is powerful and good in what we do. The Buddha did not invent them or come up with them as some kind of doctrinal contrivance. What he accomplished was to develop the wisdom and skill to strip away the neurotic and habitual ways in which these positive qualities remain hidden in the progressive stages of our actions. In fact, our neurotic and habitual patterns that either covertly or overtly display our self-centered, unenlightened perspective, are veiled, confused manifestations of these four compassions, expressing themselves in our sloth or inaction, our agitation, our pride or self-denigration, our lust and manipulations, our destructiveness. If we awaken to the truth of this and work with methods to transform the Three Poisons, when we experience these tendencies within ourselves or witness them in others, we can call forth the power of the necessary compassionate action to change them into something more uplifting, more enlightening.

Compassion in Action: Taking Up the Challenge

If you are going to embark upon a path of change in the political or social sphere, you have to prepare yourself to fight the fight, no matter what comes your way. The resistance you face will be both internal and external. In the course of becoming an activist focused on any given issue, you will have to work through your own emotional labyrinth as well as contend with those forces outside you that will test your resolve. The Buddha said to love your enemies, not because they are loveable (at least from your perspective), but because they actually give you the opportunity, as mirrors of what is unresolved within you, to manifest higher, nobler qualities in your world. They may not be your friends, but they are your gift: they test your compassion. Just think of how the face of the social and political process would change if liberals showed compassionate consideration toward neo-cons, right-to-lifers did the same toward pro-choicers, and Muslims knelt down to pray beside Jews. What could open, honest, and caring dialogue do toward creating workable solutions, as opposed to intractable positions arising from brains and hearts unwilling to change?

Standing your ground

In the face of those who might want to distract you from your course, you will need to keep your focus and relax enough to be able to maintain a steady energy for the long haul. Expending too much energy in the beginning may lead to burn-out. By maintaining your equanimity, those around you will begin to see the shallowness of their own distractions and the agitation in their own hearts.

When those who represent the forces or causes you wish to see changed discover that you are not giving up, they may try at first to ignore you, playing down your significance. Can you stand being considered irrelevant? Try to see those who pit themselves against you not as adversaries, but as potential allies, and try to embrace them. If you retaliate defensively or otherwise go negative on them at this time in order to maintain your own sense of self-worth, they will note this weakness and exploit it later. Alternatively, they may want to inflate you so that you can trip yourself up. Here you need to remind yourself of what you are doing and for whose benefit you are working.

Seeing you are not swayed from your course, these forces may also try to co-opt your energy and efforts. In such cases, you may expect ploys of bribery and manipulation, and "offers you cannot refuse." If seductive offers cannot sway you and at the same time you show love for those who would see your downfall, expect to be further tested through the ploy of embarrassment and humiliation.

If building your pride and offers of power don't appeal, your opponents will seek to find weak points in your character. When they know what your weaknesses are, they may lay tempting morsels in your way. And any vague attention you give them will be turned into a scandal. Finding and exploiting "dirt" is an old political ploy as is fabricating dirt out of thin air. (I am reminded of a political campaign in Texas where a well-known political figure in the White House planted bugging devices in his own office, claimed to have "discovered" them, and blamed his opponent. The ploy worked and destroyed his opponent's credibility.) In either case, whether one is snared by the lure, or the whole scenario you are confronted with is fabricated, you are tested to be honest about your own character. In a sense you have to be your own most loving friend *and* fiercest critic. In accepting these frailties in yourself, you build your own strength to resist. In admitting them or acknowledging them to others, much of their sting and potential for harm disappears, or at least becomes less relevant.

Embracing yourself entirely, warts and all, empowers those around you to examine their own shortcomings and points them in a direction within themselves where they, too, can let go of what sabotages their own growth. It also defuses their claims against you and, in turn, endears you to those who appreciate such honesty in the face of their own frailties. The spaciousness we create in embracing our own ambiguous natures invites others to embrace a vision of the world that is greater than they would have otherwise imagined.

If you are still standing after all of the attempts to seduce, disarm, or discredit you, your opponents may go to more extreme lengths to stop you bothering and challenging them. They may try to scare you, bring you to your knees, or even harm you. In the face of such action, you just stand your ground, because at this point you know that you are not turning back. You have the peacefulness, the power, and the charisma to withstand whatever is put in your way short of severe physical violence. You have become a formidable opponent that has turned the tables. You have no doubts, and are driven by truth to defend yourself and what you stand for.

Even if you must use force or destructive means to protect and advance a cause that benefits others, you do so not out of anger or hatred, but out of a profound love that understands that those who inflict harm on others also inflict it upon themselves as they entrench psychological and behavioral patterns arising from the Three Poisons. Because your actions are rooted in compassion, they are strategic and applied only to thwart what needs to be thwarted. With this intent and focus, "collateral damage" is kept to a minimum, sincerely regretted, addressed, and possibly willingly and publicly atoned for. As when a mother slaps away a child's hand as it reaches into a fire, the pain, fear, and upset caused is only temporary compared to the burns that could maim for life.

The inner challenge

I indicated earlier that problems and challenges arising from the outside are a reflection of our own lack of mental clarity, which in turn arises from our own fixations and aggressive attitudes and the full gamut of our own unresolved emotions. These aspects are what hinder us from using peace, empowerment, magnetizing, and wrathful compassion (see page 102) effectively. Therefore, if we want to become more effective against external challenges, we need to wake up to, and transform, the challenges within ourselves.

We may have some goal in mind, some change that we would like to see, but our mental confusion may lead us to be too attached to what we want. Consequently we may look for short cuts. Because we just want to cut to the happy ending, we may be lazy in our actions and oblivious to forces around us that really need to be addressed. Being fixated only on the goal, but not on doing what it takes to achieve the goal, we are easily prey to distractions, to being led on wild goose chases by others who perhaps actively do *not* want what we are seeking. Before we know it we may have been led in some totally different direction and our goal may be as distant as ever, and perhaps even more difficult to reach.

If we go along this path without proper attention, because we feel that our cause is justified, we may get cocky. We may act, and believe ourselves to be, more powerful than we actually are. Afraid that self-criticism makes us appear weak, we may use bravado to win others over. We try to look bigger in the eyes of others. This merely invites others to discredit or ignore us. It also makes our opponents look more appealing if our own cause appears more power-seeking, self-righteous, and hollow.

Avoiding self-criticism and trying to prove to others that we are bigger than we actually are, we may take on more than we can handle. Drunk with our own sense of power – or in denial of our actual lack of power – we may overextend ourselves and drive ourselves toward bankruptcy of means and character. Our lust for survival arises and we make poor choices.

In the end, if our world fails to conform to our goal, we may abandon our ideals and lapse into self-denigration and depression, or in extreme cases resort to a violent and destructive attitude toward anything or anyone not supporting our illusion. In other words, we may well end up manifesting all of the traits and characteristics that we set out wanting to change. On the other hand, by training our minds to understand the logic and power behind altruism, we become less self-destructive and the same ego-building neurotic tendencies begin to be transformed more and more into a foundation of true compassion. When that happens:

> You try to make the world around you more peaceful.

> You try to encourage others in order to bring out the best in them.

> You try to offer those on the edge of disaster something that can turn them in a better direction.

> If all else fails, you try to take assertive action, stopping them in their tracks or prompting them to act differently, for their own good.

The degree to which these are well-informed and skillful actions on your part will be revealed to you in time by what occurs as a result. Once you have set out upon the path of compassion, the world with all of its beauties and mishaps becomes your ally in supporting and enlightening you as an agent of change.

Wrathful Compassion – A Further Examination

The last form of compassion, wrath, is the trickiest. The reason is that we often find it difficult to distinguish between a justifiable sense of outrage at unfairness or injustice, and confused anger. There is usually so much heat and force behind both. In the first case, we are being pushed to choose a course of action that we would prefer not to engage in. All other options have been exhausted or may seem to be ineffective in addressing the severity of the situation. Maybe we have the luxury of time to explain our case. Maybe we don't. In either case delay or hesitancy may only make matters worse. In the second case, confused anger, we have not paid enough attention and our emotions brim over; we lash out, then with hindsight we try to justify our words or actions to make ourselves feel better.

But even in the case of anger unskillfully unleashed, we should not be too hard on ourselves. In fact, more than likely, in such situations, we first try to keep calm and be reasonable (peaceful); try to find common ground or give the other party the benefit of the doubt (enriching); try to convince them to think or act differently, or appeal to something inside them to draw them toward our viewpoint (magnetizing). Note that here we are going through the logical process discussed earlier – a process which, at each step of the way, could have been more informed with skill and wisdom in order to create the compassion that would abate the fourth step, our wrathful response.

But regardless of our wisdom or skill, if none of these ploys works it is only after this process that we finally give up in frustration, snap, or lash out. This sequence can happen over a matter of moments, hours, months, or years. In the end, as Bön master Tenzin Wangyal Rinpoche says, our miscalculations and failure to find a less messy path lead us to conflict, and in extreme cases perhaps even to war.

However, such failures on our part should not necessarily be seen as a negative judgment on our actions and character up to this point. How we handle any difficult situation usually takes us to the limits of our wisdom and skill. We try our best, given our current level of skill and wisdom. And it just might be that it is better to do something, to act with the right intention, in the face of injustice, than to do nothing at all. **Feeling sorry for the suffering of others, but failing to intervene just because you do not think yourself skillful enough to act without anger, is just wimping out. It is not a sign of compassion.**

Rules of engagement

Until you are a long way down the road toward perfecting and applying the first three forms of compassion, the use of wrathful compassion will more than likely be problematic. To have the presence of mind to act with the purest intention, while deploying the fiercest forms of skillful action, demands that all vestiges of malice have been rooted out from within you. If this presence of mind is not firm within, the Dharma offers the following guidelines to those who see no choice but to use such means:

> First and foremost, you must understand that those toward whom you are deploying wrathful compassion are not *bad* but *misguided.* They are confused and intoxicated by their own Three Poisons.

> As such, they are deserving of compassion and you must try not to judge them or harbor feelings such as hatred toward them.

In being minded to act wrathfully, you should feel a sense of reluctance to do so. This has nothing to do with hesitating, for you might not have this luxury.

In your heart, there should be a remorseful quality that informs your action. This will prevent you from getting carried away in the energy of your destructive means and doing more damage than is necessary.

In the end, you should not celebrate your victory, but rather show regret for actions that needed to be done.

Such an approach protects you from falling into the chasm of self-righteousness and rationalized justifications. For one thing, until you are enlightened, you really cannot tell if the person or cause you oppose *is* in error or more steeped in the Three Poisons than yourself. Thus, if you are truly trying to act with wrathful compassion, you hope for the best possible outcome, free from self-interest or partisanship. In that way, you can more easily accept and work with what befalls you as a result of your actions. For in the Dharma, there is no such thing as retaliation (see box on page 116). There is a desire to see justice, but not out of a sense of revenge or leveling the score. Aggression met with aggression just creates bad blood – and bad karma – on both sides. The Buddha would have agreed with the old Welsh saying at the beginning of this chapter.

Conclusion: Starting at Home

Before my son was a year old, many Tibetan teachers had gifted him small *phurbas*. A *phurba* is a Tibetan ritual dagger used symbolically to "cut through" the Three Poisons. Fascinated by weapons as early as he could hold one, our son reveled in being

In the face of external attacks, the Buddha did not recommend doing nothing, but warned against responding in kind, because this would keep us in a state of being rooted in the Three Poisons. These are a few things he said on the subject:

> *"Do not retaliate with anger when attacked with rage."*
>
> *"Do not retaliate with abuse when reviled."*
>
> *"Do not retaliate with criticism when blamed in public."*
>
> *"Do not retaliate with blows when threatened with physical violence."*[7]

7 From Erik Pema Kunsang's *A Tibetan Buddhist Companion.* Shambhala Books, Boston, 2003, p.155.

able to hold one of his many daggers and as soon as he was old enough, he would run in the back yard, piercing the ground every so often. He told my wife that he was "taking care of demons."

Although I have never heard a story quite like ours, friends have told us similar tales of their own children, who have grown up either to be avid Nintendo game warriors or committed to martial arts. It seems that in an age of uncertainty, where war and terrorism are the daily bread of news that our children are fed with, some children are sensing a call to warriorhood in their lives. What seems paramount in these times, therefore, is that children are not only shown how warriors behave in conflict, they need also to understand how to be warriors of peace: warriors *in* peace, and *at* peace.

Toward this end, I feel that it is essential that children learn how to resolve conflict in a variety of ways. Within the home, parents often think that they should not allow their children to see them argue. They go behind closed doors, work things out and come out smiling. If a child does not see the process by which the conflict was resolved, but only sees two mad parents go into a room and two smiling parents come out, how can they possibly understand the process?

Pacifying, enriching, magnetizing, and wrathful compassion – each demonstrates a triumph over the Three Poisons. Each is inspiring. Each seems appropriate and just. What makes this so is that they come out of a conscious, engaged attitude toward the world. This is what parents, teachers, and leaders need to model more than anything else. For if children hear only hollow rhetoric from people from whom they feel disconnected, and see themselves as disfranchised, can we really expect them to show any conscience or impetus in wanting to shape their world for the better?

"The Wheel of Sharp Weapons"

"It is an absurd assumption that religion and morality have no place in politics."

H.H. the 14th Dalai Lama [8]

Whether we have contemplated the Four Thoughts that Revolutionize the Mind; realized the implications of the Four Noble Truths; applied skillful methods at working with our minds; planted the seed of positive intention with the Four Limitless Meditations; and acted in the world skillfully applying one of the four forms of compassion; or are still caught in the turbulent sea of a confused habitual mind governed by the Three Poisons – or are somewhere in between – the world lets us know. Outer always reflects inner. If a bear stands in front of a mirror, it doesn't see a rabbit, even if it wants to. Whether we are prepared to see it or not, what is in the mirror is direct and accurate.

[8] From *The Little Book of Wisdom*. Rider, London and Sydney, 1998, p.153.

In the latter part of the tenth century, two notable books were written that address how to conduct our lives so that more and more positive qualities will naturally arise: one was Shantideva's *Bodhisattvacharyavatara*, or *The Bodhisattva's Way of Life*; the other Dharmarakshita's *The Wheel of Sharp Weapons*. A great work in the Mahayana Buddhist tradition by a great meditator and scholar, the latter is a verse text about behavior: what happens when we act in the world on the basis of our own misconceptions, greed, ambition, and other expressions of the Three Poisons; and how we can reset our way of thinking to commit to a path that is uplifting for all, including ourselves. Rather than taking the high, idealistic road of Shantideva, Dharmarakshita looks at where most of us find ourselves. Understanding with compassion that the suffering we are experiencing is something we would like to escape from, he offers antidotes to our dilemma. What I find most fascinating about its message is that the lessons it offers can be applied to individuals, groups, and even nations, depending on where we want to focus. As such, I consider it a vital text to ponder for anyone who wants to become a conscious, engaged activist.

Peacocks in the Poison Jungle

From the start, Dharmarakshita makes it clear that *not* to consider changing our motivation and action in the direction suggested is, to a greater or lesser degree, courting disaster. He explains this by using similes that distinguish the actions of bodhisattvas – those Buddhas-to-be among us who have committed themselves to a life and activity based on compassion and ending the suffering of others (see also page 100) – and the rest of us, who are more or less caught up in our own world of wants and desires. In the following extract, the world that most of us live in is considered like a jungle infested with poisonous plants that breed suffering and pain. Rather than blissfully living in the serene and healing places where there are medicinal plants that free one from suffering, the bodhisattvas chose to dwell in the jungle in order to help other beings. Here they work to transform whatever is poisonous into opportunities and situations for our awakening.

1.

"In the jungle of poisonous plants strut the peacocks,
Though medicine gardens of beauty lie near,
The masses of peacocks do not find gardens pleasant,
But thrive on the essence of poisonous plants.

2.

In similar fashion, the brave bodhisattvas
Remain in the jungle of worldly concern.
No matter how joyful this world's pleasure gardens,
These Brave Ones are never attracted to pleasures,
But thrive in the jungle of suffering and pain.

. . .

4.

Now, desire is the jungle of poisonous plants here.
Only Brave Ones, like peacocks, can thrive on such fare.
If cowardly beings, like crows, were to try it,
Because they are greedy they might lose their lives.

. . .

6.

And thus Bodhisattvas are likened to peacocks;

They live on delusions – those poisonous plants.

Transforming them into the essence of practice,

They thrive in the jungle of everyday life.

Whatever is presented they always accept,

While destroying the poison of clinging desire."[9]

One of the challenges we all face, as individuals, in collectives of societies, or as nations, is to look at our own behaviors and be able to identify clearly and admit to ourselves when we are acting for everyone's benefit or just for ourselves and our friends or allies. For along with our plans and actions often come rationalizations, which over time we may forget *are* just rationalizations, justifying what we have done. And the further we get from events, these rationalizations can become hardened or reified into doctrines with an internally consistent logic, or into religious beliefs perhaps supported by a divinity that we claim holds *us* dear and above all others.

But the true fruits of our actions are not that difficult to observe. In the Buddhist view, karma is infallible. The world we live in, and what befalls us individually and collectively, is the direct result of all our previous intentions, actions, and attitudes. If we live in a Dark Age, then as the Introduction spelled out, we have feathered our own nest to be that way (see page XVII). If we do not transform our own Three Poisons, they will not only govern our emotions and actions from within, but they can also be used like weapons by others from

9 Dharmarakshita, *The Wheel of Sharp Weapons*. Translated from the Tibetan by Geshe Ngawang Dhargyey, Sharpa Tulku, Khamlung Tulku, Alexander Berzin, and Jonathan Landaw. The Library of Tibetan Works and Archives, Dharamsala, India, 1981, pp.7–8.

without. In truth, the weapons that are used against us are made of our own hands, then given to those around us to deliver their blows. For example, if we habitually display aggression in order to get our way, why should we consider it odd or an affront to our sensibilities that resentment may one day, in turn, be expressed as aggression toward us?

Looking beyond our own personal conundrum, history is replete with leaders and nations who have thought of themselves as peacocks in the Western metaphorical sense, proud and superior to the fray, strutting through the world, seeing it as a garden whose treasures they have been manifestly destined to pluck, plunder, control, or destroy. But such would-be peacocks often pay a price in the frustration, anger, bitterness, and vengefulness felt by those who feel victimized by them. Sooner or later, the "treasures" they have gained from their behavior and treatment of others become like a poison. The victor either drowns in his own obsession or is swallowed up by the obsession of another who takes his place. Such was the fate of Romania's tyrannical leader, Ceausescu, who in 1989 was toppled and killed almost before anyone had time to think about it or reconsider. Such was the vehemence and over-whelming force of the pent-up resentment that he had provoked through his actions.

This cycle of events is, according to the teaching of the Dharma, inevitable in a world where ignorance, attachment, and aggression still inform the choices made by most people. As there are four variable aspects in any complete action – intention, thought, the manifestation of intention and thought in the action itself, and the resulting emotional response (see page 65) – what we do can have any number of possible outcomes. *The Wheel of Sharp Weapons* spells out more specifically what the logical outcomes are when the Three Poisons influence any of these variables.

The Wheel proves useful in enlightening us on many world issues and situations of our time, pointing directly to the logical, inevitable responses and consequences of how we are facing up to global problems, including one phenomenon that many Western governments are currently contending with: terrorism. The examples I will use relate to the current situation that the United States in particular finds itself in. I use these as examples because I am most familiar with them. I have no doubt that anyone looking at their own country and society will find similar examples. No country has a monopoly on the Three Poisons. To begin with, let us take another verse from *The Wheel*:

14.

"When we hear only language that is foul and abusive,
This is the wheel of sharp weapons returning
Full circle upon us from wrongs we have done.
Till now we have said many things without thinking;
We have slandered and caused many friendships
to end.
Hereafter let's censure all thoughtless remarks."[10]

Consider the harsh words in foreign media and the street protests around the world in response to US foreign policy, especially with respect to the war in Iraq. We hear Americans expressing dismay and confusion when they hear and see such protests, and when foreign governments do not stand side by side with the American way of seeing the world. Less than a year after 9/11, with much of the goodwill toward the US which that atrocity had generated ebbing away as America pursued its new

[10] Ibid., p.9.

aggressive policy in Afghanistan and the Middle East, some Americans innocently asked: "Why do people hate us?" Newspapers ran articles and editorials examining this question. Children were shown on TV discussing this issue in their schools. But rather than engaging in considered debate, the Bush administration just tried to rationalize the issue away with the answer: "They are just jealous of our American way of life."

If we follow the wisdom of *The Wheel* and look at a broader picture that includes the perspective of those who are perceived to "hate us," we will come closer to a less simplistic, but more accurate, answer to the question of why the US has generated so much hostility around the world. To start with, there is a long-standing history of grassroots hostility in the Middle East, especially in the Muslim community, toward the US because of its foreign policy in the region. For years, the US government and the corporate interests that they support, and are supported by, have masterminded resource (especially oil) exploitation as well as actions to ensure the continuation and expansion of American influence in the region. US involvement has entailed years of covert interference in the affairs of sovereign Arab nations; the propping up of undemocratic or tyrannical regimes (including that of Saddam Hussein); and a refusal to do more than benignly pressure the Israelis for their policies toward the Palestinians, much to the dismay of the entire Muslim world.

Rationalizations, rhetoric, and the skewing of history have whitewashed and sanitized a bloody history – something that may blind those who benefit from cheap oil and petroleum-based products, but enrage those who have been suppressed and disadvantaged as a result. With such a history, it does not take a stretch of the imagination to foresee such hostility manifest as it did on September 11th, 2001. To make matters worse, there is the recent US invasion in Iraq and the lies, rhetoric, and denial that went into that decision. Consider the US administration's refusal to listen to UN weapons inspectors; its belittlement of those European leaders urging caution in the Middle East; its viewing as irrelevant the cooperation of many of our most important allies of the last fifty years. The US has seriously strained relationships and alliances forged over generations.

At the same time, we should not ignore the fact that the war of words across the Atlantic has gone both ways. In recent years US administrations have sometimes been sharply critical of America's traditional friends, and the allegiances and alliances that have looked so seemingly stable in the decades after the end of World War II, particularly in Europe, have shifted over the years since America's inception. They have been rocked by scandal, and military and trade conflicts, and so on. Such incidences over time have also spawned – or reinforced – stereotypes that set people against each other at the most basic of levels; Yank, Limey, Mick, Spic, Frog, Kraut, Wop, Loud-Mouthed American – our bigotry, whose in, whose out… The Three Poisons make it impossible to think beyond self-interest and partisan alliances.

With such history to live with, and live down, the only remedy for developing international friendships that can be of lasting value into the future is to curb negative speech, to "censure all thoughtless remarks," be it at the personal or political level. *The Wheel* points to a truth that every diplomat probably knows: **It is important to be mindful of one's own tongue.** There is further discussion of what the Buddha called "right speech" in the following chapter (see page 140). For now, let us look at another verse of *The Wheel*.

13.

"When we lack any freedom, but must obey others,
This is the wheel of sharp weapons returning

Full circle upon us from wrongs we have done.

Till now we have looked down upon those who were
lowly

And used them as servants for our own selfish needs;

Hereafter let's offer our services to others

With humble devotion of body and life."[11]

If we look at American history, we see the subjugation of individuals, races, or foreign groups as a part either of culture or official policy. Witch-hunts, slavery, the conscription of immigrants right off the boats, Chinese labor gangs, the internment of ethnic Japanese citizens. Of course, nations around the world have done similar things or worse. No doubt, if we were to examine what these cultures are going through today, we would see the laws of *The Wheel* applying in just the same way. But focusing on my own culture, when we in the US begin to see a growing bureaucratic stranglehold on our way of life with more repressive and restrictive laws and law enforcement agencies; ever more suspicion of citizens in general; growing invasion of privacy and loss of freedoms as so aptly demonstrated in the nebulously written Patriot Act – can we glibly point the finger and simply blame what Michael Moore calls an elite of "Stupid White Men?"

The domination of humans over other species, however undesirable, is a fact. Because of our craving to have what we want, whatever gets in our way has to be either used or removed. This Darwinian reality only speaks to the animal, instinctual side of our nature. Because of our ignorance, domination fueled by craving seems a better bet for getting what we want than cooperation. This view is shortsighted because if we place others below us on the food chain, the chances are that whenever our

[11] Ibid., p.9.

power weakens we, too, will become food for those of greater hunger.

Great philosophers have mused over "man's inhumanity to man." During the creation of the United States, no problem vexed the Founding Fathers more than the issue of slavery. Men of great vision, they saw that a democracy could not survive if the principle of equal rights was not treated as paramount and the importance of "life, liberty, and the pursuit of happiness" not acknowledged as the wish of all human beings, regardless of race, creed, or color. But they also saw the strength of habitual tendencies and feared that to try to break the culture of slavery in a newly formed, uncertain nation would meet such hostility that it would more than likely see the dissolution of the union before it had even begun to establish itself. Not only that, because the new country was in debt to Europe, it seemed only pragmatic to let the slave trade continue as a way of paying off the debt. So slavery was allowed to remain in those states where it already existed. It was a compromise.

Though it would seem that in not confronting the injustice of slavery the Founding Fathers left the US a mess that led to the Civil War and is still being worked out today politically and socially, the awareness of the injustice was there, together with the altruistic intention to overcome it, one day. This awareness was built into the US Constitution and is what keeps alive in people's mind the idea that America is "the land of the free." Embedded in the very fabric of the Constitution was the knowledge that such dilemmas were not just for lawmakers and leaders to decide upon, but for an informed and conscious electorate to participate in solving.

In reading about the lives of such men as Benjamin Franklin, Thomas Jefferson, George Washington, John Adams, and James Madison, what strikes me is that many of their qualities and ideals are in keeping with Dharmarakshita's antidote to the dilemma set up in the above verse. These men had a strong sense of serving others in the cause of freedom. Several of them exhibited a humility that allowed them to identify with the people they served. Each of them knew that they were seen by their people as special, but wanted to avoid seeing the establishment of an American aristocracy to replace the British one they had just gotten rid of.

Raising Consciousness

The world shows us what we are up to. Dharmarakshita is not inventing what isn't there anyway. The value of his verses is that they sober us up, make us aware what we have been doing. Drunk from intoxication by the Three Poisons, it's useful to be pulled over and given a breathalyzer. In "sobering up," learning to cut loose from our "evil ways," it only stands to reason that we would have to go through an emotional and behavioral "hangover" and the painful memory of what it was we did in our drunken stupor. It is important to remember, reflect upon, and understand what we have done and what resulted – and how to not go there again. Dharmarakshita demonstrates his compassion for us in *The Wheel*.

Although our modern civilization appears to be a good distance from being enlightened, it seems to me that as more people become literate and information is more widely available, the wisdom inherent in our enlightenment potential *is* being awakened. In the not-too-distant past, we may not have known what one Tibetan monk friend said to me was the "evil that men in suits do behind closed doors." This is true everywhere, be it Washington D.C., London, Paris, Delhi, Moscow, or Beijing. We are less automatically deferential to our leaders and we do know, or suspect, more of what goes on. And because we now have a multitude of instant-access media sources, word does get out, censorship or no censorship. "The truth will out" and nowadays the consequences of unbridled ignorance, attachment, and aggression are plainer to see.

Even if we do not know how to get ourselves out of the messes we find ourselves in, and although so much of what we witness becomes sensationalized and exaggerated through the tabloid media filter, a consciousness raising *is* taking place. This has two thrusts. One is where people try to turn away from the suffering. And so through such distractions as drugs and simplistic belief systems we seek to dull the impact of the fear, anxiety, depression, and despair that we feel at the constant bombardment of suffering witnessed night after night on the evening news. In this approach, the lengths we are prepared to go in active denial, betrays the awareness, somewhere inside us, of what is *really* going on.

For those who choose the alternative path, and can use the energy that is manifest in the fear, anxiety, depression, and despair to rise above them and challenge them, one of the first tasks is to have compassion for and work skillfully with those who are in denial. **Denial and defensiveness are defenseless in the face of love**

Monitoring ourselves

Lawlessness, corruption, terrorism, and warfare will not go away by making them illegal or seeking to destroy them by equally insidious means. Violence begets violence. *The Wheel of Sharp Weapons* would attest to this, and even schoolchildren know it as a playground truth. Thomas Jefferson once made the comment that governments become corrupt when people are corrupt. In one form or another, each of us is responsible for what we are witnessing around us. How could it be any other way? And, if we understand this, we must also accept the truth that we *are* our brothers' – and sisters' – keepers. We are intimately associated with *all* life. If we see corruption in those around us, we have a relationship to it for which we must take responsibility. That responsibility begins with an honest examination of ourselves. It is a futile and wasted effort if we solely busy ourselves with trying to monitor the attitudes and behaviors of others. We may effect some apparent change in this way, but may also create a lot of resentment in the process and it may be that when we are not looking, things will revert to what they were before. Using a political example, consider what happened after the ending of communism in Romania and Yugoslavia, when various clans or cultural groups resumed old hostilities and vendettas that had merely been ignored and suppressed for decades by the communist regime that had claimed all its citizens were equals.

In the end what other people do is their own responsibility, even if we may endeavor to assist them. Similarly, it is of primary importance for us to monitor our own attitudes and behaviors, employing with the highest standards of scrutiny to which we can hold ourselves. In this way, if we are successful, we will rid ourselves of corruption and create a backbone of integrity.

Because we all share the reality of this Dark Age, each of us has a connection to its cause, its continuation, and possibly its diminishing. What we are experiencing in these troubled times is a culmination of both positive and negative causes, and therefore most of us in affluent societies need to accept that we are the beneficiaries of blood money; that each of us has blood on our hands. Many of the appliances and conveniences we enjoy come to us as the result of the pillaging and depletion of the world's natural resources and the sweatshop labor of the less fortunate. Perhaps our good karma has allowed us to enjoy a comfortable life. But being born into a position of material privilege where what we enjoy comes to us through the blood, sweat, and tears of others, we have an obligation to understand, minimize, and possibly even transform whatever has come to us from corrupted intentions and actions.

This is hard work and goes a long way toward explaining why individuals, groups, even nations go through purification, a cleansing as it were, in the process of turning harmful or aggressive tendencies into positive benefits for all to share. Buddhist history is replete with stories of corrupt individuals whose fortunes were ill gotten, but were eventually put to good use. Still, the karmic "wheel of sharp weapons" came down hard upon them and they could not escape the karma of mishaps, crises, and problems in their lives as a result of their nefarious ways. But, in the end, they triumphed in helping others.

Such was the life of the great Tibetan saint Milarepa, who, misguided by his naïve love for and obedience to his embittered mother, committed mass murder, and had to work through the karma of that before becoming a great spiritual master. Then there was the powerful Indian emperor Ashoka, who took up Buddhism and became one of India's greatest and most benevolent rulers after he had begun to question what he was doing as a leader and had been further shocked into conscious awareness and compassion after witnessing the carnage that his own armies had inflicted.

Anyone looking at noted people of wealth and influence anywhere in the world could find similar, more mundane stories. In that regard, I am reminded of an influential southern US family whose fortune was gained through prostitution and bootlegging. Today they are great contributors to many worthy humanitarian causes. And yet many in the family suffer health problems and difficulties arise in many of their undertakings. Sheer luck of the draw? Mere coincidence? Or "the wheel of sharp weapons returning full circle?"

For the most part this chapter has explored geopolitical

examples of the presence of the Three Poisons and what they can be seen to have laid at our door. But before we act too cockily about what should be changed in the world, who should lead this or that nation, we need to see *ourselves* as both part of the problem and as a possible conduit for a solution. Before we step outside our door, we have to begin with ourselves and our own responsibility for those situations in the world where we are – in truth – *never* only a spectator. To become as bold as bodhisattvas in the jungle of poisonous plants, we are called upon to uproot and transform the poisons within, so that whatever we do in the world, our intentions, thoughts, acts, and emotions will successfully digest and transform the poisons of ignorance, attachment, and aggression that we see manifest as sickness, poverty, and warfare in the world around us and convey a brighter vision of what is possible.

CHAPTER 9:

The Conscious, Engaged Activist

"The purpose of our life is not simply to be healthy, live a long life, become wealthy, get educated, or win many friends. None of these is the ultimate goal of life. Whether we are healthy or unhealthy, rich or poor, educated or uneducated, our ultimate goal is to benefit other living beings. The purpose of being alive, of continuing our present association of body and mind, is to benefit others, to use our body, speech, and mind to bring happiness to others. All our past, present, and future happiness is received through the kindness of other living beings, and our self-cherishing is the source of all our problems."

Lama Zopa[12]

[12] Lama Zopa, *Ultimate Healing: The Power of Compassion*. Wisdom Publications, 2001, p.27.

So far we have discussed general considerations, as well as particular contemplations and meditations, which we need to be aware of and work with – to the best of our ability – in order to be a conscious, engaged activist. They apply at any time, but especially in the seeming morass of the Dark Age that we live in. That being said, it is now time to flesh out our image of a conscious, engaged activist. How would they look? What would they do? How would they act?

The face and activity of the conscious, engaged activist will be different for the circumstances that they find themselves in. It's easy for someone of my age to think of the term "activist" in the context of the 1960s and Vietnam. Young men and women with long, unkempt hair, radicalized and marching. Or more modern images of serious, concerned citizens focusing on issues, getting petitions signed, emailing members of Congress. But the image and notion of a conscious, engaged activist I wish to portray here goes beyond these images, beyond left and right, beyond any sense of partisanship whatsoever.

A conscious, engaged activist interjects wisdom and skillful means into whatever field of action or endeavor they are a part of. Briefly, Buddhist tradition teaches that there is a female and male aspect to enlightenment (a bit like *yin* and *yang*, but in Tibetan referred to as *yab* and *yum*). Wisdom (*yum*, literally translated as mother) is considered the female aspect of the enlightening process that tempers our awareness with heart and directness. "Skillful means" (*yab*, literally translated as father) is the male aspect that provides us with the precision and power to act. These two aspects are necessary for any venture to be successful. If one is lacking, then problems naturally arise. If there is no skillful means and only wisdom, then there is waffling and ineffectual action. If there is skillful means and no wisdom, situations become restrictive and tend towards fascism. But when they exist together in balanced measure they produce the intelligence, conscience, and compassion to do whatever it takes to make life better and meaningful for others, beyond partisanship.

Even though we may commit to embracing the various tools and considerations that I have spelled out in this volume, more than likely we shall find ourselves drawn to various fields of action based on our own karmic inclinations, or on preferences derived (in the Buddhist view) from many lifetimes of experiences. These strengths and weaknesses are reinforced in our current lifetime by the circumstances that we find ourselves in. So for some, being the consciously, engaged activist may mean working to bring the troops home from a war we deem unjust. On the other side of the equation may be a dedicated infantryman in a war-torn region of the world whose sole intent is to manifest patience and compassion for citizens caught in the crossfire. One person may work in a social action group and choose to be out in the streets to protest unfair trade practices. Another may be a policeman dedicated to maintaining peace and order in an economically deprived inner city neighborhood. The conscious, engaged activist could be a grandmother, emailing her friends with MoveOn updates or someone sitting quietly in a retreat somewhere, generating thoughts of love and compassion. The change that is sought by one activist may be a material change of circumstances. For another, it may be a change of conscience and consciousness.

Such activists can find themselves labeled as social misfits, anarchists, fascists, revolutionaries, terrorists, saints, freedom fighters, upholders of justice, even righteous avengers. What must be understood is that if we enter and act in any given situation on the basis of the principles we have set out thus far, it does not matter what the circumstance is. The conscious, engaged activist will make that situation better by bringing into it more wisdom, skill, and compassion, thus creating the context for the emergence of something more lasting and beneficial for all.

Because we breathe in and out, because we get up in the morning, go about our business in the day, and go to sleep at night, we are active and, to a greater or lesser extent, conscious and engaged. We bring to any and all situations we encounter whatever level of understanding we have, and then engage in that situation with varying degrees of enthusiasm or reluctance. Objectively speaking, we are never *not* acting in our world. There is no such thing as doing *nothing* about a situation. We are always doing *something* – and that something extends far beyond what we may think we are doing. In the matrix of our connection to each and every being, we continually affect our world in every dimension, whether consciously or unconsciously. The more we commit ourselves to becoming conscious and awake, the more we will understand this. In turn, our knowledge puts us in touch with our own role and responsibility in the grand scheme of things. This may seem a terrible burden and lead us the point of feeling paralyzed. So what should we do?

Equally, as we grow spiritually and become more conscious in our lives, the more we begin to notice those areas of our lives where we are *not* conscious. As a group of jazz musicians in Woodstock, New York, once sang, "The confusion is endless."[13] This predicament is depicted in the Buddhist story of the life of Loving Eyes (Avalokiteshvara or Chenrezig), the bodhisattva of compassion (see page 96). His vow was to save all sentient beings from suffering, and at one point he actually thought he had accomplished this amazing feat. He soon learned that he was wrong, and in his sadness, he exploded into thousands of little pieces. Other enlightened beings,

---

[13] Lyrics from a song by Karl Berger and Friends.

seeing how vast his compassion was, decided to put him back together again, this time with eleven heads and a thousand arms so that he could resume his work, but with greater capacities. Each head and set of arms was devoted to one of the Four Forms of Compassion (see page 102). Thus the bodhisattva's activity became limitless, to match the limitless number of sentient beings he was now prepared to save.

As the story of Chenrezig is intended to imply, we have the capacity always to expand what we do. It is just that as we awaken our loving nature and express compassion through our actions, we grow more keenly aware of how much more there is to do. One of the challenges in this situation is how to maintain balance. How do we respond to the tests of our strength? How do we learn not to overextend, yet at the same time to grow even stronger?

The shortcomings we face and the unintended disasters that befall us along the way are the result of us still being partisan: not having the wisdom or skill to work in a balanced and intelligent way with our energies. Not being able to comprehend, let alone access, the amazing potentiality we possess, our focus remains narrow and we become zealous or fixated in one direction and dimension of our life at the expense of others. Only knowing limited ways of using our energies, we pour them into a limited range of tasks. There have been great geniuses and eccentrics in the course of history who have done amazing feats that have helped advance civilization and culture. But it is also true that they often had areas of their lives that were not well attended to. And, as a result, their legacies may be mixed and the results of even their greatest efforts may be skewed or used in unintended, even undesirable ways. This may have to do with the actual thing one creates, as in the case of Alfred Nobel, who invented dynamite to make mining easier, but didn't consider that it would – almost at once – be used for bombs and shells. Or, it could be someone like President Bill Clinton, who could not foresee how his effectiveness, and the fruits of his efforts domestically and internationally, would be tarnished and diminished because of his wayward personal lifestyle and habits.

To my mind, there have always been countless "unsung heroes" whose lives may not have been so exciting, but gave something of lasting value to others. Rarely do we hear of ordinary citizens who act in a conscious, engaged way in all spheres of their lives. We seem to be more intrigued by the heroes and icons of creativity, power, and spiritual attainment who may suffer in certain parts of their lives but rise to fame and universal attention in another sphere. However, the Buddhist story of Vimilakirti gives us an example of a man who was at the same time a husband, father, businessman, statesman, and spiritual teacher. We shall look more closely at his activity and legacy towards the end of the book. Suffice to say at this point, in learning methods to cut through and transform the Three Poisons, Vimilakirti's mind was open and receptive to all that he encountered. No aspect of his worldly life – such as the care for his children, his wife, his business – was considered an obstacle to some noble cause. He embraced all and saw obstacles as opportunity, rising to each situation. His wisdom and skill to act with intelligent compassion endeared him to all around him.

What is important in Vimilakirti's example is that it was in his training to awaken his enlightened potential that he developed the capacity to handle every facet of his life more effectively. He personified the Buddha's Eightfold Path, which was introduced briefly in an earlier chapter (see page 48). It made him a better, more effective person in every dimension of his life.

Doing Our Best: The Eightfold Path

"The Noble Truth of the path leading to the cessation of suffering: it is simply the Noble Eightfold Path, namely right view, right thought, right speech, right action, right livelihood, right effort, right mindfulness, right concentration." As summarized by the Buddha in the last of the Four Noble Truths, the goal of the Eightfold Path is to create a well-rounded, awakened individual, free of the grips of the Three Poisons, and hence effective at every level of his or her being and action. The eight aspects of this path engage our spirit through cultivating the wisdom of right view and thought/intention; our bodies through the cultivation of ethical conduct in speech, action, and livelihood; and our mental/emotional development through the cultivation of focused effort, mindfulness, and concentration. When we take into consideration what the Buddha suggests in each of these aspects, we become dignified, upright, and certain about how we conduct our lives and where we need to place our energies.

Of course, at this point, it is logical to think to yourself, "OK, so what do I need to do? What is the best profession or calling for me to be an effective change-maker?" or "If I get into such and such a situation, what is the best thing to say or do?" In all the vast number of books available for self-help and improvement, wouldn't it be a relief to find one that gave you the simple answers to these questions?

But, the Eightfold Path is not about convenience. The Eightfold Path does not necessarily focus on what you *should* do. Much of that has to do with the particular situation you find yourself in. For certain, in the category of "Right Livelihood," there are some professions or career tracks that are more problematic and necessitate more skill than many can muster. Beyond these, however, the Eightfold Path is pretty wide open. The

Buddhist teachings on each aspect of the Path have less to say about exactly how you *should* be and act than about how *not* to be and act. The reason for this is simple: If you begin to live your life with the considerations we have outlined thus far, your speech and actions will clear themselves up. You will awaken more and more wisdom and skillfulness in your actions and, increasingly, you will know what to do in each situation as it arises. At the same time, as imperfect beings, we shall periodically lapse into our old negative patterns of speech, thought, and action based on our unresolved, nontransformed emotions – residues of our Three Poisons. Thus, the Buddha spends a little more time providing us with a thorough understanding of these negative emotions and their resultant actions, so we can be more aware of the usefulness of avoiding or minimizing them.

Much of the discussion up to now has focused on the spiritual and mental/emotional components of the Eightfold Path. Let us now focus more closely on the ethical components: right speech, action, and livelihood. We shall begin with right speech – how to communicate with integrity and clarity.

Right Speech: Communication

The Bible says: "In the beginning was the Word." God first manifested in the unformed cosmos as an act of communication. The divine Word was the very agent of creation, the means by which everything in the universe came into being. It was also the means by which God related to Creation. Likewise, we shape our own personal universe, and ultimately the wider world beyond, through how we communicate.

It used to be said that a person was known by their word. Their word was a sacred bond and meant something, because it carried the intentions and the vibratory qualities of its speaker to the listener. In this light, effectiveness in speech, or any other form of communication, goes far beyond words and their specific meanings. That is why corporations, politicians, and organizations hire speechwriters, public relations professionals, or spin doctors who are paid to charge the words to create as positive, and memorable an impact as possible. A person's sincerity, intent, and "vibe" can make words powerful. As words, whether spoken or written, are commonly what set actions in motion, we need to be clear and speak from the heart if we stand any chance of getting the most out of what we say. If we want our words to be valued, the Buddha makes the Four Recommendations for Right Speech, as follows:

> **Do not lie or deliberately deceive others;**
> **Do not slander or speak maliciously of others;**
> **Do not use harsh or hurtful words;**
> **Do not gossip.**

In the next few pages we shall deal with each of these recommendations in turn.

Do not lie or deliberately deceive others

This is actually harder than it seems. With respect to lying, due to our Three Poisons, more than likely our ignorance will ensure that what we say is not entirely accurate. As beings in a relative world filtering everything we look at through our subjectivity, we can skew just about anything; data is never objective, facts are never objective facts. Because of our subjectivity, what we communicate is immediately and always open to a vast array of interpretations. That is why the legal oath "to tell the truth, the whole truth, and nothing but the truth," is an impossibility in a reactive, litigious society such as currently exists in the US, and leads to the legal hairsplitting that gets criminals acquitted and innocents condemned. This is probably why Tibetan masters generally encourage people to stay away from the legal profession and litigation if at all possible. They believe that the law of karma will usually take care of people's misdemeanors better than we can.

Considering the number of frivolous or unnecessary lawsuits and the booming "compensation culture" that we are famous for in the West (especially in the US), and how we have all seen certain cases blown up into hysterical media circuses that preclude sober common sense reflection, the advice of the Tibetan masters seems warranted. The same masters will also tell you that two careers worth not pursuing are acting and politics. They consider both careers to be focused on creating illusions in the minds of others. And as for lawyers and actors becoming politicians…

Because we are social animals and communication is vital to our survival and the quality of our lives, the intention behind our words can be of far greater importance than the truth or accuracy of the words themselves. The Buddha was once asked about the matter of lying and told the following story as an example. A man is walking home from the marketplace and sees a fire in the distance. As he gets closer to the smoke, he sees that the fire is in his own home. He looks up at the second story window and sees his children playing, unaware of the danger that is engulfing them. Wanting to get them out of the house quickly, but without alarming them into a state of panic, he calls: "Children, come downstairs. I have brought each of you a beautiful present from the market!" Excitedly, the children run down the stairs to find what their father has brought them and as they reach his side, the house crashes to the ground in ruins.

At one level this father blatantly lies to his children. He has no gifts from the market and he is fully aware that he is deceiving his children, who are expecting toys or sweets or something similar. On another level, he *is* giving them a far greater gift –

their lives – but understands that they are too young to grasp the magnitude of this. But in the few moments he has before the house's imminent collapse, an act of deceit is the only means by which the father can fulfill the more important task of preventing his children from suffering terror, pain, and certain death. In this case, the harm that comes from lying – his children's disappointment – is overwhelmingly outweighed.

The issue in lying and right speech, therefore, has more to do with the *intent* behind the deceit. We should try being honest about our intent, but there are times, as in the last story, when that might not be appropriate.

On this subject of honesty, we should remember that **it is easier to be honest than it is to be truthful.** We can be more frank about our thinking process, our biases, perhaps the emotions that are fueling our reasoning; the more honest we can be about what our assumptions are, about what lies behind our words, the more we show our openness and invite openness from others. And in that spirit of openness, we come closer and closer to what is true.

In the context of this thought, I will take a brief look at post-9/11 America and the use of speech by the current US administration. On the one hand, US citizens have been encouraged to relax and go about their business, travel, go to the malls, and so on. But alongside these reassurances there are periodic orange alerts, warnings about travel, bomb threats to malls, and so on. With such a schizophrenic message, what can the administration think is a reasonable response on the part of the people? And, more to the point, I look at the timing of such warnings and ponder what the intent really is.

The great British psychoanalyst R.D. Laing once said that if the average person knew what was really going on with respect to the forces operating behind the scenes in foreign relations, most of us would commit suicide. Similarly, governments have *always* lied to their citizens. At times, when war was wanted, fear was woven into the dialogue. When peace was wanted, platitudes and reassurances put the citizens back to sleep. As Goering well knew (see page 7), this has been one aspect of how leaders manipulate their nations since the beginning.

I think that a digression at this point to look at the events in the times that I am writing will highlight the Buddha's concerns and guidelines.

With regard to the War on Terror, it is interesting to learn that in the prosperous 1990s, President Bill Clinton was carrying on a covert war against the likes of Osama Bin Laden. Periodically, such news made its way to the forefront, but most of the time it was played down. And the country had a more positive, upbeat feel to it. Other than the "millennium bug" scare, the twenty-first century was generally anticipated with optimism.

But since 9/11/01, under the Bush administration, this covert war has gone public. Of course circumstances are different in that terrorism finally and officially made it to American shores. It would logically be more in the forefront of our minds and concerns. However, I cannot but feel that this fact is being used as a weapon against US citizens; a weapon to manipulate forces and funds to benefit some more than others, and to secure those benefits for years to come. The "Downing Street Memos," the "Plame Affair"(the outing of a covert CIA operative to get back at her ambassador husband, who had published the simple truth that there were not uranium deals happening between Niger and Iraq) – these and other controversies let most who wish to see such things know the transparent truth, that the war in Iraq was fabricated. And when no-bid business contracts with ties to the US administration were in place without there being an "exit strategy" following the "liberating" of Iraq, it is not a matter of rocket science to deduce that a small number of powerbrokers and their friends played the American public and the "coalition of the willing" like a well-tuned fiddle. I have gone to political meetings where people have wanted the US government to announce when they will leave Iraq. My answer to them is simple: The US will pull out when the contracts with these private companies come to an end. In the meantime, the soldiers that are there act as mercenaries for private moneyed interests.

In the pre-9/11 American press, an attention to politicians' words seemed to be matched by an observation of their body language. Body language communicates how clearly and honestly we are behind the words we utter. Post-9/11, the media seem to have suspended commentary on this and focused on words alone. Speeches by the administration have been "good" if the "right" words are being used and provide some choice, newsworthy "sound bites." Even though the furtive glances, grimacing lips, and defensive postures might be telling a different story, few in the media have been willing to comment on body language. As in the story of "The Emperor's New Clothes," those wanting to believe the bullish, upbeat words of the Bush administration, have continued to take their claims about the threat of terrorism and America's success in fighting it, at face value. Sharp observation or criticism from astute political analysts willing to separate fact from rhetoric has been sorely lacking. Of course, in a highly charged political atmosphere, one may think that the reason few people stand up and ask questions is that they fear being deemed "unpatriotic." This may make some people cower, but for the most part, the reason for the absence of serious critical analysis in the American media is simple: Along with building a monopoly over energy sources and large world commodity interests, the same small group has invested its money in the media. What Americans have come to hear more and more on the "news" is less news and more spin.

State-run or monitored media outlets are nothing new in most countries of the world. Friends from Eastern Europe told me that one thing that seemed to distinguish Americans from themselves was that Americans tended to believe what they heard or saw in the news. A free press was the hallmark of a young America. Over time, this has been eroded to the current sad state of affairs that many in the US lament. Still, this doesn't stop the administration's apologists defending what a small but growing group has become more and more suspicious and concerned about.

But with the passage of time, deceit always begins to wear thin and the strings holding the marionettes become plain for all to see. In the end, the results of this deceit may actually prove beneficial and bring us back to a Jeffersonian-like suspicion of government. In the end, it may mature the American citizenry and hone their discriminating awareness by making them more conscious, more observant, and less likely to be seduced. Like the citizens of our western European allies, who have witnessed the folly and devious machinations of their governments for centuries, Americans may become more conscious, critical, and engaged in the political process. As this happens, the issues that bind cultures and economies around the world will, more than likely, enter into our consideration and we shall, once again, cooperate with the international community as equals rather than try to bully the world into following what America wants. However, knowing that we are in a Dark Age, I believe this process may take longer than many of us would like.

For the conscious, engaged, activist the challenge becomes how to advance a cause or issue without undue exaggeration, and in a way that does not cause harm. There are certainly times when one needs to employ great skill to grab the attention of others and get your message across, but if we remember that "what goes around comes around," if we "spin" something one way we only ensure that in the future, things will get spun in the exact opposite direction, to our disadvantage. If we do lapse into spin and then get caught out, the only protection we have in such situations is to be honest about the intent behind our spin. For some reason, officials and those who get caught in the spotlight often forget how forgiving human nature can be in the face of honesty. How often have we seen people who, in their reluctance to demonstrate such transparency, have come to be haunted by their words down the line? It is better not to "spin" or misrepresent things in the first place.

Do not slander or speak maliciously of others

The Buddha's second recommendation for right speech warns of the damaging effects of slanderous speech: speaking maliciously or with ill will about others. These damaging effects are not only to others but to ourselves, because such behavior, in the end, destroys our own credibility. One aspect of this is rumor-mongering: deliberately infecting other people with negative, hurtful beliefs about someone. What is interesting about rumor-mongering is that, seen from the perspective of The Wheel of Sharp Weapons, it may be that the rumor itself is not wholly untrue. But the point is, again, what is your intention in spreading information about a person that is likely to make others think less highly of them? Or, if their reputation is already poor, what is your true intent in reinforcing it? Think on your reason for getting involved in spreading some negative piece of news or information. Is it really to draw attention to yourself? There is wisdom in the childhood expression, "Nobody likes a tattle tale." In the end, your own reputation can be on the line just as much, if not more, than the person you are tattling about.

To speak ill of another with the intent of helping a noble

cause, protecting lives, and so on, may perhaps be justified in certain circumstances. But you must carefully monitor your intent to ensure that it is truly altruistic, in order to respond firmly to any accusation of acting maliciously and with ill will.

Do not use harsh or hurtful words

The Buddha next admonishes us to be careful of the words that we use in speaking directly to another person. He warns of the damage that can be caused by harsh, hurtful words. When we deride or belittle someone, or use angry and aggressive words toward them, that is often a defensive reaction that reflects our own unresolved issues. Unable to deal openly with what we see or hear, we may lash out in aggression and anger. According to the Buddha, though, anger destroys virtue. The positive rapport we may have established in our communication with someone can be destroyed in an instant. And the weakening effect of "lashing out" not only harms our relationship to the person we have attacked, but it can infect other relationships, too.

However, there may be times when we need to shake someone up, confront them about their own actions or behavior, for their own good or for the good of those around them, and our words can seem harsh in order to get through. Again, this boils down to the question of *intent*. There is of course a difference between defensive, ego-centered *anger* and the sort of compassion-centered *wrath* discussed earlier (see page 104). Shaking someone up with compassionate intent aims to provide an opportunity for self-reflection and honesty. Harsh words said not out of anger, but with concern and care, are likely to be less damaging to a relationship in the longer term, even if the immediate fall-out is a personal rift. Indeed, confronting someone with an honest appraisal of their conduct may well have a healing effect that makes a relationship closer than before. In this respect I reflect upon the falling out of friends, neighbors, nations who have, over time, come back together, even stronger. However, the choice of this form of communication always carries a risk, unless we are certain that the Three Poisons played no part in our motives.

With respect to the harshness of words, one additional point needs to be added. This has to do with a more sociological perspective, taking the Buddha's advice and looking at it from a more macro-perspective. I mention this because within circles attempting to be more conscious, there is, I believe, a movement toward taking the concept of *ahimsa*, or nonviolence, too literally and too far. In a nutshell, the admonitions and recommendations in the Buddha's teachings on Right Speech are the essence of nonviolent ways of communicating. This is the basis for such techniques as "Nonviolent Communication," or NVC, that are taught today. For certain, I have seen the benefits of such techniques in the lives of individuals and couples. But we must understand that, as mentioned earlier, everything is empty of intrinsic, independent existence. All words and actions may be positive, negative, or neutral depending on the perceiver. What may cause harm in one situation may be beneficial in another, and vice versa.

What that implies is that there *is* a place for harsh words, for painful frankness, for inciting those to act who would otherwise remain on the sidelines of life. These are hard judgment calls. But, they should not be wholly discarded as means that can be used when necessary by the conscious, engaged activist. As one Tibetan monk friend used to say to me, "Sometimes you need to call black black." Even the the proponents of NVC recognize this, but add – and rightly so – that with harsh words, with confrontations where there is a lack of mutuality and one side prevails over another, there is always a price to pay. And sometimes that price is unavoidable.

The discussion here focuses on power differentials and

legitimacy. Such factors do influence what type of speech is most effective When a power is perceived as legitimate, for example the head of the class, the CEO of a company, the ruling party or class, the words and actions initiated by that power can often be rationalized away or sanctioned by what appears to be a higher authority of some sort, be it historical precedent, God, or whatever. If what they are doing or how they are acting is questioned by others, those in power can often respond in a benign, understanding manner that can descend into condescension toward those levying the challenge. More than likely, because those who have the legitimated power have more access to people's opinions, the news media, and so on, anyone justly challenging that power may need to become more provocative in their message to overcome their lack of legitimacy in the eyes of others.

This is why the words of radicals and revolutionaries often deliberately set out to appeal in a very direct, emotional way. One of the future Founding Fathers of the United States, the young Thomas Jefferson, concurred with the French anarchist, Denis Diderot, who was quoted as saying that "The last king should be hung by the entrails of the last priest." We may never know how literally Jefferson was willing to consider Diderot's statement. Other equally provocative statements were made by the circle of men and women responsible for inciting the population of America to go to war to cast off what they defined as tyranny. John Adams, the second president, was quoted as saying, "I must study politics and war that my sons may have liberty to study mathematics and philosophy." Benjamin Franklin said at the signing of the American Declaration of Independence: "We must all hang together, or assuredly we shall all hang separately." And there are the famous words of Patrick Henry: "Is life so dear or peace so sweet as to be purchased at the price of chains and slavery? Forbid it, Almighty God. I know not what course others may take, but as for me, give me liberty or give me death!"

No doubt, if we gathered the words of other radicals, revolutionaries, and "insurgents" around the world over the course of history, we would hear similar sentiments. The point here is that in the absence of being under the mantle of what is deemed circumstantially legitimate in the eyes of God or man, a biting turn of phrase or well-crafted pronouncement from a charismatic leader can stop people in their tracks, incite comment, raise questions. In times when wrathful actions seem the only option to effect change, the speech that is necessary to set in motion those actions will also be wrathful.

All this having been said, confrontational or provocative speech need not be filled with vitriol and harmful intent. Of course, those whose legitimacy or authority is called into question may feel the sting of words against them and claim that they are being treated unfairly or worse by their challengers. This is just a political matter. But it is not infrequently the case that the rhetoric that is used by those wishing for change also includes comments that are demeaning or degrading to their opponents beyond what is necessary. I am reminded of various left-wing or liberal talk show hosts in America in recent years who seem to think nothing of going head to head with their right-wing or conservative counterparts when it comes to slanderous comments that really have nothing to do with the matters at hand. Such words uttered in a noble cause will degrade that cause, lower the bar, so to speak. They indicate that the consciousness of those using such tactics is not too dissimilar to that of those whom they rage against. In the end, there is cause for concern that if the tables were turned, those who sought change would become just as recalcitrant and problematic as those whom they sought to oust for the better – it would be the same soap opera with different players

Do not gossip

Lastly, the Buddha talks about the **damaging effect of gossip.**
Gossip may seem benign, but in fact it is probably the most
devious and destructive form of communication. There is a
saying, "Loose lips sink ships," and there is truth in these words.
Gossip has to do with poorly monitored communication. It is
idle talk – unthought-out, ill-considered, lazy language. Behind
the seemingly harmless banter of gossip is usually some poorly
defined driving force. Are we speaking because we are nervous?
Are we saying something so we get noticed, don't feel left out?
Perhaps we are blabbering on just to make the other person feel
at ease. What can follow is the passing on, with only partial
consideration, of inaccurate information. A vague, unfounded,
theoretical notion that you don't give much attention to can slip
off your tongue, pen, or keyboard and become an idea "out
there" that someone else takes seriously and acts upon.

Gossip creates collusion and conspiracy. Among friends, it
creates a secret society of those who are "in the know" and
those who are not. It can spread information in such a way as to
make something insignificant into a big deal, a rallying cause. Or,
as modern day spin doctors know, you can also make a big
problem go away by just making something else seem more
important. (I think of the days when Enron was falling and
the CEOs close to the US administration were falling prey to
scrutiny. Suddenly, everyone was chattering about two notorious
criminals, Winona Ryder and Martha Stewart. And we all but
forgot about Enron…)

Whereas rumor-mongering is direct and has more
immediate consequences, gossip creates a nexus of confusion
that can be the cause for the acceleration of rumors, harsh
words, and other forms of ill-conceived communication.

It is probably because gossip is the greatest source of our
communication problems that the Buddha recommended silent

retreats and times when we sit silently so that we can quieten the banter of our minds. It is interesting to note that some of the most successful corporations in the world are run by Quakers, who are reputed to start their business meetings with several minutes of silence. What this does is to clear the space, and prevent anyone from coming into the meeting on a roll. And, if there are prior ideas or intentions, having them come out of silence exposes them to greater scrutiny, both from within and without.

As we become more conscious of the cacophony within our own mind and see how it steers our communication one way and the other, we have more compassion in understanding the willy-nilly nature of what most people go through in their own minds. We can then make the ecological decision not to pollute the world with our own confusion.

Some thoughts on the media

Knowing the Buddha's teaching on speech and actions that damage reputations, wreak havoc in people's lives, and lead to karmic repercussions, further down the road, it becomes painfully obvious that much of our media and news focus almost exclusively on just the sort of thing he warns against. The media are constantly churning out exposés and personal dramas that have as their central themes lies, deceit, murder, corruption, sexual misconduct, and so on. Some would like to argue that focusing on human depravity and immorality actually encourages it, by advertising its existence. Others feel that the entitlement to free expression, as enshrined for example in the US Constitution, guarantees the right of the media to put out such material, and that those who do not want to watch it or read it do not have to.

I look at such material in the context of gossip; the media rarely has a well-defined moral purpose for putting something out into the public domain, but rather observes what people currently seem to be fixated on and feeds those fixations in order to maximize profits. As the media and news services grow in importance in our lives, it is only logical that issues of morality, ethics, and intent become part of the dialogue in discussions about regulating them. This dialogue should not favor one ideology over another. An overly liberal media can be just as problematic as an overly conservative and restrictive one. In the ambiguity of relative reality, all we can ask of those who have the power over media services is that they occasionally think about providing just that – something that genuinely *serves* their audience.

Right Action

In the chapter on compassion, intent was considered as the driving force behind action and indeed synonymous with action when deployed for the benefit of others. What we now address, as with the discussion of speech and communication, are those actions which should generally be avoided.

In discussing "right action," the Buddha again broadly summarizes what he means in a series of admonitions:

> **Do not cause deliberate harm to others or yourself;**
> **Do not commit theft;**
> **Do not engage in sexual misconduct.**

Do not cause deliberate harm to others or yourself

The Buddha's first admonition under Right Action is against us causing deliberate harm or taking life, including our own. As I have said repeatedly, there is an endless cascade of events spawned by whatever we do. If we were enlightened, then not only would we know how our actions would be interpreted and responded to by others, but we would have the omniscience to see how they, in turn, would act upon others. Until cleared of the force of the Three Poisons, we have limited control over the possibly harmful effects of our actions. However, when it comes to our own actions, we can hone our intentions to ensure that what we do, even if it seems hurtful, is not done with a vengeful, spiteful, or retaliatory attitude. Thus, defending oneself or others from harm is acceptable. It may even be that in such a situation you need to use deadly force. From a Buddhist point of view such acts will have karmic repercussions, but they are mollified by the intent from which you were compelled to act and an attitude of regret to have done so. However, if you step beyond the minimum necessary action to prevent harm and act out of a desire to punish or exact revenge, then you will have crossed a line and the consequences, karmically speaking, are more severe.

The word "deliberately" in the Buddha's admonition is important. There are, of course, situations where one accidentally or unintentionally harms, maims, or kills another being. Someone may run out in front of our car; machinery fails on a job site; we accidentally tread on worms. The Buddhist understanding of karma sees a subtle link between those who find themselves behind the wheel, operating the machinery, and so on, and those who are harmed or killed. Our Western tradition seeks to exonerate of guilt those who end up as inadvertent killers in such situations, but does not go far enough in recognizing how infinite the repercussions of such events are in the wider cosmos. This probably has to with our general cultural denial of the truth of impermanence, and our limited understanding of the interconnectedness of all life.

My friend Lama Ole Nydahl works a great deal with European Buddhist students. World Wars I and II are still vividly in the consciousness of most Europeans, as war was a direct reality for many people who are still alive today. Lama Ole has looked closely at these wars and has found evidence that demonstrates that our basically loving nature was not suppressed even amid the brutality of those conflicts. One statistic he often brings up is that of the millions of rounds of ammunition that were fired by infantrymen during World War II, it is estimated that less than twenty per cent were ever aimed directly at another person. *We are not, by and large, natural born killers.* Most of us prefer peace and cherish life. And the disparity between this basic fact of human nature and what is demanded of soldiers in armed warfare is the foundation for the Post-Traumatic Stress Disorder suffered by many former combatants.

There are those among us who, in their darkness and confusion, somehow think that harming or annihilating others is justifiable. Even leaving aside clear cases of mental illness, there are people who see it as their duty, their destiny, their right, or whatever rationalization they use to themselves and others, to take life in certain circumstances.

Beyond possibly the examples of "enlightened assassins" and others who can see that their actions will protect the many (see the Tibetan story recounted on pages 17–18), it is difficult to justify any intervention that deliberately ends life. A good intent may lack the component of sufficient remorse, turn vengeful, or go further than strictly necessary. History cites countless examples of battles that went too far, or happened after treaties had been signed, leaving behind a legacy that precipitated hatred in the future.

In our everyday lives, few of us have to consider whether or not we are going to enter a situation where we may have to decide whether to kill someone or put ourselves in harm's way. For those who do, such as agents of law enforcement or the armed forces, it would seem both prudent and necessary to encourage a mindfulness that addresses this dilemma, and sharpen the skill to be able to use deadly force sparingly and with genuine regret.

On the issue of taking ones own life, Buddhism naturally does not encourage suicide. It is considered, for the most part, a demonstration of a lack of compassion toward oneself, rooted in rigid beliefs. The Ven. Khenpo Karthar Rinpoche once said that if a person deliberately shortens their own life, then that person's consciousness will re-enact the suicide day after day until the time that their karma would otherwise have determined as the end of their life. In other words, we may want it all to be over, but that's not what we get. (I shall not discuss here euthanasia when a person is in extreme pain; my views on this are expressed in *Perfect Endings: A Conscious Approach to Dying and Death*).

But then there are examples of Vietnamese monks who willfully burned themselves in protest of a war in their country. In this case, using Buddhist logic, these monks no longer saw their bodies as personal. Their intent was to use their body as a vehicle of expression, to create images that would provoke reflection and dialogue. It is hard to know if the impact they desired made a difference one way or the other in the course of the war. But it certainly demonstrated a fierceness of spirit that left its mark on the minds of many an American GI.

Another example is the self-induced death of Tibetan monks when facing Chinese execution squads. These monks, adept in the yogic conscious dying practice known as *phowa*, elected to eject their consciousness out of their own bodies. The Chinese thought that these monks died from fright. But, in fact, they chose to cause their own deaths out of great compassion for their executioners. The Dharma teaches that it is a crime with serious karmic consequences if one takes the life of a person devoted to spirituality. Thus, their executioners were spared these consequences.

In recent times, we have become sadly familiar with those who commit suicide in the pursuit of a military, political or religious objective. In itself this is nothing new, as the world has long had its share of willing martyrs. However, whereas these acts have often been carried out against perceived aggressors ("enemy" troops or police, the predominant targets in the Iraq war, for example), many suicide bombers of today, such as those of 9/11 in New York and 7/7 in London, often choose to attack defenseless civilians in order to influence political outcomes.

Of course, such suicide bombers of today (notably in Iraq and Israel-Palestine) usually hold the religious or ideological belief that what they are doing is noble, an act of redressing injustice, for which they will be rewarded in heaven. However we may recoil in horror from the outlook of such people, it is naïve, foolish, and insensitive to dismiss them as beyond the pale, or to think that the only action we can take against such misguided souls is, in the words of President George W. Bush, to "hunt them down and bring them to justice."

Religious zealotry and the seductive words of dangerous and malicious charismatics is usually most effective in places where there is poverty, unemployment, and poor education. Where do the young and disfranchised in such places find ways of displaying their nobility, their higher purpose? Taking these common human desires and coupling them with anger, frustration, and a sense of futility is one recipe for creating people who are willing to strap on bombs to make a point, to further a cause, to proclaim the glory of their God. In addition the stark truth is that many of these same people have also been direct or indirect witnesses to the effects of the civilian "collateral damage" of bombs dropped on military targets; of covert operations; and of martial law, often imposed by Western "aggressors" or the regimes they support.

In some respects, acts of terrorism and suicide bombings are the weapons of those who, once again, do not have legitimate power, or feel cut off from it. Their presence is a leveling of the playing field. Consider dropping a daisy wheel bomb into an area from 5,000 feet above the ground. You never see the faces of those you kill with the countless bits of flying shrapnel. Then consider what it takes walking into a crowded market, seeing the faces of those around you as you detonate your bomb-laden vest. Perhaps those who do such acts are trained to be dispassionate or cut off in the moment so that they do not back down, do not hesitate. If so, this is actually a testimony to our loving nature and the fact that, in order for us to do such harm to others, we need to override our sensibilities through extreme belief, charged rhetoric, and brainwashing. Thus even if, in the act, suicide bombers are numb or out of touch other than with their mission, their choice comes out of a fierceness of purpose.

The resolve of these men and women, therefore, is very powerful. As such, we cannot simply "root them out," because the root causes that create them are perpetuated, both from within and without, by a mind confused with the Three Poisons and living in a world which, karmically speaking, is of their own making and is reinforced by others who, caught in their own Three Poison and, lacking the wisdom and compassion to know better, support or encourage them to act atrociously. And if they *do* know better, it is doubly worse for them.

(As a side note to this discussion, I cannot help but ponder how different the training of terrorists is compared to those who are trained as special forces and those involved with covert operations. To get people to do what would be, in "normal circumstances," heinous would seem to require a similar overriding of normal decency and sensibility. Thinking of such fierce and abnormal devotion reminds me of a conversation I had many years ago with an associate who knew the leaders of US Strategic

Air Command. While at dinner and getting very drunk, senior commanders – who were directly under the order of the president of the United States – began to weep in an expression of their devotion to the office of the president and believed that the president was carrying out the will of God on Earth.)

To counter terrorism of this nature therefore, we need to look more closely at our own behaviors and actions. It is more than "hunting" the terrorists and bringing them to "justice." We need to think about bringing justice to the lands where terrorists are bred. What can we do to end poverty, create opportunity, and educate people? What can we do to challenge our own governments and leaders not to march to the tune of corporate greed and avarice that leaches the life blood from countries and peoples all over the world? What can we do to stand in the way of another daisy wheel bomb being dropped? These are the issues we must address if we want to see an end to terrorism.

The bottom line in this whole discussion about harming others is that we should generally try to avoid situations where harming or killing are the options laid before us. And even if we have no choice but to elect either action, there is no escaping the karmic repercussions that harming or taking of life has. Even if the reason seems justified or enlightened, there will be some hell to pay – and that is part of the equation we need to accept.

Do not commit theft

The Buddha then addresses the damage done by robbery, theft, and fraud. We want what we do not have and under the influence of the Three Poisons try to get it by deceptive and dishonest means, often because we cannot think of any other way. However, our motivation for doing so may not always be negative. Perhaps we pilfer to get money or food for our starving children. Perhaps our family is on the verge of being evicted. Not seeing any other option but to steal, the intent is to keep the family fed and safe.

But the truth is that such actions usually invoke someone's negative response. Few people thank you for stealing from them. Most people respond with disappointment, fear, or outrage; they recoil and hold on to what they have more tightly, or desire reprisal or getting even. Thus the poverty in one mind that leads to the unskillful act of stealing encourages negative responses in others. It is a self-perpetuating "lose-lose" scenario.

There is the old saying "Property is theft." We can all think of historical examples where robbing, stealing, fraud, looting, and so on have "seemingly" paid off. The seizure of land by one group or another, be it a clan, a landlord, a church, or a nation state. The bankrupting of natural resources of entire regions by fortune seekers, or governments in search of more resources. In recent years we have watched the greed of powerful executives misleading shareholders and employees, bilking their own corporation of billions and leaving thousands of people without pensions or retirement funds. And whereas a breaking and entering charge against an inner city person on welfare may see them in jail almost immediately, the crimes of such executives have yet to be looked at with the same level of scrutiny.

Witnessing such events, it is not hard to see that more often than not, those who have the power and the money lay down the rules (the golden rule of "he who has the gold makes the rules.") Empires, kingdoms of religious and secular nature are founded on the blood and backs of others.

Because those who feel left out or wish they had more are fixated on poverty and the feeling of not having their due or entitlement, most look at the rich and mighty with awe. It is they who seem immortalized most in art, song, literature: the rich, powerful, and famous. Especially in our Dark Age, where material wealth is the measure of success, magazines, TV entertainment exposés, and newspapers focus on the lives of such people. We are supposed to be entertained by how they dress, where they go, and who they are with, and we revel in their scandals. The simple fact is that when wealth is ill-gotten or disproportionate to what our being can embrace or handle skillfully, mishaps, disasters, and scandals are bound to occur. If we look into the history of families who have ascended within society by such means, we often see that they, too, suffer. And if the laws of karma are to be believed, part of their suffering results from having taken what is not theirs to begin with.

The Buddhist mind training slogan says, "Don't reduce a god to a demon."[14] In our poverty, in our feeling somehow deprived, we should not wish to see the downfall of those who have more than us. We may think they deserve it, that they have got it coming, but, their falling or not will be determined by their karma. And our karma will just be made worse by harboring negative thoughts about others.

On the other hand, if we admire the wealth, success, power, or influence of others we should not mimic their misdemeanors, thinking that if they do it, why shouldn't we? I have heard such an argument by those who cheat on tax forms, or lie on legal forms. For one thing, this usually doesn't work well for those who do not have a wall of accountants, legal professionals, or armed protectors. But more importantly, such actions weaken us. Even if we steal or rob for seemingly altruistic reasons, the act of stealing brings us down, lowers our standards of behavior, leaves us open to reprisal. If nothing else, we subject ourselves to self-denigration – which does more to disconnect us from our loving nature than anything else.

In matters of property and finance, it behooves the

---

[14] *The Great Awakening*, by Jamgon Kongtrul. Shambhala Books, Boston, 1987, p.34.

conscious, engaged activist not to invoke the enmity of those who would like to scrutinize our actions in order to weaken our efforts or for other negative reasons. Within any society there are rules around property. Even if we are not in agreement with these laws or regulations and we consider them to be unfair or unjust, to challenge them overtly by not adhering to them will – in most situations – create two problems. For one thing, the collective mentality around us, the reified cultural reality of which we are a part, *does* have its impact on our mind. It can, therefore, be quite difficult to justify our lack of compliance – our bending of the laws to suit our needs – even to ourselves. The result can be nagging thoughts of doubt, and the energy we need to expend in order both not to think negatively of ourselves and to live in the rationalization of what we have done, can take its toll. As a mirror to these doubts, there will appear from the outside those who consider us a cheat, a scoundrel, someone not to be trusted, a criminal.

By not giving in to these tendencies and "rendering unto Caesar what is Caesar's," we stay under the radar. It also gives us a firm foundation upon which we can then address the injustices that we see around us. For disparities we see do more than just factually bespeak God's, or karmic, justice. It is a call for those with the resources to practice such virtues as generosity. And the power of doing so and the benefits yielded thereby do far more to ensure the constancy and growth of what one has, than the hiring of accounting book-cookers, attorneys, and private armies.

It is admittedly hard to stand by and watch people with power and wealth ignore, oppress, or seize the rights and property of others. When this happens, some may feel compelled to become active rebels against legitimated authority. But such efforts risk perpetuating the cycle of haves versus have-nots, if their goal is simply to even the score, to seize for ourselves what others possess. A Buddhist – the Dalai Lama is a famous example – would always advocate nonviolent action and dialogue, so that when change is achieved, those who are perceived as having disfranchised others do not in turn become disfranchised. This is the only way to guarantee a solution that is truly fair and does not leave a legacy of resentment and envy. Nonviolence and dialogue are also a way of ensuring that changes in wealth patterns are nurtured gradually. When generation upon generation has reaped the rewards of materially exploiting others, it can similarly take time to alter habitual patterns and set things on a new course. In our impatience or outrage we may want to see things happen tomorrow, if not today. But the risk in such haste is to alter the entire fabric of society so radically as to bring chaos, disorder, and suffering.

Do not engage in sexual misconduct

In the discussion of compassion, I spoke of acquiring an unshakeable charisma and an ability to influence others. This is based on overcoming the seductive power of craving and attachment and becoming equanimous. A possible problem is that as our power increases, we have to beware of becoming attached to an erroneous belief in our specialness – a belief that in our case, the ordinary rules of mortals no longer apply.

When one engages in sexual relations with another, especially intercourse, be it consensual or otherwise, Dharma teachers say that there is a bond that is created on the level of the etheric between the two people. Thus, while you may think nothing of a one-night stand or a well hidden tête-à-tête, the fact is that the person you have had sex with is stuck to you, energetically, like glue. So when your spouse or special friend thinks that you are being distant or that something has changed, they are right, even if you proclaim your love, protest vehemently, and so on. You are also stuck like glue to the other person. And, more than likely if your mate or theirs sees the two of you together or just saying hello to each other in passing, the bond or history that you share will get noticed. Beyond the duplicity in the most intimate of your relationships and the damage this will eventually have, suspicion will begin to have its effect in your other relationships. Illicit or harmful sexual relationships will always weaken, if not destroy, your credibility. That is why, beyond all of its various karmic implications, it can be used as an effective political weapon. For when the cover is blown and the illicit affair is in the open, it will usually create all-out scandal. Even if you are not actively setting out to destroy your own credibility by tempting fate, those who know the seductive side of power may place sexual temptation in your path.

Beyond such cases, which for some may seem confined to the antics of high-flying politicians and those in the espionage business, the simple truth is that sexual energies always form a part of the mix of any group that comes together. I have seen many organizations come unglued as a result of an affair between key players, sexual harassment, and so on. Thus, if you want to remain effective as an individual or you want to see a cause move forward more smoothly with less distraction and dramatics, the Buddha suggests gaining some control over your own sexual energy and its display. This is not about being prudish, but rather prudent. (Note: A detailed discussion of sex and what is meant by sexual misconduct is presented in my book *The Passionate Buddha: Wisdom on Intimacy and Enduring Love.*)

Some thoughts on mindfulness in action

Acquiring the ability to bring mindfulness to what we do and say comes about in a variety of ways. Our history can show us the skillfulness or lack of skillfulness in our actions. But, as we are habitual creatures and tend to repeat our actions rather than reform them according to the lessons of history, the Buddha offers us advice about how to steer clear of certain major stumbling blocks that will always thwart our actions, and gives us meditative methods to dismantle the habitual mind that finds itself continually lured into the same traps.

In the Japanese meditative art of archery, or *kyudo*, the mind is observant, poised in the moment prior to the arrow being set free. Freed from the Three Poisons, the mind is intent upon the bullseye, and the arrow is the connection between the two. If the mind is not freed of the Poisons, and our intention is mixed, then the arrow will miss the mark. The arrow lets us know this in the moment of its release, and where the target is hit shows us how far we have gone astray. Of course, as in life when something demands to be done, in kyudo one cannot wait forever. You place your arrow, draw your bow, rest your mind on the target, and release. It is like breathing in and breathing out. The next arrow is like the next cycle of breathing. You boldly let go, accept the consequences, then take another arrow and make a commitment to be even more mindful – even freer of the Three Poisons.

The German writer and philosopher Goethe once wrote: "Whatever you can do or dream you can do – begin it. Boldness has genius, power, and magic." The magic and power that is transformation happens when, in the present moment, you trust your loving nature and let go. This usually requires conscious work on our part, even though it is in fact the most natural thing in the world. To find the "middle way" between "too loose" and "too tight," – to become natural in our actions – is the realization of this aspect of the Eightfold Path.

Timidity stifles creativity and possibility – and usually yields a mediocre result with an assortment of regrets. But the polar opposite of timidity, recklessness, is equally problematic. The problem we face is that regardless of how conscious or not we are, act we must. Perhaps our greatest challenge in effectively doing whatever we do is knowing how to move forward in mindful action between the looseness of recklessness and the tightness of timidity. We risk falling into a state of paralysis – not wanting to act at all – as if that were some kind of solution. But it is not, and we *shall* have to act, one way or the other, which is why to have the willingness to step forward in the first place takes boldness. **Having the boldness to put full heart and intention behind what you do ensures that you will learn the most from your actions. Properly observing the results of what it is that you have done, guarantees that your future actions will be even more effective.**

Many contemporary Buddhist teachers have written about mindfulness in action, especially when it comes to ordinary, everyday life. One such text that I have found immensely useful is Tarthang Tulku Rinpoche's *Skillful Means*. Tarthang Rinpoche looks at the pitfalls each of us can get into in the course of embarking on a project or cause. Probably the single most useful idea he puts forth is following through; following the course of action from beginning to end and trying to stay on task until you see it through.

This may seem obvious, but it is interesting to see how the mind strays in the process of doing any one particular task; group dynamics, sexual inklings, boredom and wanting to change track or approach prematurely. Distraction and wanting to be entertained often get in the way of doing effectively whatever we want to do, even if it is important to us. In effect, we are looking at how we can apply our meditative mind, come back to the breath, and translate that into coming back to the intention, to the task at hand. In the process of doing this we learn about endurance, patience, and generosity, and so on. **In mindfulness, we learn what it means to care.**

Right Livelihood: Being Practical, Pragmatic, and Useful

The Buddha saw that it is a natural part of growing as a human that we learn to take our place and make some kind of contribution to the world around us. This helps us to develop the independent state of mind that is a feature of enlightened being. There are no dead-beat Buddhas or Bodhisattvas. Each has their job, which is synonymous with their being. Until our mere presence is all that is needed to transform a situation in an enlightened direction, the rest of us will grow from having an ethical livelihood.

Livelihood takes action and translates it into how you will support yourself and take care of your responsibilities to others in an ethical way. When looking at a career, calling, job – however you want to define what you do on a day to day basis to secure the lifestyle you wish to lead – what choices can you make in what you do that will have a positive short- or long-term impact on those around you? This naturally includes activities related to social and political activism.

Please bear in mind that I am not saying that your livelihood needs be the focus of what you do as an activist. Those for whom it is, usually see their work as their calling: how they get their livelihood and their heart's interests to happily coincide. On the other hand, others make a living in order to have the time and resources to devote their thoughts, intentions, and actions to a different activity. The conscious, engaged activist is not someone who can be solely judged by looking at one dimension of his or her life, such as livelihood. Rather, it is the intelligent use of their resources and skills, focused on their intention to benefit others which matters most. At the same time, an ethical livelihood can support the energy to accomplish this, while a livelihood of more questionable deeds and aims can detract, if not negate, the good one is trying to accomplish elsewhere.

To accomplish the good that he or she seeks, the conscious, engaged activist requires self-knowledge. The Dharma teaches that this is primarily achieved through contemplation and meditation – the various methods I have presented earlier. As you familiarize yourself *with* yourself and discover what potential you have and the roadblocks that you habitually place in your own path that hinder that potential, you begin to lighten up, become more pliable, see ways of being that help you to access new skills within, and more resources without. Whatever your personal circumstances, attributes, and available resources may be, all can be turned into assets to help you along the way. If you are rich, you can learn to use your wealth wisely so that you create more opportunity and enrich the lives of others. If you are poor, knowing how to live without in a dignified manner can inspire those trapped in a mindset of poverty to give up the negative attitudes that create jealousy, greed, and other emotions that limit possibility and keep people in their place. If society deems you beautiful, you can often magnetize people to listen to you, and hence contribute to something that is worthy. If you are strong, you can engage in activities that physically protect others.

Of course, you may well have other internal attributes that you value in yourself more than these external ones – your honesty, your depth, your sincerity, and so on. You don't want to be recognized as the cute blond, the rich kid, the poor kid from the ghetto, the jock. But the truth is that, karmically speaking, you have been graced with whatever attributes are attached to these labels and to align your inner qualities with these outer attributes gives you added resourcefulness. It also helps us to break through stereotypic thinking that constrains us as much as it does others.

With respect to action and livelihood, how do you know where to put your efforts and energies? More than likely, based on your karmic inclinations, you will find yourself pulled in a particular direction. Your loving nature will bring out your affinity to this or that particular cause, plight, and so on. Trust this, "You cannot be all things to all people." Even the peacocks, the noble Bodhisattvas, have their specialties. These were not given to them as assignments. Rather, there was a calling they felt from within that they then perfected in opening up to their loving nature and their Buddha-potentiality. Thus your job in becoming a conscious, engaged activist is to develop the wisdom, skill, and compassion to use your inner and outer resources for maximum benefit.

And even if society becomes so repressive as to limit how and what we can do with the resources and capacities we have – for example nullifying or canceling elections, taking away personal freedoms in the name of patriotism or national security – unless each of us is lobotomized or restrained by mandatory psychotropic medicine, we always have our own mind. **And, we should not underestimate the transformational power of a thought well formed and directed.**

Rather than giving the student or reader a rundown of the *best* careers to choose, the classic Buddhist texts on right livelihood prefer to elaborate on those career choices that fundamentally help no one and, in the long run, cause harm that can last for generations. These careers are discussed here mainly because to be engaged in them while also claiming to focus on doing good in the world is either a blatant contradiction or a very uphill battle that few, if any, can win. On the contrary, it is an extremely worthy cause for an activist to work consciously and in an engaged way to curb or alter such practices, or halt them altogether, because of their global consequences. Again, the particular calling or work chosen in order to accomplish this may differ from person to person.

Wrong livelihood 1: The arms trade

The first of the wrong career choices is **being involved with the dealing or selling of arms.** Soon after the first Gulf War, His Holiness the Dalai Lama was visiting Albuquerque, New Mexico. In a full auditorium, he was asked what he thought about American involvement in Iraq and his opinion of Saddam Hussein. His Holiness said that while it may be true that Saddam was not a good person, it must be remembered that it was the US and other foreign governments and weapons corporations that had supplied him with the weaponry to invade Kuwait in the first place. We gave him the tools to act on his worst impulses. In this light, His Holiness felt that those who supplied the weapons were far more immoral than any action Saddam could commit, because his Western suppliers knew he would use the weapons he was sold. They just did not anticipate that he would use them against his own people, and against allies of the West.

It is problematic enough to possess one's own weapons with the intent, according to one's own ethical standards, only to use them in self-defense. We see this dilemma daily in the blurring of the line between self-defense and the idea of "pre-emption." What is the difference between a pre-emptive strike as a means of self-defense, and out-and-out militaristic aggression? Beyond the current debacle around the US' (and the "coalition of the willing") invasion of Afghanistan and Iraq, history is replete with despots and tyrants who whipped their populace into a frenzy based on fear of others, in order to justify invasions.

Bringing our discussion back from foreign policy to the act of making money from arms sales, I discussed earlier the fact that war is the failure to find other, more peaceful methods of settling our differences. To be engaged in the manufacturing and selling of weaponry, therefore, is cashing in on humanity's failures. Encouraging someone to buy your AK-47s, tanks, and missile launchers is basically pushing for a worst-case scenario to come about. Success in this endeavor usually breeds more worst-case scenarios – a win-win scenario for the arms industry.

On a personal note, I recall teaching at an international holistic health conference where great healers, speakers, and proponents of spirituality were invited to present. The conference was poorly attended and there were endless problems with staff, facilities, and funds. Only later did we learn that the company responsible for organizing the event mainly did conferences for weapons dealers.

Of course, nothing is ever entirely black or white. Applying the new nuclear technology to create the atomic bomb may or may not have shortened the Second World War. After the first two were dropped on Japan and the world recognized their horrific effects, some wanted to see a ban on such weapons. But for years they have continued to proliferate worldwide and the desire to acquire them is the aim of many governments convinced that to hold such destructive capability generates respect and acts as a deterrent. The problem is that when one has a nuclear arsenal, what temptations are there to go one step further? How often has time erased the memory of the sins of our fathers only for new generations disconnected from the nightmare of earlier history to go, once again, down the road of doom?

Rarely do we stop in our tracks or reverse course. The pride of the powerful and those seeking power is hard to tame and easy to capitalize on. And no matter how ethical a weapons dealer may want to be – claiming to balance the forces of opposing sides, or whatever rationale they may try to convince themselves and others with – their ethics and reasoning will be warped, as the demand for their goods and potential profitability inevitably lead them down a path that few, if any, can negotiate skillfully.

Seeing the heinous effects that the marketing of weaponry

can have, the courageous step of being involved with, or supporting, groups that work to stop nuclear proliferation, ban land mines, and seek stronger laws regulating gun and weapon sales, is surely a worthy cause for a conscious, engaged activist.

Wrong livelihood 2: Trading in other living beings

The next of the worst career choices, from a Buddhist viewpoint, is **to be involved in the direct manipulation of the lives of others.** Here I am speaking of slavery, the sex trade, and raising animals for slaughter. All sentient beings want happiness and the causes of happiness. None want to suffer, to be used or manipulated against their will. Few if any of us need to be lectured on the nonvirtue of the sex and slave trades. If nothing else, we can look at history and see the negative social and cultural effects of these practices and institutions. Such negative fallout comes as no real surprise.

However, as far as the treatment of animals for slaughter is concerned, I believe this issue is a karmic powder keg that deserves far more attention than most of us have probably hitherto given it. In my discussion of this matter, I will include the actual slaughter of animals.

It could be argued that with a growing human population and the dwindling of open land for animals to range freely, raising animals for the sustenance of one's family or village makes sense. We can argue about the virtues of vegetarianism all we like. The Buddha saw the virtue of it, and orders of the Theravada tradition of Buddhism are exclusively vegetarian, as are many Mahayana orders. Even in those traditions where eating meat is accepted, there are practices and meditations that encourage becoming vegetarian for a time.

However, more human beings eat meat than not. Therefore, as this is an activity that most people participate in either directly or passively by consumption (directly through the slaughter or eating of meat and other animal products, and indirectly by consuming animal by-products such as leather for shoes, coats, and so on), it seems relevant to come up with moral and ethical standards for it. Most traditional and indigenous cultures have such an approach. But in our society, the commercialization and industrialization of the activity leads us away from such sensitivities by disconnecting consumers from the animals they consume. This in turn takes us down a very slippery slope where we more and more risk losing our connection to the sacredness of life itself.

The animal rights activist John Robbins has said that one of the legacies of our time will be that we were extremely cruel to animals. Although there are exceptions, commercially raised animals these days usually lead a tortured existence. They are often raised in close quarters, which increases their stress levels and creates the easy spreading of disease. Rather than change these living conditions (giving the animals more space would mean raising fewer animals), the owners just feed them antibiotics and other medicines that swell their bodies (good for pound per dollar ratios) and leave residues in their blood and muscles which we eventually consume (and probably accounts for more and more people being resistant to the benefits of certain antibiotics). Stressed, underexercised, and bloated, the beasts are then slaughtered with little thought that they, too, have consciousnesses and if degraded and killed with no regard for this fact, the pain, confusion, and fear that they experience in dying will be infused in their meat and byproducts. Animal stress hormones form part of the legacy we partake in at our dinner tables. So if we eat pounds and pounds of meat from distressed, frightened animals, why should we not expect our own state of mind to be affected, our own consciousness to go to similar places?

Our consumption of meat is disproportionate to our needs.

Few of us live in climates, or do the physical labor, that would warrant the volume of meat we consume daily. As our healthcare systems corroborate this, perhaps this will have an impact on how much land is assigned to creating animals for slaughter and how much used to grow grains, fruits, and vegetables. But this is more than a healthcare issue. It is an issue with global economic, political, environmental, and moral consequences. It is one of many issues raised by those protesting agri-business, genetic modification, and proposals for cloning for consumption.

It is possible (and there are some groups already demonstrating this) to raise animals in healthy environments, to feed them well, and take them to slaughter in ways that minimize their suffering. Native American slaughter practices, Jewish Kosher practices, and the Tibetan tradition of butchers knowing *phowa* so they can eject the consciousness of the animals before slaughter, demonstrate that it is possible to bring consciousness into a meat-consuming nation.

To my mind, this is an area where activists can be extremely valuable, even more than against slavery or weapons sales. As we all eat daily, to bring consciousness into this area is to encourage consciousness and conscience across the board. As we value the life we take in order to sustain our own, this may lead to greater consideration in other dimensions of our lives, and hence curb the attitudes that encourage slavery and weapons dealing in the first place.

Wrong livelihood 3: The trade in intoxicants

The last of the careers that the Buddha would consider as anathema to a life that is conscious and engaged is to deal, market, or sell intoxicants, those substances that, in fact, are designed to make one *less* conscious and engaged – drugs and alcohol. Generally speaking, the Dharma frowns upon intoxication, a state where one loses mindfulness and consequently can find oneself wandering unchecked into the minefields of the Three Poisons. In the interest of health, consciousness, and desirable behavior, we are encouraged to "drink responsibly" as it were: to know our limits. In that regard, the Buddha was not necessarily against intoxicants per se, but it is a rare individual who can maintain their clarity while partaking in them, let alone resist overindulging. And, as someone who sells intoxicants is more interested in making a living and expects the buyer to beware and to monitor themselves, more than likely they will encourage us in directions few of us would really want to consciously take ourselves. **To sell intoxicants is, therefore, an assault on the mind itself.**

When it comes to other nonvirtuous professions, it is interesting to ponder their interrelationship – how alcohol and drugs fit into the arms trade, gambling, prostitution, and so on. To think that the money that is generated by such businesses is not tainted, again, flies in the face of karmic law. In my own experience, I can think of several examples, some personal. My great-grandfather was a rabbi whose sons chose nonreligious livelihoods. My grandfather became a dentist, but several of his brothers became bootleggers and went west during Prohibition. As they got involved with bootlegging whiskey and such, they soon found themselves embroiled with organized crime syndicates. Scandal or tragedy ruined many of their lives and the lives of their families. Again, this is much the same as the well-known American philanthropic family that I mentioned earlier (see page 131) whose money came from alcohol and prostitution. Despite all of their grand contributions to various causes in society, this did not prevent family members from suffering a disproportionate amount of mental illness and disease.

Of course, one can argue that at least *someone* wanted to take these dubiously gotten fortunes and put them to good use. Indeed, such actions can be virtuous and stop a habitual process that may have further negative consequences in the future. But this does not avert negative consequences incurred up to that point. Karmically speaking, someone still has to pay the piper. And I do wonder if even the most humanitarian projects funded by such philanthropy will not find themselves at some point in the future in crises that are somehow directly related to the means by which the donated money was earned.

In modern times, the issue of intoxication needs to be addressed beyond the traditional/historical/cultural intoxicants we all know or have addressed in our schools, churches, temples, mosques, and homes. We need to look at ways in which we have culturally sanctioned intoxication *as a normal state of being*. By this I am referring to the vast array of psychoactive drugs promoted by the pharmaceutical industry and the allopathic medical community that it serves.

In "The Spectrum of Life" program that I teach to teens, I talk to them about the failure of the DARE (Drug Abuse Resistance Education) program in American schools. This program has been in existence in American elementary and middle schools for over twenty years. Statistics seem to indicate that despite such education, the use of illicit drugs in a younger and younger population increase year after year. DARE fails not because the message is not a good one. It fails because it does not recognize that *we are a drug-taking culture*. I tell these kids that the theme should not be "Dare to get kids off drugs," but rather *"Dare to keep parents off Prozac."* The use of psycho-pharmaceuticals in the West is pandemic. We need not be so worried about keeping our kids away from dealers and peddlers of drugs and alcohol. For one thing, so many homes already have alcohol available as a matter of course – albeit supposedly for the adults. And then there are Prozac, Valium, Librium, Elevil,

Xanax, Zoloft, Ativan, and a host of other mood-altering substances, that more people are addicted to than to any drugs that can be found on the street. These are legal and prescribed. Thus we model addiction to our children. They don't have to learn somewhere else.

We are living in a Dark Age where denial of the Three Poisons running amok in our lives leads us to be very intolerant of any mood that bespeaks our dissatisfaction, our alienation, our suffering. And rather than look at the causal factors, rather than begin the process of dismantling the Three Poisons, we are offered, and choose, substances that blur them, keep us synthetically in an "OK" gray zone. And this leads to our intolerance of slightly more active children in the classroom who "obviously need Ritalin" to agitated old people afraid of dying who "need" to be "snowed" with morphine. In between there are the intolerable ups and downs of conditioned, everyday life that show the cracks in the illusion of everything being OK, 24/7. We are looking at the fulfillment of Aldous Huxley's vision in *Brave New World*, where citizens are kept tame and in-line with *soma*.

To me, the culturally-sanctioned drugs sold to those who have not been given any mind training to learn how to relax and cope with what life throws at them, can be just as devastating in their effect and just as difficult to overcome or withdraw from as illegal street drugs and alcohol. The social consequences of the latter may be more dramatic, but in the end, a consciousness denied is a consciousness denied; and the profits made by the socially-sanctioned drugs corporations far exceed the money generated by alcohol producers and illegal drug cartels. To date, pharmaceutical companies rank as some of the top producers in terms of commodity profitability in the world, making some people who work for them wealthy almost beyond imagination.

Admittedly, many pharmaceutical drugs are produced for other purposes; and even those psychoactive drugs that I have mentioned do have their place and merits. But the degree to which money is generated by the sale of these drugs, without there first being much attempt to develop consciousness-enhancing methods for social unmanageability, is the degree to which these corporations reap the consequences that are not dissimilar to those facing the drug runners and bootleggers among us. Thus, as with other bad career choices, I believe that people should be wary of involvement with the pharmaceutical industry. And I also think that **the monitoring of such enterprises is another noble endeavor for the conscious, engaged activist.**

Another culturally sanctioned enterprise that encourages our intoxication is the marketing/advertising industry. **Because we are basically good, we also have the tendency to be basically gullible.** It may be true that everyone is doing the best based on what they know, but that does not mean that everyone comes to what they do with the best of intentions, wisdom, or skill. Part of enlightenment, and becoming a conscious, engaged activist, is losing our gullibility by developing discriminating awareness, the source of compassionate action. But, while we remain blind and unable to perceive things for what they are, there will be some who will capitalize on our frailty. Such people know the mechanisms of craving and seduction and will exploit them to lead us by the nose.

This is nothing new. Whoever sold the first donkey or chicken to another person had to have some marketing skills. The art and skill of influencing has always been a two-edged sword. Thus, the marketplace has always been rife with tantalizers, snake-oil salesmen, con artists, and confidence men and women. But as we learn more about psychology and the mind, we also learn the mechanisms by which we become influenced and make choices. This information can be used with integrity by teachers effectively to leave deep, positive impressions in our minds. But those with less noble, ethical and moral standards can use the same information to enslave us – to brainwash us. It really depends on intention. Neurolinguistic programming (NLP); visual and auditory subliminal messaging; spin-doctoring by repetition; and "operant conditioning" – all are part of the weaponry used by the media and advertisers to get their messages across – whether it is for us to buy soap or a car we can't afford, or vote for a particular candidate, *or go to war.*

To be involved in a livelihood and industry that promotes hyperbole and distortion for self-serving aims, or generally leads people away from their sensibilities, is exploitative, hence a questionable choice of life-direction. **To be actively involved in supporting organizations that are consumer watchdogs and promote truth in advertising seems a warranted endeavor for the conscious, engaged activist.**

Sickness, Poverty, and Warfare

In the Dedication of this book, I used a line from the vow of a Bodhisattva about being committed to seeing an end to sickness, poverty, and warfare. If I were in any way to narrow the definition of what I would consider to be the most appropriate livelihoods or causes for conscious, engaged, activists, I would say that these three issues are the most central.

Sickness, poverty, and warfare are closely interconnected. Each has influenced or contributed to the other two over the course of history. Depending on your inclinations and what you see around you, therefore, addressing any of these problems in what you do will have merit and probably a positive effect on the other two problems.

At the same time, if I were to reduce the definition of right livelihood even further, I would focus on poverty. I say this not out of any great love for socialism, but rather, from a Buddhist sense of logic. The Buddhist laws of karma teach that if one is born into poverty, there has to be a personal cause. If we are to trust the examples and logic presented in *The Wheel of Sharp Weapons* (see Chapter Eight), if one has been cruel to others and deprived others of what they need, more than likely the wheel will come around and one will find oneself reborn into a situation where you too experience a lack of resources, similarly created by others, repaying the favor. Whether you accept this idea of karmic retribution or not, it is a concept that leaves out no player in terms of allocating responsibility for the circumstance of poverty. This is the key point. It is too simplistic and too sentimental to see people who live in dire poverty as solely victims or pawns of clearly identifiable "perpetrators" of poverty. We have to look not only at the role of the "perpetrator" but also at that of the "victim" to see how causes and conditions come together to reinforce poverty on both sides.

Craving, as we have discussed, is the greatest cause for our suffering. Not knowing the way things are, not understanding reality or how it works, as beings of desire, we crave. Rarely are we satisfied, regardless of how good we have things. And, as mentioned previously, there are those who in the most impoverished situations can demonstrate a spirit of generosity far greater than those living in wealthy iron-gated communities.

But, let us say that we are not so wise or enlightened. We live in situations which most would agree are impoverished in the relative sense. If we have little education, we may be receptive to forces within society, perhaps state-sanctioned religion and religious education, which praise the virtues of poverty and the evils of wealth. Perhaps they encourage us to be fatalistic about our place, as in the words of the old hymn: "The rich man in his castle, / The poor man at his gate, / God made them high and lowly / And ordered their estate." Or we may be susceptible to radical forces within society saying that we are poor because of other people, such as corrupt officials, corporate tycoons, foreign invaders. Add to this mix the growing access to media: along with useful information, it presents us with images of what others have that we do not. When we have little and see that others have a lot, it would seem to be a rare individual among us who is able to embrace a moderate approach to transforming their predicament – the moderate approach that teaches the middle way of personal responsibility and the need to change both the inner and outer causes of the difficulties you find yourself in. In craving an end to suffering, both in the ultimate and relative sense, it stands to reason that the habit patterns of greed, jealousy, and a host of other emotions associated with dissatisfaction arise strongly. When the habitual mental patterns that help to breed and reinforce poverty are coaxed to a higher state of agitation by those who see or can sense the energy and force of the frustration beneath the surface, then it is not hard to see how one might motivate those who are poor, starving, homeless, or feeling disfranchised to join *jihad*s, the ranks of suicide bombers, and so on.

Of course, this is a very sociological interpretation of a very complex phenomenon. But such an interpretation generally makes sense, and policy makers would be well advised to pay attention to sociologists, social psychologists, anthropologists, and others who spend their time examining the intricacies of societal interaction. However, we must also bear in mind that only a tiny number of people actually do join *jihad*s or become terrorists. Does this mean that they are brainwashed by those who wish to keep them subdued? Or is it because people are basically good and really do not wish to cause harm in their lives or in the lives of others?

Ultimately, helping all beings, through mind training, to overcome the strong craving that leads them to suffer is the greatest gift you can give them. It is especially helpful if it can turn the mind of someone who has considered violence and wants to try another way. Mother Teresa once said, "To a starving person, God comes in the form of a loaf of bread." Similarly, unless we help to lift vulnerable people out of their immediate material distress, it will be very difficult for such people to feel a motivation to make changes to more fundamental levels of consciousness.

Although, from a karmic point of view, such people may find themselves in such conditions by their own hand over the course of lifetimes, the fact that these conditions exist in the world is a call to us to grow spiritually, to use what resources we have to lessen the suffering we see. Some will benefit from food, some from education, some through programs like Habitat for Humanity, and so on. In some instances, forcibly ending civil war and strife may be necessary. Perhaps political and economic reforms will need to be put in place, and you will find yourself wanting to work with a lobbying group, seek political office, or join organizations that feel called to protest actively or directly challenge the powers-that-be in more wrathful ways.

So, there is plenty of work to do and each of us has the capacity to do *something*. What matters is that we make love and compassion manifest in a practical, useful way. For if we do not, then it's like the saying, "use it or lose it." Karmically speaking, the benefits that we currently have are because of positive deeds we have done in the past. To just hoard what we have and turn a blind eye to the suffering of others around us is to squander a precious opportunity that has the potential of in turn opening the doors of opportunity for others. In the end, actively using this opportunity will do more to bring us to a deeper level of peace and happiness than the pursuit of any real or imagined trinket.

To work truly on poverty, then, the conscious, engaged activist must not only put his or her efforts into whatever worldly organization or cause inspires them, but must also spend time meditating on the power of craving and attachment. For as we understand the power of what we crave and loosen our own attachments, a greater understanding for what needs to be done will arise in our work.

The Daily Life of an Activist

Most of us possess a blend of habits that are good, bad, and somewhere in between. Throughout our lives we then create well-trodden routines that will either consciously and willfully or unconsciously and seemingly capriciously reinforce our habits, for better or worse. In consequence, when we have established the thought and intent to reinforce what is good and eliminate what is harmful or of little value, putting that intent into action will require effort. If we want to become more conscious and engaged in what we do and in the lives of others, we need to go beyond just making that wish or holding that intention. We need to do something on a day-to-day basis that focuses our thoughts and actions on bringing us closer and closer to the awakening, enlightenment potentiality that we each know is our birthright. Therefore, setting some kind of daily activist schedule is useful.

What is presented here is not a template for what *must* be done. Be flexible. At the same time, recognize the value of each of these components as part of making our daily lives more meaningful and productive. Hold each aspect in your mind. Do the things you can and acknowledge the significance of the others to maintain a thread.

1. Upon waking, tradition teaches that we should appreciate that we have woken up to a new day. Each day holds the promise of transformation. What makes our day look predictable and end predictably has more to do with our

habitual mind than what is lying in wait behind each corner. To shake us from our complacency and the humdrum of our minds, there are the Four Thoughts That Revolutionize The Mind (see pages 30–40).

2. Orienting our day with the recognition of the preciousness of what time and space provide us, we come to the Four Limitless Meditations (see pages 58–69) that link our happiness and wellbeing with the happiness and wellbeing with all whom we encounter. Such an altruistic focus takes us beyond our obsession with ourselves, lightens our load, and makes us more open to our own loving nature and the potential it conceals.

3. With such thoughts and intentions in place, it is good to take some time to center the mind with some form of meditation or mantra that helps to dissolve the Three Poisons (for example, the meditations and mantras given in Chapter 6). Dissolving our fixations and residing in a more natural state of being, we are immediately put in touch with our resourcefulness.

4. We then go out and meet our day. We perform our livelihood or whatever activity we do in a day. Regardless of what that activity may be, we try to feel some direct or indirect connection with others and the world around us. In a mindful, relaxed state fueled by positive intention, we strive to be compassionate in our actions: sometimes peacefully; sometimes needing to empower others; sometimes exerting more influence and charisma; sometimes confronting. We try our best to do what we feel is most beneficial with the greatest amount of wisdom and skill we can muster.

5. As the day is drawing to a close, we can spend some moments reviewing what has happened. We should look

closely at our successes as well as our failures. When we feel we have fallen short, we should admit it clearly to ourselves and recommit our efforts for the days to come. When we feel we have been successful, imagine that the value and merit of that success spreads out to more and more people.

Structuring our days in this way makes life like a *sadhana*, a deepening ritual that enriches each moment, and nothing that is done is ever wasted. In emphasizing what is positive and committing ourselves to act accordingly, we begin to steer our lives in a direction that will naturally dissolve whatever barriers we have in our path. This does not mean that this process is easy. But it is more rewarding. And when we embark on anything with a reward at the end, we embark on a journey.

The Journey of the Conscious, Engaged Activist

The world that we see and experience around us is the sum total of all previous intentions, whether good, bad, or indifferent; their resulting actions, whether skillful or not; and the ensuing emotional reactions and responses, which prompted a cascading of other intentions and their actions – and so on throughout time to the present. Our interpretation of our world is filtered through our cognitive and perceptual filters. If we are awakening to our enlightened potentiality, we see a world in suffering that beckons us to action. If we are more steeped in the Three Poisons, we choose to ignore what we see, put on rose-colored spectacles, and try to pretend that it really isn't happening; or we fight to get our way or that piece of the pie we think we are being deprived of. Apathy, endless distraction in limited *material or mundane* pursuits, frustration translated into self-destruction, war-mongering, and terrorism are naturally spawned by our lack of intelligence, skill, and/or willingness to actively engage in new ways of being and acting in the world. It is the dominance of this mentality that determines a Dark Age.

Regardless of how enlightened we are – or not – we would all like to live in a world that is peaceful and safe, whether it be for personal or collective happiness. When we think of the world around us and wish to see changes in foreign policy, a change of cultural or social imperatives, or economic reform, we often do not see our part in the picture. Many place the lion's share of such jobs and responsibilities upon officials – those who have or presume dominion over our lives and nation. Regardless of whether such officials are elected or not, if we do not ourselves actively participate in the processes that determine the course of what our world is to become, is it reasonable to assume that the actions of others, even if supposedly on our behalf, will yield the consequences we want?

Certainly, as we have seen again and again throughout history, those leaders who detach themselves or feel themselves to be different from the people around them, create circumstances that often lead to something other than what many had hoped for – even the opposite. If we live in a society where we can elect our leaders, they are charged to do the will of those by whom they have been elected. We may also have the seemingly peaceful choice of influencing legislation and changing government policy through the election process. Those living under less democratic systems, where the powers-that-be derive less of their legitimacy from the will of the citizenry, may need to seek allies and other ways of influencing how change can be initiated. Situations where the powers-that-be control by manipulation or intimidation may require someone of great charisma, who can magnetize and galvanize people around them to deal with an issue that needs to be addressed, to emerge as the force behind change. In a situation where people live in terror of a dictator, if all other peaceful means to ease the suffering of those at the hands of such a ruler seem ineffective, it may be necessary to take up arms and rebel.

Regardless of our situation, change is always possible. We can always participate more fully in effecting change. And the wisdom and skill we need to apply will be different depending on the individual circumstances we are facing. More profoundly, the circumstances we are facing are a mirror reflection of who we are. And if they appear to us as circumstances that need to be changed, then the resources that we need to call up from within are the ones most necessary for our own development and enlightenment. **Our world tests us and perfects us.**

The Last Straw: Saint, Sinner, Martyr, Madman, Hero...

In a world caught up in the Three Poisons, we may get the illusory idea that being a conscious, engaged activist would invite praise, admiration, adulation. After all, if we all possess enlightenment-potential, wouldn't we all want to celebrate someone who demonstrates these potentials in their life and is doing great things to change social systems, policies, governments, nations, and so on?

The fact is, however, that the Three Poisons, true to their name, "poison" this perception for many. Hence while some may well honor your courage and effort, there will be many others who see what you do as an embarrassment, creating tension and awkwardness. Deep down, people know that *they* can do better, but the habitual patterns that dominate their thoughts and actions bind them to an illusion of impossibility. And your actions are an affront to this reality.

The conscious, engaged activist is someone who strives to live according to higher, spiritual principles. The joy that we discover from within through living and acting in accordance with these principles must not be dependent upon what is outside us. In this light, I am reminded of the words of two of my closest teachers from the mid-1970s and early 1980s. At one teaching, in 1978, the Venerable Bardor Tulku Rinpoche was speaking to a class on making the choice to follow the Dharma, the teachings of the Buddha. "When you enter the Dharma," he said, "you will be treated lower than a dog in the street."

What his words were driving at was the fact that even though the Buddha teaches that we all have enlightenment-potential, most beings live in a state of mind governed by self-centeredness and self-preservation. When an individual makes a commitment to opening up to this inner potential and living in a way that demonstrates universal love and compassion, such light creates embarrassment to those around, who feel the same potential inside themselves, but somehow do not know how to pull themselves away from their habit of trying to have the world just the way they want it. And so, the "dog in the street," the spiritual aspirant, may be viewed as different, delusional, crazy, heretical, and perhaps even worth crucifying. In secular terms they might be viewed as "unpatriotic," as they are not a patriot according to the preferred, culturally reinforced paradigm.

Thus, to commit oneself to a life and a path based on spiritual or higher principles and practices is noble, but fraught with emotional turmoil and the distinct possibility that unpleasantness, even danger, will be part of the process. At a minimum, don't expect gratitude. In the face of hostility or condemnation, it may prove difficult to maintain equanimity. Your defenses, the Three Poisons attempting to ensure your sense of importance, at least to yourself, may translate into an attitude of superiority. This will only lead you to feel more isolated and probably give you a condescending air. It can even translate into a sense of feeling like a martyr. History has very few examples of truly noble martyrs. Let's not make the list any longer than we have to.

Along these lines, but in a more pragmatic vein, remember what was said earlier about rendering unto Caesar what is Caesar's. All too often, those who seek change are struck down by their own inattentiveness to the social and cultural norms around them – paying taxes, curbing the dog, participating in their own children's education, and so on. Not that you have to kowtow to morals and mores that you sincerely do not approve of, but consider: what would the ideal citizen look like? By not (or not overtly) breaking the rules that most people around you see as reasonable, and by participating in your community in ways that make you seem less alien, you can set a remarkable example: someone committed to principles of change and growth who, at the same time, exemplifies that which is upright in the eyes of those around you. Presenting people with such a quandary will invoke less wrath and more inquisitiveness.

Several years after the teaching with Bardor Tulku Rinpoche, I attended a group interview with the Venerable Khenpo Karthar Rinpoche. A rather distraught woman asked him why her life was so hard, even though she did her meditations faithfully and daily and tried to help others wherever she could. In answering her, he also turned to the audience and posed a rhetorical question. Why would we think that entering on a spiritual path would be easy? If we are truly committed to stopping the self-perpetuated nonsense of our lives, wouldn't it stand to reason that "the buck would stop here?" **Once we commit ourselves to stopping ways of being that are unhelpful to ourselves and others, isn't it logical that the momentum behind such habits would come crashing in on us all at once? That there will be a quickening, an acceleration of the resolution of the karma created, as it were, which demands our utmost attention if we** are not to backslide into negativity and the old habitual knee-jerk responses from which we are trying to liberate ourselves?

By committing ourselves to a life of becoming more and more conscious and engaged in our actions, we run into the protests from within of our own Three Poisons, and the protests from without of others whose Three Poisons wish not to be disturbed by us. If we are to stick to our convictions, we must be prepared to tread a path not dissimilar to that of the Buddha's. To make a difference in our lives and the lives of others, we need to accept internal and external resistance to our intent and actions. As we face down the habit patterns that lead to sickness, poverty, and warfare, we must be prepared to be tested at every possible turn and to view these challenges not as grounds for turning back, but as confirmations of the value of our struggle.

Of course, because we are human, we can only exhibit human behaviors, whether we are delusional (caught in the web of the Three Poisons) or on the path to awakening. Either way, our actions may lead some to cheer us on, while others point the finger at us, accusing us of various crimes and misdemeanors. If we are committed to a path of awakening, rather than reacting by isolating ourselves, creating more disconnection and the likelihood of more confusion, we openly step forward and embrace those who challenge us along the way. This doesn't mean we necessarily become friends, kiss, and make up. Perhaps they will remain adversaries. But, in being willing to listen, to remain open to communicating, there is a greater likelihood of a resolution that makes things better for all.

Treading the path of a conscious, engaged activist as laid out in this chapter can be lonely. But because we are all interconnected, change within ourselves or in the world around us will not happen in isolation. Along with those who challenge us, there will also be friends and helpers along the way. They are indispensable in the changes and transformations to which we are now committed. In the next chapter, I move on to address the issues of community and support – the "pockets of light" mentioned in the Introduction.

Pockets of Light, Sources of Inspiration

Whatever work we set out to do as conscious, engaged activists, we can never succeed by our own efforts alone. The simple truth is that because we are all inextricably interconnected, there will have been those who go before us and pave the road; well-wishers providing support as we pursue our goals; skeptics and others who challenge us to live up to our dreams and visions by their negative input; and those in the future whom we hope the seeds of our actions will inspire, so that the good that is done carries on. Thus, the past, present, and future, and all of those who we come into contact with along the way, provide the context of our efforts and always contribute to them.

All that being said, we *do* make choices with regard to whom we associate with. Generally speaking, we prefer to be around those who agree with us, try to avoid those who annoy us, and care little one way or another about everyone else. Such is the nature of the Three Poisons. Even if we have the equanimity of a Buddha, as in the earlier quote of Gampopa (see page 68), it *is* nice to have a few good friends. This is who I am referring to when I speak of "pockets of light and sources of inspiration."

Unless our minds and hearts are stable like those of a Buddha or bodhisattva, more than likely we shall not have the veracity and courage to endure and prevail in situations where all we get are challenges and negative feedback for our actions and our desire to transform ourselves and the world around us. We can learn to love our enemies and those who challenge us for the gifts of molding our character, even become Bodhisattva-like peacocks who learn to thrive in the Three Poisons that they offer us. But, for the most part, and especially in a Dark Age, it behooves us to seek out those who inspire us and those of a like mind – friends and helpers along the way. This is not a cop-out or a sign of weakness, it is a sign and testimony to the human way in which we most effectively manifest our loving nature.

Refuge

In the Buddhist tradition, there is the notion of seeking refuge. Refuge is like seeking shelter, protection, succor, a place where one is nurtured. In a sense, we do this in relative ways all the time through associating with what we like and staying away from what we don't like. We seek refuge in our friends, our favorite foods, in acquiring what we think will make us feel more complete as a person. The Buddha saw this human tendency and translated it into a path with more ultimate goals in mind. Seeking refuge in the Buddhist sense is about identifying and associating with those persons and things in our life that encourage us to grow; that help us to cut through the Three Poisons that imprison us and develop our enlightened potential.

In the Buddhist tradition, there are three primary dimensions in refuge that contribute to accomplishing this goal. This is called the Triple Refuge, or seeking refuge in the "Three Jewels": the Buddha, the Dharma (his teaching), and the Sangha (community of practitioners). They are called "jewels," because the Buddha saw them as precious and invaluable to our growth and development. In a broader sense, we are speaking about what I have referred to as sources of inspiration – learning and practicing methods that help us to transform our Three Poisons so that we can be more effective in what we do – together with some form of community support. All three of these jewels come together in a tangible way when the third, a supportive community, is present; this coming together is what "pockets of light" specifically refers to, and explains why the Buddha saw and emphasized the importance of "*sangha*" or community. That being said, let us look at each of the dimensions contributing to these "pockets of light."

Seeking refuge in the Buddha

To seek refuge in the Buddha is the desire to make a strong connection with all of those who manifest their full enlightened potential. We do this not out of a sense of worshipping them like a god or gods, but rather because they represent, and can show us by example, what it is we can accomplish in our own lives. In the Tibetan tradition, living people may indeed be recognized as incarnations of Buddhas and bodhisattvas. Called *tulkus*, these special individuals are often lamas or monks, but not necessarily so. There are also laypeople who do work in the world in a variety of ways. They can be ordinary people or those of note in history.

With this in mind, who inspires us? If it is true that nothing is ever lost, then those who have gone before, our ancestors, our nation's forefathers, the mothers and fathers of various humanitarian causes, those who have been sainted – are more than just historical figures. What endures is more than the memory of their actions. We can feel their energetic signature: their intentions, thoughts, and actions well focused and released in time and space that carry on to this day. When we reflect upon them, visualize and meditate upon them, and try to emulate them, we forge a direct connection to their cause, their being.

Tantric Buddhist tradition formalizes this in various visualization meditations. The Buddhas or bodhisattvas meditated upon express qualities that we wish to identify with and manifest in our own lives, be it compassion, wisdom, the ability to protect others, heal, and so on. Because these meditations have been done for centuries with great success, they are, according to tradition, reliable and guarantee results. But whether one does these particular practices or not, **the act of invoking and seeking refuge in the example and energy of a source of inspiration, identifying with that being or person and seeing ourselves becoming just like them, can be done regardless of whether it is a saint, a national leader, or any very powerful figure. In this way we connect with and become a conduit for a worthy way of being, cause, or goal, and by taking it forward one more generation, we can deliver something of value to the future.**

Spending a little time each day showing appreciation for those who inspire us is valuable and creates connection. This may be done as formal meditation. We might make a special space where we have pictures, artifacts, books, or other reminders invoking our connection to what and/or who inspires us. Going on a pilgrimage to where such people lived or taught – be it Bodh Gaya in India (where the Buddha found Enlightenment), Rome, or Washington D.C. – and meeting, spending time, or studying with those who continue their work or example, can strengthen our qualities and appreciation and give us a deeper resolve to do the work we are inspired to do.

Seeking refuge in the Dharma

The second refuge in Buddhist tradition is the Dharma. Most appropriately translated, Dharma means "the way things are." As mentioned earlier, the Dharma is what the Buddha taught – an entire cosmology and explanation of how things are in this world and beyond. But this is not so unusual because all cosmologies and philosophies do the same, and proclaim themselves to be true.

The fundamental teachings of the Dharma do not in any way contradict any of the world's great wisdom traditions, of East or West. At the same time, as a pragmatist and one who respected science and experiential learning, the Buddha did not want anyone to take what he said about what was going on in blind faith. He wanted people to know things from the inside out. And so he gave methods of contemplation and meditation that worked with dismantling the Three Poisons, the root causes of our biases and prejudices. In that way, people came to knowledge of the world through experience and intimacy. Many other traditions in the world have similar methods and practices of enquiry, contemplation, and meditation. It is interesting and refreshing to note that once people get beyond their sectarian biases, there is often a sharing of methods and information that enriches all traditions and those who practice them. (I recall doing some work for a Trappist monastery in Kentucky where the brothers of the order did yoga and meditation as part of their spiritual practice. As far as they were concerned, any method that got them closer to God was fine by them.)

Seeking refuge in such wisdom traditions is the conscious, engaged activist's commitment to employing methods that always cut to the chase; that always aim to dismantle mechanisms that create partisanship, boundaries, suspicion, or barriers to peace and harmony among people and nations. The methods outlined throughout this book, employed with skill and wisdom to accomplish the noble intention of the Four Limitless Meditations on love, compassion, joy, and equanimity, fit well with any of the great wisdom traditions or with any other positive, life-embracing philosophy to which one may feel aligned.

The term Dharma is usually classified as either "absolute," or "ultimate," and "relative." Absolute or ultimate Dharma has to do with the meditation and contemplative methods that aim directly to counter our intoxication in the Three Poisons. This will help us in whatever endeavor we apply skillful means and wisdom. Relative Dharma has to do with the information and practical day-to-day things we can do in the world in order to foster a positive and encouraging environment for us to engage in the practices of absolute Dharma. Among the fields of knowledge that were considered part of relative Dharma, the Buddha spoke of philosophy and dialectics – pondering the world from a broader perspective and understanding some of its underlying mechanisms. Thus there are great treatises on Buddhist philosophy, cosmology, earth sciences, and medicine which help us to see how the Three Poisons play themselves out in the world as the Five Great Elements. These elements are common to virtually all wisdom traditions as the matrix that comes together at all levels in manifest reality. There is no room to elaborate on such a vast topic here. But the point is that if we do *not* know how these elements come together and function in the normal run of things as they unfold, then we shall be less able to know what to do for ourselves or others.

In all the ages humans have existed on this planet, there have been seminal thinkers and visionaries who – steeped in the forms of prayer, meditation, and contemplation of their own spiritual and cultural context – have examined their world at the level of physical science, philosophy, linguistics, political and social sciences, and economics. They have presented models of understanding that at times have brought stability to uncertain times, and at other times challenged people with revolutionary ways of seeing. The works of such thinkers have stood the test of time for good reason.

So we should not be satisfied with reading books only on spiritual matters. How spiritual awareness is translated into the "affairs of the world" – the daily realities of the average person – as presented by philosophers, historians, economists and the like, while perhaps not being entirely "enlightened" are worth reading, contemplating, discussing. At the least, they can take us out of the ivory towers of spiritual refinement and put us back in the trenches with the nitty gritty realities of *samsara*, giving us some grist for the mill so that we can test our awakening hearts and minds in the practical matters of the day. Along with the classics of antiquity and other distant times, there are any number of modern thinkers whose perspectives are worth considering, such as Marilyn Ferguson, Noam Chomsky, R.D. Laing, and even the political reflections of former presidents and world leaders.

Of course, we *can* always just focus on spiritual matters and on our own transformation – then step into the world wherever we like, raising the consciousness where we are. But, more than likely, we shall gravitate toward those figures whom we feel close to or identify with. The world as presented by great thinkers and visionaries may not be entirely complete or accurate, but it can offer us a wider context from which we can choose how and where to deploy our efforts. Even someone like His Holiness the Dalai Lama recognizes the necessity of this, which explains the often very political content of his writings.

Seeking refuge in the Sangha

Finally we come to refuge in sangha. Sangha is about community – forging a connection between us and those who exemplify what we are trying to accomplish in our lives or who, like ourselves, are also trying to figure out how to manifest conscious, engaged activism in their day-to-day lives. In Buddhist tradition, there is a distinction drawn between "noble" sangha and "ordinary" sangha. This distinction is worth looking at as it can clarify several issues, including jealousy, competitiveness, and personal disappointment.

For now I will focus exclusively on spiritual matters. As I have said at other times, regardless of whether our intentions are clear and pure and whether or not our actions are wise and skillful, we shall continue to breathe and act in this world. Thus until we have reached a state of enlightened awareness where our clarity and purity create only wholesome results in the world around us, we can expect mixed outcomes – some good, some not so good, even some bad – with the hope that the greater weight goes to what is good or at least not harmful. In other words, we should not be too surprised that things don't work out exactly as we envision them, and that there is some karmic fallout and kickback that lets us know that we are not as smart, or compassionate, or selfless as we would like to imagine.

At the same time, this does not mean that we should not strive over the course of our lives toward clarity and purity as the most noble of goals. In fact, one can argue that for some of us, a path that is more active and involved in the world is the fastest path to clearing things up for ourselves and others – providing we are given the tools, the time, the space, and ability to work with our mindfulness in the course of things.

I say this for pragmatic reasons because, generally speaking, few of us have either the luxury or inclination to devote all of our time and mental, physical, and spiritual energies toward a solely contemplative life in a monastery or cloistered retreat. But it would be erroneous for us not to value and appreciate those who *do* have such time and opportunity – who have a single-minded focus on spiritual matters and can create the energy and openness that not only contributes to their own awakening, but also creates an energy vortex that can inspire and create opportunity for others as well. This is the value of monasteries and the treasure of saints, hermits, and practitioners of faith who dedicate their lives and express their conscious, engaged activism in this particular manner.

There are many such men and women around the world, who most of us have never heard of. Of course, such an exclusively religious life may, for some, seem rarified, cloistered, impractical – a way of avoiding the big responsibilities of life. In some cases this may be true. Even the great Tibetan saint Milarepa once said that "A monastery is where driftwood gathers." At the same time, there are those whose abilities are best trained and honed in such environments. And to have the opportunity to retreat, to have a place to go to which is exclusively focused on deepening our understanding and experience of transforming the Three Poisons can be invaluable for everyone; such places are "pockets of light," and it is for these reasons that it is worthwhile supporting them and their practitioners.

And then there are those whose spiritual practices and lives as spiritual elders and guides lead them to up the moral and ethical standards in practical walks of life beyond "spiritual" ones alone. Such is the case with such spiritual adepts as Mother Teresa, the Dalai Lama, Gyalwa Karmapa, or Zalman Schacter, whose impact on wider world events should not be underestimated.

In more mundane matters, it is also true that there are causes or issues we would like to spend more time or energy on, but are limited from doing so for any number of reasons. There are others, however, who have the inclination, time, resources, or a combination of all three, to devote their energies almost exclusively to worthy causes, to making a difference. We should celebrate and admire those who are willing to spend their time and energy in this way as they are often the ones who keep social movements and political action groups alive over time. For the rest of us, contributing our time, energy, or resources whenever we can keeps us connected and can demonstrate our commitment to such causes and issues.

Beyond the mutual support and benefits that are derived from supporting those dedicated activists who are "minding the fort," so to speak, it can be just as important, if not more so, for us to find those around us on a day to day basis who share a similar path. And by sharing a "path" I mean more than just an interest in particular causes or issues: even more important is to find those who are committed to *inner* as well as outer change, and can support our own commitment in this respect. Basically, we need to find others who are similarly interested in treading the path of a conscious, engaged activist.

To come across teachers and associates committed to such a path is rare in the normal course of our daily lives. These days, however, there are any number of spiritual groups, Dharma centers, psychotherapeutic groups, and so on; if they do not yet exist in your area, the chances are that there are other people also looking for them who would, if the opportunity arose, be willing to join together. That being said, it is not necessarily likely that such a support group, spiritual organization, center of activity, or gathering will be harmonious, blissful and nurturing in the same way one might expect a group of quilt or dog enthusiasts to be bonded together. This has to do with the very nature of such groups.

Generally speaking, what matters most in a "pocket of light" group or community is that all agree upon what it is important *to aspire to*. There needs to be a *shared intention*. This intention centers on each person's commitment to transforming their Three Poisons. With that in place and agreed upon, the complex and often messy entanglements of human interaction can then be played out and worked on, and each member's personal transformation is hopefully accelerated in the process. For in the process of committing to that intention, each person will be dragged backward into their own Three Poisons. Each person's personal commitment to work on transforming their Three Poisons is mirrored in their tolerance or intolerance, patience or impatience, compassion or lack of compassion for everyone else in the group. Naturally, everyone in the group will be at a different stage of inner growth, which is why such groups are complex and personally sometimes fraught. The aim of the group is for the whole to collectively help each individual member toward his or her goal.

While it may be true that our interaction with each and every being we meet will mirror what is going on inside of us, the people in a "pocket of light" community are *committed* to being mirrors. This is very different, and in a way trickier, than "normal" social discourse, where we try to cover for each other, turning a blind eye, if at all possible, to what we find embarrassing or awkward. Here, we refuse to turn away from one another. We tell it how we see it. And in being committed to openness in this way, of course, we also subject one another to the sum total of our own confusion and enlightenment. Our ultimate aspiration to benefit others, and our relative wisdom and ability to do so, are tested in a well-focused "loving-nature laboratory." This can make such groups at times feel quite claustrophobic and at other times quite liberating. A wide range of emotional responses needs to be embraced and accepted if one is to harness and work successfully with the intensity of such groups. If any group member begins to feel smug, or noticeable "in-crowds" or cliques start to appear, it is a sign that partisanship is emerging and the group is becoming a social club that needs to be shaken up. This will inevitably happen, one way or another. The reification and ossification of behaviors into personal styles and mannerisms can stifle true growth. For this reason, *all* groups need their heretics, or those who are willing to shake things up, to redirect the group back to its original purpose: being a pocket of light, for the benefit of all, not just a few.

Pockets of light and sources of inspiration may be found at the types of group mentioned above, which we can contact, be a part of, pay membership dues to, and so on. However, I would suggest that we also need to be quite flexible in our expectations of how a pocket of light might appear. Our sources of inspiration and community can be an informal, unorganized association of close friends from over the years, people whom we occasionally talk with or email. However such sources of refuge in our lives appear, it is valuable for us to visualize them and try to manifest them. For without their support, generating the enthusiasm, discipline, patience, focus, and other qualities we need to be a light-bearer in a Dark Age is far more daunting a task.

Recognizing the importance of these "jewels" for our lives and our work as conscious, engaged activists demonstrates not only our interdependent relationship with all those around us. It is a sign of our spiritual maturity and understanding that, in order to get things done – to muster a force more powerful than our own person or personality – we don a mantle of enduring inspiration, arm ourselves with the skill and wisdom born of discriminating compassionate mindfulness, and step forward into action with force and the protection of all those who support our unabashed attempts at authentically being who we are: a conscious, engaged activist wishing to benefit all we can by our efforts.

Pockets of light bring together the refuges of sources of inspiration and methods to transform our own lives and the lives of those we touch, into a tangible social group or culture that we surround ourselves with. This powerful trinity of refuges constitutes a unity that is indispensable for true and lasting change, within and without. As we open up, surrender our sense of personal ego and advantage, and learn to trust and be reliant upon these sources of support, our field of action and effectiveness grows. Our refuges then also become bases, which foster and develop natural born leaders for future generations.

A Conscious, Engaged Civilization

In *The Buddha at War*, I concluded the practice portion of the book with the chapter on "Pockets of Light," intimating that if we were in or were about to experience the ravages of a Dark Age, the practices outlined would not only help us to grow saner and stronger, but would also help us to develop resourcefulness to pass onto future generations. I have also made it clear that we need to do this with the help of friends. In *The Wisdom of The Buddhist Masters: Common and Uncommon Sense*, it became apparent to me that teachers from the East were more convinced – based on their understanding of human nature and a long historical view – of the inevitability of a Dark, or darker, Age becoming the reality that most of us alive today will have to endure. Conversely, some Western teachers, raised in the American fields of dream and possibility, conceived that it was possible to create a more peaceful and enlightened society even in the midst of the uncertainty that we face. In the long run, there is a great deal of practical personal, social, and global work to be done to if we are to collectively – or as a large proportion of our human family – overcome some of our most base and self-centered tendencies in order to survive these times and develop a conscious, engaged, and sustainable global community.

The paths you can follow in accomplishing the creation of

such a society are so many and varied: where you live, what resources you have materially and/or spiritually, the time you have, your needs for the present, your needs for the future, and so forth. In the chapter, "Pockets of Light," I speak of groups or communities of awakening individuals, committed to personal transformation whilst remaining or becoming engaged in supporting change and helping others in the "troubled times" that we face. Beyond the work we need to do within our human family, there is a similar need to repair and develop a more holistic, equal, and reciprocal relationship with all sentient life on this planet. It's not just about us in the small sense of the word "us," i.e. humans. It's about the big US – all of what works and interacts in animal and plant life to create a sustainable harmonious planet.

Although as an American I tend to think of such transformation in a more *laissez faire* manner, there was a model presented to me by Bonpo teacher, Geshe Tenzin Wangyal Rinpoche, in my last book, *The Wisdom of The Buddhist Masters*, that I can see as an overarching spiritually oriented framework that is – to my mind – both vital and indispensible in tending to all that needs to be addressed in creating such a world. This has to do with what he called the principle of The Four Guests which I would like to explain as best I can and – if the reader will indulge me – expand on.

All of the Buddhist traditions teach us that there are levels of sentient existence, seen and unseen, with which we need to have good relationships in order for there to be harmony amongst and around us. Although it may also be true in the other Tibetan lineages, the Bonpo speak of Four Guests, each being a manifestation or representative of the different levels of sentient life with whom we need to relate and who we need to honor in the most appropriate way. To do so is a sign of a civilized society in proper relationship with all of – if you will – creation. Knowing our place in relation to the Four Guests and in the spirit of loving kindness and compassion for all, we learn that for us to fulfill our human destiny, we need help and we need *to* help. Furthermore, when people in a society have respect for and attend to their relationship to the Guests, tradition teaches that the perfect environment is created for spiritual growth, peace, and happiness. Conversely, when one of the Guests is honored at the expense of the others, or there is a general disregard for any of the Guests, there arises an imbalance and the environment becomes more challenging to these good qualities.

Succinctly put, the Four Guests include, but also go beyond, what we normally define in our three-dimensional reality. By the same token, they can be taken as principles, archetypes, or roles at levels of our consciousness both individually and collectively, that need to be addressed in order for us to feel and be integrated and whole. The traditional way of speaking about the Four Guests describes them as Transcendental Beings, Protectors, local spirits and our "karmic" family, and those less fortunate than us. All of these will be explained in full. With respect to the first two Guests, in our three-dimensional, materialistic secular culture, it may seem primitive, silly, or irrelevant to pay attention especially to the first and second guests as they are more spiritual and essentially unseen to the normal eye. However, because they represent important levels of critical thinking, openness, and skill in learning how to properly engage the world around us, I feel compelled to spell them out in traditional terms as well as more experiential terms and leave each reader to decide how they can best honor these guests or levels.

Honoring the First Guest

From the Buddhist perspective, The First Guest has to do with Enlightened Beings – Buddhas, Bodhisattvas, as well as Enlightened representatives of the natural world, i.e. the Space Goddess, Fire Goddess, Earth Goddess, Air Goddess, and Water Goddess. For those who are not of a Buddhist persuasion, think of a transcendent, ineffable reality; a level of reality that would include God, Allah, and such beings as Moses, Jesus, Mohammed, the Saints, as well as inspirational men and women of history who exemplify the qualities we seek to aspire to in our own lives. To this level of existence and to the transcendental beings who exist in and/or operate from that ultimate reality, we show honor and deference. Tenzin Wangyal Rinpoche says that we open ourselves up for blessings, guidance, power, and support as a gesture that we are willing to connect with something larger, grander than ourselves. Doing so provides us with a whole new level of confidence. We can feel a more profound sense of place and purpose. It can help us to leap beyond our boundaries.

To dismiss this level of reality because it is not materially tangible or too idealized (if we are speaking of honoring extraordinary souls in history or in our midst), or to grab onto it with fanatic zeal and use it for myopic, prejudiced ambitions would be a tragedy. With respect to agnostics and atheists, I feel saddened, but not alarmed by their view. They are smart not to fall for the big daddy in the sky mythology or superhero cults which so often make people abdicate their personal power and responsibility. But, as a result of their refusal to accept the First Guest, I think that sensitivity and wisdom are lost. What is of more concern to me are those people who zealously create a materialistic concept of who these beings are and how to relate to them. Such people often spend time justifying their overly conceptualized reality by recruiting others to join them in their exclusivist fundamentalist ideology. Such people are a problem for all of us.

In honoring the First Guest, part of our responsibility is to be ever watchful of such distortions and to commit ourselves to developing the skill and will to prevent future incidences of extreme political correctness in our religious tolerance, which have in the past led us to turn a blind eye to people with corrupted perspective ascending to dangerous levels of power.

Superheroes aside and focusing more on transcendental beings, whilst the deities and beings of this enlightened or transcendental reality may be intangible, these guests hold dominion over creation: from a Buddhist perspective, the natural world and the five elements. This world, nature, and the elements of which all things are a part, are the very context in which we live. Without these, we would die. By disrespecting them, therefore, why should it be any surprise when greater harm and suffering arise in our lives?

We do not honor SPACE, the source of all creativity; that within everything arises and disappears. We territorialize space, yet encroach on others' space. We move too quickly to fully appreciate space. We have to keep ourselves busy, always preoccupied with one thing or another, or go to the other extreme of spacing out and abdicating our roles and responsibilities. Through ignorance of how to properly work with what is around us, being attached to and defensive of our wants and desires, we have polluted the air and water and rendered the ground infertile, to a large extent with our abuse of fire in the form of nuclear radiation, petrochemical byproducts and exhausts, electromagnetic smog, and with a host of fertilizers and chemicals which we use every day. All of these have a fiery quality that contributes to global warming, not only by the way they impact the atmosphere and the ozone layer, but by the way they also burn up all of the other elements. The food crisis, including droughts and floods that prevent and create conditions that make it impossible to grow food, and the resultant starvation, malnutrition, and our increased confusion and incompetence in knowing how to actually feed ourselves properly is a manifestation of this improper relationship with the elements.

Looking at this food issue as a perfect example of our not honoring nature and the elements, there are two problems created from the Judeo-Christian assumption of our being God's agent on earth and of our dominion over this planet. The first has to do with what I believe to be a misunderstanding of the Ten Commandments and the primacy of the one God.

"Thou shalt have no other god before me," *does not mean* that there are no other gods. It just puts one god on top. This hierarchy is not a problem; it is not necessarily a bad thing. But, if we attribute and rely upon one god for all things, then we are missing the point and making God's job too complicated. This is the first problem.

The second problem is related to the first problem. We have come to believe that we are the stewards of the planet (with God being the CEO) and are thus the managers and intermediaries in mastering the natural world as God has duly elected us to be. Thus we have shown disregard for the elemental goddesses and other enlightened beings by thinking we can do their jobs. Clearly we cannot. For the most part, we have strayed so far away from the natural world that most of us really do not know what we are doing and what we are creating as a result of our rush to modernize, to force nature to comply with our technological designs and our desire to make things happen according to our own limited plan.

It would be foolish to think that the step that non-Buddhists with a monotheistic perspective should take is to accept pantheism and start praying to other deities, and so on. What is most important is for us to re-establish a sacred bond with a world that appears to be in rebellion against hubris, our excesses, and our corporate wants and timetables.

We need to re-learn a sensitivity to the rhythms of nature. It is wonderful to see the growing interest in organic foods, permaculture, and other philosophies and approaches that emphasize sustainability. What we must bear in mind is that going "back to the land" cannot be done by following the ways of our ancestors. At the same time, with respect to the subtle and unseen beings and forces of nature, there is so much to learn from shamans and spiritual elders who call upon these beings and forces to support our efforts. I have seen time and again the power of calling on the land, releasing prayers into the air, of floating offerings in the oceans and rivers. I have watched Hopi elders call on rain spirits and seen it rain from a cloudless sky. I have been with Tibetan masters when they called rain, sent it away, trapped the wind, and made the earth open up. We may not have such abilities. But it is worth making efforts to re-establish a sacred bond as a first or at least a necessary step in receiving the help and cooperation from these invisible beings to use our resources wisely in the circumstances that we find ourselves in. For some, this may involve invoking the elements through ritual. These rituals may come from our own heritage or from another culture still in touch with these forces and their representatives. Or we may feel inspired to come up with our own way of doing this. Whatever ritual one chooses to do, focusing together with others in a collective is more powerful and effective.

If this is not your thing, then consider "reducing, re-using, and recycling" and encouraging these practices among your children and your communities.

And then, look at the bigger picture. Don't be oblivious to corporate behaviors. Learn about your world, your environment. Watch documentaries with your children. Pay attention to how your lawmakers act and what goals they are supporting or not supporting that impact our land, water, and air.

Respecting the Second Guest

The Second Guest is a guest we often bump into when we hit roadblocks or feel pressured to act when it might not be comfortable to do so. In Tibetan tradition, such beings are called protectors and guardians. In Eastern astrology, the stars and planets are considered Second Guest entities. They appear in our charts as strengths and challenges. Tenzin Wangyal Rinpoche says that angels from the Western traditions would fit into this second guest category.

Such beings are ever vigilant and influential in our lives, often in very subtle ways. For example, there are times when we would like to do something, but some kind of neurotic impulse stops us from following through and we only learn later that our inaction was a good thing. Or, perhaps we are gung ho to do something that we have not really thought through, and we get in our car and find that the battery is dead. Conversely, we are hesitant to make a change, to confront a situation, and suddenly that situation is right in our face and we need to do something about it immediately. When we look at this in hindsight, we usually find that we had the strength and ability, but not the will to carry it through. But, somehow, something happened and what we thought we could not do we have done. These are all examples of the protector function in our lives.

Protector deities and guardians in the Tibetan tradition look demonic from a Western point of view. When Westerners first saw pictures and iconography of these beings, they were thought to be proof of Eastern devil and demon worship. In Tibetan tradition, however, these bone-crushing, blood-spattered, skull-wearing beings represent a wrathful manifestation of compassion. When we disregard our higher nature, when we take advantage of others or abuse our natural world, these beings are there to show us that we've blown it and call upon us to straighten up and get it right. They will hold us to the awkwardness and difficulties we have created through our ignorance, attachment, and aggression. There are any number of stories in mythology, Eastern and Western, where a hag or ogre confronts the hero. Inevitably, what happens in these stories is that the hero changes direction, whether it is in their heart or mind, or in what they are doing and the ogre turns into a prince, the hag into a beauty. In indigenous and pre-modern societies, there are a host of wrathful or mischievous demi-gods – all of whom are invisible (or not so easily seen) beings with a direct connection to and responsibility for helping to maintain and support nature and the five elements. In the shamanic and esoteric traditions on every continent of this earth, there are teachers, shamans, medicine men and women who understand how to summon and create a proper relationship with this guest.

Of course, you may have doubts about praying to or honoring scary-looking deities and fairies at the bottom of your garden. But, basically, what this level and this guest most calls on us to do is to raise our ethical and moral standards and be accountable for our actions. If I were to think about this level with respect to human roles within society that represent this protector function, I would consider educators, watch-dog organizations such as the ACLU and Sierra Club, conscientious elected officials, and well-trained warriors – be they policemen or soldiers – to be Second Guest emissaries. An education in critical thinking skills is the first safeguard in ensuring that thoughtfulness goes into how we act in the world and treat life around us. And when things get out of hand, when ignorance, attachment, and aggression get the better of us individually or collectively, at home, in the office, or in our relation to other cultures and nations, we need those who can check, confront, even destroy what will lead to greater harm. In some ways, however, these roles are some of the trickiest and most abused and thus require – to be effective – a higher, if not an impeccable standard of ethics in concert with the society they are entrusted to protect.

To stick to higher principles, to take risks, and to stand for something that you know runs counter to the norms and expectations of consumer culture today takes power and courage. You need to be willing to take what is thrown at you, and break down some doors periodically when others create harmful circumstances and suffering in other beings' lives. Such an attitude and effort shows a sense of decency and respect for who we are and what we are a part of.

If we are willing to do this, then we earn the right to request these protectors and guardians to imbue us with their qualities and to support us in removing obstacles in our path. To support our requests, an integral part of the honoring of the Second Guests is the respect we show them. They are not there as enforcers, although enforcers they may need to become to fulfill their role and lead us away from self-destructive tendencies. Showing respect for them should, therefore, not come out of fear, but a humble recognition that we need help to do what we – in our better moments – know needs to be done.

The Second Guests – whether we understand them to be the protector deities in their non-human form, or our friends and neighbors who take on the mantel for the benefit of us all – are an essential and powerful ally when it comes to trying to affect social and political change.

Loving Kindness for the Third Guest

With respect to the first two Guests, I mention an honoring and deference for the First Guest and respect for the Second Guest. It demonstrates at the level of our understanding and intention that we have an appreciation for the larger design of which we are a part and the humility for us not to take ourselves too seriously. In this I am reminded of Jeremy Narby's book, *The Cosmic Serpent*, where he takes ayahuasca offered to him by a Brazilian shaman and finds himself looking at two serpents who say to him, "Remember, you're only human."

When it comes to the next two Guests, the third and the fourth, the situation becomes more intimate and interactive. It thus calls upon us to apply what in Buddhism is called *bodhicitta* or "awakened heart." The two "prongs" of *bodhicitta* are loving kindness and compassion.

The Venerable Chogyam Trungpa Rinpoche used to look at words and phrases and play with them to find their deeper meanings. Honoring his spirit, I have come to think of the term "loving kindness" differently from how I had heard and thought of it for years when I heard teachers mention the phrase in Dharma discourses.

If we take the word loving to be a verb rather than an adjective, it comes alive. Similarly, if we take the word "kind" and use it not as an attitude, but rather as a descriptive noun, we can take it to mean that – at least in the stretchy quality of my imagination – something that we are a part of. What are we a part of? We are a part of sentient life. In the spirit of the fourth of the Four Immeasurables ("May they dwell in great equanimity, which is beyond passion, aggression, and prejudice." Chapter 5), therefore, this phrase can mean **loving kind-ness**, i.e. loving and feeling an equal connection with all whom we share sentience with. Having a body and mind like all other sentient beings and knowing from a Buddhist perspective that all sentient beings possess Buddhanature, we make an acknowledgement and are willing and joyful in putting ourselves on an equal footing. With respect to the Third Guest, honoring, therefore, is characterized by a demonstrating of this loving kindness.

The Third Guest principle includes both invisible, more local spirits of a locale or region and what are known as "karmic" beings; our mothers, fathers, family, friends, and neighbors. As it is said that we have all been mothers, fathers, brothers, sisters, and so on in various forms and incarnations for lifetime after lifetime, there can be other forms of sentient life with whom we share a similar kinship, i.e. animals – perhaps even the pets we chose. As this may seem a stretch or improbable for some readers, when speaking of those with whom we have karma, I shall stick to our human family.

Briefly and with respect to local spirits, Buddhist teachings mention the spirits of the mountains, the streams, the land, and so on. Of course, from a Western "sophisticated" point, it may seem primitive to make offerings to or to try to connect with nature's spirits. Such local spirits and deities are not like the deities referred to in the description of the First Guest. They are more tied to the place or location in which we live. They are our invisible neighbors with whom we may be sharing our property and homes; whose lease or ownership policy on the turf we want to call home may stand up in a different kind of court. With respect to these beings, respecting and not ransacking our environment is the most significant way we can honor the spirits intimated at this level. This also has to do with making peace with and being able to accommodate them.

Tending to nature and the spirits that inhabit her is crucial when it comes to honoring the Third Guest. But, because of our closeness to our karmic family, the other humans of whose societies and cultures we are a part, the remainder of our discussion on the Third Guest will focus on them.

When I listen to some Western Buddhist teachers, and read the reflections and predictions of others who claim that a new, more enlightened society is on the rise and that an old way of seeing and being in the world is dying, I feel cautious. I would like to show more enthusiasm, to be more optimistic. But, in looking at spiritual gatherings (be they Buddhist Dharma groups, Hindu satsangs, people interested in Kabbalah, Sufism, or progressive Christianity), information groups and gatherings like Noetics, or progressive peace and political action groups and parties, for the most part I see bald, white, and gray heads. There are very, very few children, teens, or young couples with families in these groups. Consequently, the conclusion I draw is that if there is a growing circle of people interested in raising consciousness and establishing a progressive, more enlightened society, that circle may be wider than it has ever been in recent memory, but it is not deep. It is attracting the "usual suspects;" i.e. the same demographic. It is not reaching the next generation as much as we would like. And, if this does not change, if consciousness-raising individuals and groups cannot solicit or entice more youth to join its ranks, then Ajahn Amaro's interpretation of the sutra's timetable of the end of a mini-Golden Age in a Dark Age around 2050 will come to pass.

Personally, not wanting to see this come to pass, I think it is important to understand why such groups are not reaching young people, and then come up with a way of changing this reality.

In the ever-increasing pace of industrial and technological advance and the rush to become modern, to free ourselves from the limitations and restraints of a more provincial life, I believe we have lost some very basic human skills. In Western society, where the dominant family model is the nuclear family (frequently even more nuclearized into a mother-and-two-children family), connection to local and extended family have broken down. If, as Hilary Clinton writes, "It Takes a Village" to raise children, then few of us have a connection to such. Relatives, friends, and neighbors used to be the matrix that made a village. But, so many of us have moved away from our immediate families. We may have great neighbors around us, but as the saying goes, "Blood is thicker than water." Those with whom we have a blood bond can be meddlesome, but they can also be called upon in a more unconditional way. In general for most of us, aunts, uncles, and grandparents are not around to be supportive, to offer their wisdom and guidance. Multi-generational households in the modern world are rare. Retirement communities exist where there are restrictions on who can live there and how long children can visit. And there are nursing homes where a growing number of our elders, our family sages, are parked, and tended to and medicated by strangers.

In the circles of friends around both of my daughters who are in their late twenties, few of their friends, male or female, know how to cook or take care of where they live. Domestic skills are disappearing fast in a culture that is more concerned with how well we keep up with material acquisition than with learning how to discern the quality of, to treasure, savor, and maintain what we already have. In fact, I would say that by and large, the hip and sexy Hollywood model of reality, for the most par, mocks domesticity. "Suzie Homemakers" may know how to bake a pie. But do they look good in a Victoria's Secret lingerie? And guys, well aren't they supposed to be domestically challenged?

What I find interesting – or paradoxical – is that Christian fundamentalists in the West (even if I cannot accept what I perceive to be their overly simplistic views and exclusivity) seem to show a genuine concern for and place a high moral value on the support of family and community. They get involved in school boards and local politics. They tithe to their churches, which generally have after-school programs and camps for youth. They may have strong, sometimes very repressive definitions in terms of male and female roles. But, they take family very seriously. I have noted that some of the most progressive thinking about food, exercise, relaxation and wellness can be seen daily on fundamentalist TV networks.

For the most part, I think that many of the Western spiritual, new age, and progressive teachers that I have met come out of either an elite or fragmented family structure or society. On an ultimate level, they have much to contribute when it comes to introducing wisdom principles to a culture so lacking in them. But, few of them have, or have practical lives, or lives that bear much resemblance to the ordinary day-to-day lives of people in search of place, meaning, and purpose. In the circles where I teach, I have seen how poor the Buddhist community has been in offering teaching to, or including children. During a Feng Shui conference I attended in Zurich, I heard a well-known Chinese master chastise the audience of budding Feng Shui teachers by telling them that it was impossible for them to offer anything of value in Feng Shui if they did not know how to take care of their own relationships.

If we want to see the re-establishment of honoring the Third Guest and in particular our own human family, whilst it is noble and worthwhile to give profound teachings and fight to free people from persecution and uplift their circumstances (something we shall talk more about when it comes to the Fourth Guest), it is crucial to start at home.

If the future begins with our children, I would like to comment first on what we need to offer our children.

The first point here is that – whilst it would seem irresponsible and contrary to general concern for the world's population – I encourage well-educated, affluent couples to have children.

As a general rule, this particular social group tends to elect against having children, or at least more than one child. For a start, they are better educated, have easy access to birth control, want to be free to travel, explore, get their careers on track, and have a concern for global issues (including population). Also, seeing the disastrously high divorce rate and often defining their own nuclear family living history as dysfunctional, many young couples have decided not to have children. After all, the world is over-crowded and times are dangerous. Wouldn't it be irresponsible to bring one more child into such a place?

I think that this view is misguided. There may be some who are altruistic about not wanting to have children. But, as our affluence has created an almost responsibility-free and overly-extended adolescence, I think most young couples are scared, traumatized by their own personal history, and/or are more self-involved and do not want the responsibility of raising another being. I also think that this view is reinforced by the schizoid perspective of Western religions where our sexuality is so demonized in the early years of our development, that when it comes to matrimony and the blessing to "be fruitful and multiply," the damage is already done. The result is a cultural ambivalence towards child bearing which – in my mind – is the spiritual foundation behind the ineptitude many feel about raising children. I think that there is also a view that if you really, truly want to be spiritual, you wouldn't have children. You would be celibate, a monk, a nun, a renunciate. And even though the Reformation faiths wanted to dispute this view and encourage a more "in the world" perspective with respect to religion, clergy, and family, the duality between sacred and profane, the world of spirit and flesh persists. Even amongst those who are attracted to Eastern faiths, this view creates a distortion which in turns creates a longing for a monastic, otherworldly life – just like the monks and gurus.

When it comes to population, the matter isn't entirely about numbers. Part of the issue is balance and quality. I agree with Lama Ole Nydahl that the wealthier nations should pay the poor and disadvantaged to not have children. At the same time, they should also provide education so that these people can climb out of poverty and lead more healthy, productive lives where the number of offspring is not a necessity or sign of prestige. On the other side of this equation, if people who are educated and have resources to raise children in safe, healthy environments, and provide them with the kind of education and resourcefulness to make positive contributions to the world's future, they should be encouraged to do so.

Of course, we could just sit back and watch the population continue to sky rocket, in which case it will be disproportionately poor and uneducated – the types of disenfranchised individuals who will overly burden health care systems and be the drones who swell the ranks of armies at the beck and call of tyrannical characters. In the past, where the herd gets too thick and stressed from lack of space, food, and other life-supporting amenities, there have been ways in which nature takes care of the burden – such as the plague. Macrobiotic teacher, Michio Kushi, once said, "Civilization is the disease and cancer is the cure." As we continue to damage our environment and food supply and weaken our psycho-physical condition, then perhaps cancer and AIDS, and other diseases to come, and rising oceans and other catastrophic climate changes will thin out the herd. But, do we want to succumb to such solutions to a problem we can at least make efforts to get a handle on? Can we manage the size *and* **quality** of our own population?

In the raising of children, I think there are a few basic factors that must be included beyond organized or formal education. These points will directly or tangentially contribute to the development of their critical thinking abilities.

First: Give children good food and educate them in where food comes from, how to grow it, and how to cook it. And, *eat it together.*

Second: His Holiness Kunzig Shamar Rinpoche was once asked what was the most important thing parents could teach their children. His message: Teach them to be less materialistic. Although critical thinking skills will go a long way in helping your children to discern what is and is not of value, the best way to teach being less materialistic is to model it yourself.

Third: Teach them about IMPERMANENCE. After the student massacre in Littleton, Colorado, in the late 1990s, I listened to and read commentaries about what could have been the causal factors in young people being willing to take lives; not only those of others, but their own as well. From the outside, what could be concluded was nothing particularly dramatic. However, it did lead me to look at features in American (and Western European) culture that may not be addressed fully, if at all – especially in relationship to youth. There are certain inevitable facts that we need to appreciate regarding life in general and pass on to our youth. These facts may seem self-evident, but rarely do we talk about them or operationalize them in terms of making their factual nature viscerally real:

That we are born into this world

That we shall inevitably experience various forms of stress and disease, be they physical or emotional, over the course of our lives

That we will age and, as a result, go through various changes in life – no matter how long or short our lives may be

That we shall die as do all things born into this
world

It is in appreciating change and impermanence that we are able
to more fully appreciate the *preciousness of our lives*. It makes us
become appreciative of what we have and who we are. It helps
to temper our behaviors so that we act more realistically and
responsibly. It also gives us a much deeper appreciation for
people around us. The ones we love will experience these Four
INEVITABLE FACTS as we do. The same is true for even those
who we dislike or have problems with. If we understand this
more fully, then we are kinder to others and more considerate.
If impermanence and these inevitable facts are not taught or
discussed and, furthermore, if children are not exposed to a
world they can witness, talk about, and learn to integrate into
their hearts and minds – the truth of birth, sickness, old age, and
death – then they will develop an unrealistic world view.

Sadly, these four facts of life, which we all experience, are
poorly attended to or managed in our modern industrial
societies. To start with, we live in a culture that has medicalized
both ends of the life cycle. Most of us are born behind hospital
doors and most of us die there as well. Thus only in rare circumstances do we see each other going through these life transitions
which define our mortality.

In a culture that is focused on immediate gratification and
youthful energy, aging is considered an enemy that must be
fought. We create a world of pop and beauty icons that we
compare ourselves to. Thus we lose our ability to value who we
are and the changes we need to go through in our own time. Any
signs that contradict this artificially frozen reality are ignored,
put to the side – as we have placed our elders behind closed doors
as well. Thus we are losing touch with the wisdom of age.

We also try to medicate every experienced discomfort. We

have painkillers and medical procedures to eradicate our physical pains and use a wide psycho-pharmacological arsenal to modulate our moods on a day-to-day basis. And if we don't look the way we want to, if there is a telltale bulge or wrinkle, there is always liposuction or botox. There is no particular virtue in suffering needlessly. But, we must also be aware that there are times in life where the pain that we experience, even the perception and realization that we are not "perfect," actually help us to grow into more mature, caring individuals with greater empathy.

Looking more specifically at teenagers, and young adults, a section of the population which does not tend to witness firsthand the preciousness of life beginning (i.e. birth), or the ending of life (i.e. death), there is a tendency on their part to believe that they are immortal or at least untouchable with respect to the Four Inevitable Facts. Not being truly in touch with the life cycle and its impermanence, these young people may be aware of it intellectually, but it doesn't really touch their lives directly. Thus, they experience these events vicariously through TV and other media. And in a culture that denies these truths, there is a good likelihood that these same youth will become obsessed with what they cannot experience directly – video games and movies which demonstrate in more and more detail graphic ways in which people are maimed, killed, slaughtered.

There are also those children who *have* witnessed such events; the birth of a child, the death of a friend or parent. However, because this is not the norm, such experiences do not feel normal and, as such, cannot be shared with others, making these children marginalized. In order to fit in, they try to deny their impact, and this can also create alienation and disconnection from the Four Inevitable Facts.

We become obsessed by that which our culture forbids us to look at realistically and honestly. This precipitates an increased level of risk-taking behavior in general. For between the two ends of the life spectrum, we do everything we can to eliminate the pain that is the consequence of our lifestyle habits or actions. With respect to drugs and alcohol, when children and young people see their parents and authority figures modulating their moods with the use of alcohol or prescription medication, a message is sent to them that it is not necessary to face how we really feel in this world. It only stands to reason, then, that these young people seek their own chemical means to modulate their own moods as well. As parents go to their peers – doctors – for medications to obliterate the pain of living, it stands to reason that youths, who do not have access to the medical system in the same way, will seek those who can supply them with the necessary pain medication within their own peer group. Although one example is legitimate and the other is defined as illegitimate or illegal, the behavior is the same. Thus, in this matter, the problem is not a "peer" problem. It is a *modeling* and parenting problem.

Several years ago, to address this lack, I instituted a program within a local state-run program for difficult-to-manage youth. It was called The Spectrum of Life.

The purpose of the Spectrum of Life program was to help students develop a sound appreciation of the Four Inevitable Facts, thus reducing risk-taking behavior and facilitating a greater level of caring, consideration, and community participation.

To accomplish this, there were a variety of experiential learning opportunities arranged with the cooperation of various community-based organizations. These included but were restricted to the following...

- placement in a maternity unit for a day
- if possible, attending a birth and/or be around newborns
- spending time helping at a neo-natal intensive care unit

- going to a home for developmentally disabled/handicapped
- spending an evening at an Emergency Room
- visiting and attending a group at an AIDS project
- visiting people on a hospital cancer unit
- spending two days assisting at a nursing home facility
- being encouraged to spend an entire day with their grandparents
- receiving some limited training as a hospice volunteer and going out on 2–3 calls
- alternatively, going out on assignment with a hospice volunteer
- visiting the county morgue
- spending a day at one of the mortuaries

Included with these placements were presentations made by experts in each of these areas and the related disciplines. After each one of these learning experiences, group time was arranged with one of the Spectrum of Life counselors to process the experiences. Also, students were encouraged to keep a journal throughout. To measure the effectiveness of such a program in positively impacting the lives of youths and student, a pre- and post-questionnaire was administered to determine any changes in perspectives and/or attitudes.

The results of running The Spectrum of Life program have been impressive. These results included…

- Significant changes in pre- and post-questionnaires. Youth showed changes in priorities (how they would like to spend their time, who matters to them in their life) and expressed interest in new fields that they wanted to pursue as possible careers in the future.

- Agencies throughout the community thoroughly enjoyed educating, showcasing to young people what they do.
- Students who had not yet done the program requested to join it.
- Agencies who had participated looked forward to new students joining future programs.

I would encourage parents, educators, and lawmakers to consider introducing such programs into their communities.

Finally, we need to honor and re-establish an ongoing relationship with the most revered of all of the Third Guests: our own elders; our parents and grandparents. No matter how educated they may or may not be, whether we agree with them and their values or not, if we can go below the surface of our own issues to understand how they were raised and what events shaped their thinking, we can gain a sense of personal history which will help us to appreciate them. It will also allow us to be easier on ourselves, giving us a much greater understanding of our seemingly intractable habits and their accompanying thoughts and feelings, and of the time it will take to transform them.

The fact of the matter is that, yes, raising children and tending to elders is challenging and demands us to be willing to take on responsibility. But, unless we take care of our own homes, unless we are able to show loving kindness to our own mothers and fathers, unless we are willing to raise children of conscience, then all of our prayers for the benefit of others, and – I contend – even our actions that seemingly benefit others and their concerns, will be less realistic and less able to stand the test of time. There is no finer laboratory in which to develop the patience, generosity, and forbearance needed to act effectively and responsibly in the world than our homes.

Compassion for The Fourth Guest

The concept of the Fourth Guest relates to honoring, caring for and tending to the needs of those who are, by our or society's standards, less fortunate than ourselves. In Tibetan tradition, this can include anyone who does not aspire to or comprehend the significance of awakening to their enlightened potential: to be a fully engaged being manifesting love and compassion effortlessly and endlessly. This can include a lot of beings at all levels of existence seen and unseen; gods, demi-gods, fellow humans, animals, ghosts, and hell beings – the Six Realms of Existence according to Tibetan philosophy. Buddhist tradition says that encouraging and supporting changes to awaken a being's curiosity and desire to connect with their own Buddhanature is the ultimate gift and source of all good things, spiritual, emotional, and physical. Regardless of whether one feels up to this task, we should not dismiss or minimize the significance of becoming more conscious and engaged in helping our fellow humans in dire circumstances, as well as animal species who, like us, want to be happy and free of suffering.

It is said that developing and working with compassion is the most powerful vehicle in awakening our potentials. If compassion is the force behind an intention to do good in the world, then, more than likely, the fruits of such actions will prove positive and successful. Compassion can have many faces, however.

Summarizing what I elaborate on in previous chapters, there are times when, in order to help another, we need peaceful, calming actions to soothe their pain, which can be spiritual pain as well as tangible pain. Such acts are charitable. This is what most people think of as compassion.

But compassion can also be an enriching and empowering act, as in the spirit of "Give a man a fish and he will eat for a day. Teach him how to fish, and he will be able to feed himself for the rest of his life." Here we are looking at education, encouraging people to rise up in their own power.

Then there are those who, because of either a lack of access to better education or difficulties in embracing a philosophy of inclusivity, find themselves habitually, or through being seduced or convinced against their own better judgment, to do things that can harm themselves and others. In these cases, you may need to use more influence, charisma, and a well-crafted marketing strategy to prevent individuals, groups, even nations from such harmful acts. If the power and momentum to do harm is something they are unable or unwilling to stop, then you may have to stop them yourself. This is the fourth act of compassion; wrathfulness, which can conversely be the situation where you defend someone from being attacked or harmed.

There are endless ways in which these Four Acts of Compassion (pacifying, enriching, magnetizing, and wrathful) can manifest; sending canned goods to food drives, sending money to organizations that fight for prisoners' rights, volunteering to teach, sending letters to lawmakers compelling them to do better and think of others, being involved in the political process or doing whatever you can to promote justice and end poverty, sickness, and warfare. And sometimes, you may even need to take on the role of a more wrathful warrior; to sit in front of a tank, make yourself a nuisance, or take up arms to stop corruption and the abuse of power when others who may have the power to do so do not.

If we are to sow the seeds for a future enlightened society, all Four Guests need to be honored and cared for. In an interdependent universe, how could it be otherwise? Still, each of us may be more aware of or inclined to feel an affinity or connection with one Guest more than others. Some may feel that the most important relationship they have in this world is with

God. Some may feel that way about nature. Others may feel the same way about their family. And then there are those who feel a greater connection and joy in helping those in need.

But, if one truly wants to see sustainable changes, one must be willing to recognize and make good the relationships with all of the other Guests as well. For to disregard or deny the significance of any one Guest, as we grow individually or as a society, will make all of our actions lopsided and less effective.

To honor the First Guest, to respect the Second Guest, to show loving kindness for the Third Guest, and compassion for the Fourth Guest creates a state of mind free of alienation. Being aware and having the clarity and intention to live to a higher standard for ourselves and others; being willing to stay focused, engaged in body, speech, and mind in order to bring happiness to others, all indicate that we are in touch with our own inherent loving nature – our Buddhanature, or whatever you want to call that part of us which most values the altruistic spirit of service.

To be involved in co-creating a conscious, engaged society – an awakened civilization – may sound like a difficult, improbable path to put one's energies towards. But, if it was unachievable, then wisdom that tells some masters that it is possible, and the dreams of utopia that have danced on the fringes of society and tempted us with a better life, would be more myth and hold less of a real possibility in our minds.

Are we willing to encourage such a vision of our world? As conscious, engaged activists, do we have the resolve to employ all of the tools that we possess to eradicate any vestiges of the ignorance, attachment, and aggression in oneself and the world that stands in the way of this vision?

If we are to look to the future at all, whether we see a better time in our own lives or not, such efforts are not only worthwhile and noble. They seed our world for generations to come.

Salvation – saving ourselves, saving our world for the ever-awakening and happiness of all beings – is in our hands. And even if we do not feel capable of acting in accordance with our clarity and intentions, we can at least dream with such a vision in mind.

Furthermore, we should not underestimate the power of dreams.

CHAPTER 12:

The Buddha at Peace

"We must be the change we wish to see in the world."

Mahatma Gandhi

In the first verses of the classical Buddhist text, the *Vimalakirti Nirdesa Sutra*, the historical Buddha, Shakyamuni, is sitting among countless disciples, bodhisattvas, goddesses, and gods, all experiencing in their own way the splendor of his field of enlightened energy – the "Buddhafield" that radiates from the enlightened being at its center.

All seemed so perfect. However, in Buddhist lore it is said that when beings are stuck or in need of further teaching, a Buddha will telepathically influence the mind of a disciple to pose a question. In this way, Shakyamuni prompted his disciple Shariputra to raise the following question about the Buddha's Buddhafield or enlightened realm: If an enlightened realm is a perfect, splendid place, why do some beings residing in it suffer? Why are there beings suffering in sickness, poverty, and warfare? For indeed, beyond the enclave of blissful gods and disciples, this is what Shariputra saw in the world outside.

To this the Buddha replied, "What do you think Shariputra? Is it because the sun and moon are impure that those blind from birth do not see them?"[15] The Buddha was referring to the Three Poisons that blind us to the splendor of the world. To demonstrate beyond a shadow of a doubt the world's splendor, the Buddha touched his big toe to the ground. Everything was transformed into precious gems blazing dazzlingly beautiful light in all directions. Thus the Buddha revealed to Shariputra and every other being present the full splendor of his Buddhafield – the true nature of the world around us. And then, to show Shariputra once more what the world looks like under the influence of the Three Poisons, the Buddha removed his toe from the ground.

The message from the Buddha here is that, **on an ultimate level, everything is fine. There is, absolutely speaking, *nothing really* to worry about, because what we *do* worry about is *nothing that is real*.** What makes it seem real are the Three Poisons – our ignorance, our attachments, our aggression.

The Buddha's war against the Three Poisons does not require him to suit up for battle. In fact, it requires nothing of him at all. In his love, compassion, joy, and equanimity he effortlessly creates the context and the methods that can give beings the time, space, and opportunity to unravel the mystery for themselves. However, like all of those with common sense, the Buddha knows that "You can lead a horse to water, but…." He knows that for us to manifest our enlightened potentiality and become free, independent, conscious, and engaged activists – to become Buddha – requires work that is rooted in our own intention, our own motivation to change.

[15] *Vimalakirti Nirdesa Sutra*, translated by Robert Thurman. University of Pennsylvania, 1976, pp.6–7 (online version).

Beyond Hope and Fear

The Venerable Khenpo Karthar Rinpoche addressed this issue in a talk about the Medicine Buddha, a being we met in Chapter 6 (see page 95). The Rinpoche said that if all it took for us to become enlightened was grace – being blessed or blasted with *shakti* or fairydust by some divine being – then we would all have become enlightened a long time ago. But this is obviously not the case. If, however, we hold onto such a belief or faith, that grace is all that is needed, then it is easy to find ourselves caught in a cycle of hope and fear: hoping that it will happen to us, that things will just change by themselves and everything will be fine; or fearing that it won't happen at all, or that it doesn't matter what we do.

The late Venerable Chögyam Trungpa Rinpoche also warned against hope and fear. Hope, he argued, can make us lazy and cause us to lapse into inertia, believing that "the universe will provide," or some similar manifestation of predestination or a dualistic belief in some outside force or being coming to our rescue, making everything all right. Fear, on the other hand, causes inaction in a different way, by creating paralysis and a resistance to change – the groundwork for the devastating dualistic notion of nihilism, the belief that nothing is worth doing because nothing makes a difference. Whether we are too loose or too tight, in either case we lose the will to move forward and end up wallowing in self-absorbing indulgence, self-denigration, or apathy. But if things are to change for the better, move we must. And, **if we really want to change, we need to get behind ourselves in the moves that we do make.** We need to choose between extremes of looseness and tightness. We need to seek a middle way that allows us to thread our path around all the illusions that the web of the Three Poisons casts before us.

The Buddha's demeanor does not change in peace or war. Enlightened beings are always available to us. In their intimate connection to everything – having awoken to the illusion of separateness – they appear in accordance with our needs and perceptions. In either guise, he and other enlightened beings – of all traditions and times – are there to inspire us to use our resourcefulness to undo the dark times in which we suffer. For, like everything else, what is this Dark Age but an illusion?

In a similar fashion, in "becoming Buddha," the conscious, engaged activist may appear in any number of guises, and act in any number of ways, depending on the circumstances. In the course of history, even in the course of our own lives, we see that what we are called to do, what resources we draw on from within, do change. There is a slogan in Buddhist mind training: "Don't be consistent" (or "Don't rely on consistency"[16]). In a world that fears the truth of impermanence, such a slogan is illogical and threatening. Our social and cultural mores emphasize certain behaviors as being more acceptable than others. On the one hand this is reasonable, but only to a limited degree. For, in the long run, too strict a prescription of how we are supposed to be is stifling and can drive us away from trusting the wisdom inherent in our loving nature. As beings of the human realm, bound by the energies of our passions, awaiting transformation to their enlightened potential, we are not, nor can we ever really be, consistent. What is demanded of us to grow and act in the world, here and now, requires us to draw deeply from the limitless resources that are within each of us.

As we revolutionize our minds and come to an understanding that for one of us to be liberated, all must be liberated, we become more conscious, engage each situation with greater wisdom and clarity, and employ whatever skills or actions the

[16] Jamgon Kongtrul, *The Great Awakening*, p.31.

situation before us demands. As love, compassion, joy, and equanimity become the motivating intentions upon which all of our actions are based, the peace and stillness of our minds – the mind of the Buddha at Peace – will not be disturbed by whatever action we are inspired to take. **It is said that the end point of Samurai training comes when the warrior moves through the day in a state of perfect peace and equanimity and then, as he lies down to sleep, notices that there is blood on the edge of his sword.**

In the End...

Whether or not we accept the truth that the dark time we currently face is a Dark Age, what we are facing – what humanity always faces – is the shared illusion that arises from our previous actions and emotional responses to all the dilemmas we have faced over the course of human history. Conversely, our future will be determined by how we respond to *today's* dilemmas. If our responses come out of anger, then we shall see the fruits of anger in the future. If we respond with despair, likewise.

The only option to consider if we truly want to start contributing to a better today and a brighter tomorrow is to commit ourselves to living and acting from our loving nature, doing whatever we can to minimize our reaction from our Three Poisons, and ultimately transforming them. We commit ourselves to acting compassionately with the clearest intention that we can muster.

If we want our world to look different, to see it as the Buddha sees it, we need to undertake the transformation of ourselves from within. This task is at least equal in importance to our external actions in the world. Otherwise, in the face of the sickness, poverty, and warfare that still rages within us, a lasting world peace is not possible. Whatever we do and whatever we create will be undone and, like a house of cards, is not worth betting on. We have no choice in such times but to accept and operationalize our birthright. *Becoming Buddha* is what we need to do, for ourselves and all beings. And we need to support others in their efforts to do the same.

And even as more enlightened awareness grows and expands from the "pockets of light" that continue to shine, the work of making such awareness real and applying it practically to today's conflict and strife remains an immense task – a task that men and women of courage and virtue have wrestled with since the dawn of civilization. Even to focus on less ambitious goals intended to transform social and political policy, and to support more enlightened behaviors in the world will not be accomplished in a few short years. It would be foolhardy and downright naïve to assume that one or two election cycles, even in the most progressive, democratic nation can effect a transformation of deep-seated, historical patterns of greed and self-interest. Habitual patterns reinforced over generations do not easily fade; they easily resurface by the sheer weight that they carry, if the efforts to change them are not carried through with similar force and determination.

In this context I am reminded of a Tibetan teacher who presented us with a startling look at Tibetan culture. Tibetan belief includes a tradition of detecting and identifying great teachers from the past who have been newly reincarnated. Once recognized, usually at a very young age, these *tulkus* or *Rinpoches* ("Precious Ones") are often installed as heads of sects, monasteries, and so on, with full responsibility for, and access to, the material and spiritual treasures passed down through the ages, so that they can be used to benefit the world they currently live in. At the same time, Tibetan culture is clan- and family-oriented. So even if a child is identified as a high lama and is raised to hold a position of high ecclesiastical authority, they are still beholden to their family and clan, and those who head them. Consequently, if there are conflicts or problems in the community, these highly evolved and spiritually-oriented teachers are expected to go along with what the clan and family leaders tell them to do.

They may know better and yet, because they understand that "blood is thicker than water" and that the reinforced habitual patterns of families, clans, and the culture in general affect a number of beings all at once, they are very conscious of implementing or encouraging change in ways that do not disturb the overall beneficial functions that the family and clan may perform. This is very much in keeping with the Native American "seventh generation" principle – the principle that, before any action is taken by the clan, its implications not just for now but for the next *seven generations* must be considered. In our own instant, quick-fix cultural milieu, not only does such an attitude seem foreign. It seems painfully slow, and not *exciting* in the least. But that is the challenge we face if we want to steer our cultures, our civilization, our fellow humanity in the direction of embracing compassionate, enlightened principles in all it does.

What we ask of ourselves is no small thing. The enlightened ones who walk among us, the "peacocks" who manage to demonstrate skill and wisdom in creating change around us in whatever capacity they can, have not achieved their skills over a weekend, perhaps – in the Buddhist view – not even in one lifetime. Yet, because it is our birthright, we cannot help but strive toward this awakened state and act accordingly. Until then, we must accept the fact that unless we are an enlightened being and can act so flawlessly that there are only *intended* effects from what we do, in the present through to the future, our actions will lead to unintended and unwanted effects, even "collateral damage." No situation we walk into is clear-cut. A multitude of forces – positive, negative, and mixed intentions, and actions skillful or otherwise – come together to present us with the situation we want to make better. We can have the best intentions, act compassionately with the wisdom and skill derived from practices that focus our mind, and dedicate our efforts with the hope that something of lasting value will persist.

But as the endless moments keep coming, it is difficult to know what, of that which we have done, will endure. So while we may derive happiness or satisfaction from the victory of our cause – our candidate being elected, a policy changed for the better, our adversary vanquished – something new and different will always emerge. Our work in one sense may be done, but in the endlessness of time marching on, new work will be called for. We may not choose to address that work. The skills we employed to do what we just accomplished may not even be needed or called for in what needs to be addressed next. But we cannot ignore, or dissociate ourselves from, what follows in the wake of our actions by reveling only in what we have done up till now. To do so is to ossify our hearts and minds, to lapse into nostalgia and a very tenuous self-satisfaction. **Smugness is not an admirable trait in anyone and is especially inappropriate, and a gross miscalculation, for the conscious, engaged activist.**

For, long after we have influenced the course of any given event directly, we can learn about cause and effect, see the skill or error of our ways, by witnessing what has endured and what has fallen away. This deepens our spiritual awareness and places us in the position of sage – someone who has been there, knows the path and the pitfalls, and thus can contribute through passing on the wisdom of our age and experience to those who are now more keen or able to continue with the work that needs to be done.

It is sad if those of younger, more agile abilities do not seek out this wisdom. But when the wisdom-holders, or "elders," themselves choose not to stay engaged, then, the culture of sharing available wisdom is lost, and this is sadder still – and is, in fact, one of the causes of history repeating itself and of people needing to "reinvent the wheel" again and again. But as tedious and futile as it may seem repeatedly to bring about changes which in turn get undone for any number of reasons, it takes much longer to change consciousness than it does to change external events. As has been said earlier, it is in the consciousness of humanity where the fundamental changes need to occur before we can expect to see the external improvements that we may desperately fight for persist.

In the very end, whether we stay engaged or turn away from honestly looking at the fruits of our actions, on our deathbeds we shall look around and see that while we may have made a change to improve our world, things could be even better. We shall die with unfinished business. This unfinished business will, according to the principles of karma, be the cause for our return. Those capacities that we have developed in this current lifetime will continue in our next life, but so will any traces of our Three Poisons that remain untransformed. The circumstances that mirror what we have not transformed within us will manifest as the circumstances we show up to in our next life. As in the saying, "Wherever you go, there you are," **we never, ever get away.** Our sentience, our consciousness, and the desire to manifest our loving nature present us with perpetual moments of unfinished business, which are, at the same time, endless moments for awakening. From the Buddhist point of view, this awakening becomes less and less personal and more and more transpersonal and transuniversal. In the end, our enlightenment is not an "escape" from it all, but rather a total 100 percent immersion into the stream, radiating love and compassion overtly and in inexplicable ways to countless beings whose Three Poisons create the illusion of separation (which includes the illusion of escape) and are the causes and conditions for sickness, poverty, and warfare.

To be, live, and act in such a way is to be love incarnate. The Venerable Chögyam Trungpa Rinpoche, Lord Ösel Mukpo of Shambhala (see page 10), often said that being a warrior of Shambhala was to be a "darling of the world" – having a soft front and a hard back, a balance of wisdom and skill to care, to love. Thus, **love is who we are and love is what we are destined to do.** This is what being conscious and engaged is truly all about, and if we focus on this here and now, we implicitly understand the logic of both "getting our own house in order" and attending to our world as best we know how.

The roads that activists follow may look similar, contradictory, or in direct opposition to one another. Some will walk arm in arm. Some will take up arms against each other. This does not matter. For if each is working with the highest possible intent, based on a commitment to mindfulness, and dedicated to the betterment of all, regardless of the actions taken, there will be a confluence of pooled goodness that will reveal itself in a future possibly more glorious than any of its contributors could have imagined possible.

Even if we feel overwhelmed at times, when our wisdom fails to provide us the ultimate view of a world shining with possibility and we feel lacking in the skill to be able to make effective, lasting change, we should try to visualize and hold in our hearts the images of a world free of the Three Poisons and the sickness, poverty, and warfare they inevitably create. For if we focus solely on thoughts of gloom and doom, what is wrong, and how hard it all is, we shall be weighed down from within and never fully be able to claim the power, joy, and compassion that we truly are. To be an effective agent of social and political change, the conscious, engaged activist must train himself or herself to see through the pessimism, the illusion of solid darkness, and remain steadfast in a vision of light and promise.

Dark Ages do come to an end. In truth, they never were, are, or will be anything other than the illusion that conceals an unending light. In truth, each of us knows this to a greater or lesser extent. However, the conscious, engaged activist commits to putting an end to the illusion – no matter how long it takes.

"How to React as a Buddhist to the September 11th Tragedy"

A Statement Made by His Holiness the 14th Kunzig Shamar
Rinpoche on September 24th, 2001

"During the past two weeks as I have traveled in the United States, many have asked me to explain the horrible acts of the terrorists on September 11th, and to suggest a course of action from the Buddhist perspective. I offer the following thoughts for guidance.

The terrorists who brought about this senseless tragedy are afflicted by ignorance and, consequently, can be deceived by a blind faith in a belief system that distorts the true spirit of Islam. They do not have the wisdom and proper sense of judgment to determine what is right or wrong. Because of their ignorance and blind faith, people with evil intentions have manipulated and misused them. Therefore, just as we should show compassion for the victims, we should also have compassion for the terrorists due to their ignorance.

When governments and individuals set a future course of action, their motivation or aim is the critical determinant to what is appropriate and morally correct. The seeking of revenge clearly is not acceptable in Buddhist terms. However, if a government or individual must take an action that has harmful effects, but is done for the purpose of preventing evil and benefiting the majority, then this is acceptable.

According to the Buddha's teachings on ethics, I believe there are four different combinations of aim and intention and action. Listed from the most evil to the most compassionate, they are:

Bad or evil aim with negative or hurtful action;
Bad aim with benign or positive action;
Good, realistic aim with destructive or harmful action;
Good or pure aim with benevolent action.

In order to counter terrorism, governments of the world and their leaders must pursue this goal only with the aim of benefiting everyone, including the ignorant terrorists themselves. If purely benevolent acts are inadequate to achieve this goal, then there is no choice but to engage in narrowly targeted acts designed to root out the evil of the terrorists while inflicting the least amount of harm to the innocent. This can be accomplished through the use of wisdom and compassion which we find through logical analysis that is a part of human wisdom. It is important not to make decisions based on our obscured emotions.

On a personal level, we should not dwell in our sadness or fear over this tragedy. Instead, we should use it as an inspiration to develop our compassion. We should make wishing prayers for the victims, but also expand our wishes to include all beings who have suffered throughout the world. This tragedy must inspire us to achieve a vast compassion for all beings."

Shamarpa.

Essay on the 2008 American Election

On November 5th, 2008, I was landing at London Heathrow when it was announced that Barack Obama had won the presidential election in the United States. Soon after, I drafted this letter which, in my attempt to be a conscious, engaged activist, I sent around the internet.

"Barack Obama is now the 44th president of The United States. I am deeply happy and relieved about this, for he is the first truly elected president we have had in over eight years. Still, I do not want to gloat or be so carried away in my joy that I forget what made this all possible for us in America. We *all* co-created this election. We dreamed a truly American dream; that it is possible to have a person of high integrity, intelligence, and energy as our next president. Barack Obama manifested as the personification of that dream. And, it became so.

Now what? After the celebrations, the tears and cheers, the balls and cocktail parties, do we stop there? Can we now return to our lives and be once more complacent and go back to sleep, nestled in the security that all will be – once again – right with the world?

When I wrote my book, *The Buddha at War*, one of the reasons why I was turned down by several American publishers is that they did not think that Buddhists and spiritually inclined readers were all that caught up in politics. They argued with me and my agent that when John Kerry was to become president, all the political hoo-ha would die down and the Buddhists and other spiritually distressed people would go back to their cushions, their mantras or whatever bliss bubble they lived in. Well, Kerry won. It did not matter because the election was stolen right before us and four more years of George W. Bush and Dick Cheney inspired a number of Buddhist and other spiritual leaders and writers to start writing about activism and political engagement. There was now a chorus, both spiritual and secular from all segments of society, telling us that we were not allowed to go back to sleep. We had to stay awake. And – to my mind – the sum total of this call to awaken and to action is what we are living today.

In that regard, we have to thank George W. Bush and his administration. Disaster has always been mankind's best teacher and the American administration under Bush's leadership sufficiently highlighted the failing and follies of ignorance, greed, and aggression run amuck over the geo-political, monetary and environmental landscapes. We are now teetering on the brink of the collapse of civilization as we know it and it was in the clarity of the adrenalin rush that made us gather our wits, that we decided to finally act and do something about it. We should all rejoice in this.

The American dream as conceived by our founding mothers and fathers was founded on the notion that life, liberty, and the pursuit of happiness was possible only if we educated ourselves about our world and took action on the knowledge gleaned. Only then could democracy truly benefitting all not tailspin into despotism. But, even in those early days of our republic, there were those who wanted to fashion themselves in the image of the ruling elites of Europe. They did not want democracy. They had just won a continent and wanted to capitalize on its riches. For them, education was problematic. Power-mongers – budding tyrants – can only rule if fear bred from ignorance is encouraged to flourish. The Founding Fathers knew of such men and formed the constitution so as to make their ascent less likely. And, for over 200 years, the power-mongers and those of selfish ambition have worked their hardest to overcome every possible barrier to their ascent – which brings us to what many of us hope is the pinnacle of their ascent in the manifestation of the Bush administration. As we co-created Barack Obama, we *must* also accept the responsibility in co-creating George W. Bush and Dick Cheney. Over the past 200 years, by focusing more on material acquisition as the hallmark of success and the most significant contributor to happiness, we began to lose our connection to the land, our innate sensitivity to each other, and the inner fortitude and outer strength that is necessary to forge our reality with our own hands. We may have abolished slavery, but spawned carpetbaggers, war-profiteers, drunken corporate moguls, greed-driven corporate outsourcing and foreign policies supporting tyrants around the world, and have thus both wittingly and unwittingly built our lives on the backs of millions who still wallow in less-than-subsistence reality. Sickness, poverty, and warfare are the natural by-products of our lack of attentiveness to the source and suffering bringing us our material comfort. Thus, it is only logical that we would fashion an administration single-mindedly focused on giving us exactly what we wanted.

In the chaos and destruction of our times and in witnessing an ever-growing chasm between the haves and have-nots of this world, we have awoken. And in this election, we have brought about the single most significant event in the possible creation of true democracy on this planet. The physical manifestation of these efforts is Barack Obama. And so to Mr Obama I want to say, "Welcome." We are so happy that you are here. And, you are right. This is as much about us as it is about you. So, I want you to know that we are watching. But, more than just watching, we are with you and will continue to be with you whether you like it or not. For we cannot afford to fall asleep once again. You have been given a bankrupt country in the midst of war and the threats of terrorism and environmental collapse. You need us every bit as much as we need you. We need you, not as an answer, but as a beacon, and the degree to which you shine brightly and inspire more to join the great awakening to the tasks at hand, is the degree to which the American dream and the possibility that it promises is being lived out in intention and action by all of us.

And to Mr Bush we say, "Thank you." You and your secretive administration have slapped us out of our complacency and reminded us of what our Founding Fathers wanted for us. Unwittingly you have re-awoken us to dream of America. In that awakening of heart, mind, and hand we shall be vigilant and intent on co-creating that dream with the Obama administration.

President-elect Obama, we look forward to working with you for the next 4 or 8 years. We don't expect things to get better by going back to the way things were when we were more asleep. The world cannot afford this. And indeed, to climb a different hill or to get out of the gully that we find ourselves in at this time will not be easy. But, we do have the resilience. We do have the "Yes We Can" genes of the American spirit. It might not mean that it looks all that rosy for us, but there are future generations to think of – our children and children's children. None of us can be so selfish as give up on our or their world anymore. Mr Obama, stay healthy. Stay clear. Stay focused on boldly acting for the benefit of all with the mandate we have handed you. And remember. We are watching. And we shall continue to watch, not only you, but all who follow in your footsteps for years to come.

I Remain, *Robert Sachs.*

BIBLIOGRAPHY

Chödrön, Pema. *The Wisdom of No Escape*. Shambhala Books, Boston, 1991.

Chögyam Trungpa Rinpoche. *Great Eastern Sun: The Wisdom of Shambhala*. Shambhala Books, Boston, 1999.

Dalai Lama, H.H. the 14th. *A Policy of Kindness*. Snow Lion Publications, Ithaca, NY, 1990.

Dalai Lama, H.H. the 14th. *The Little Book of Wisdom*. Rider, London, Sydney, Auckland, Johannesburg, 1997.

Dharmarakshita. *The Wheel of Sharp Weapons*. Translated from the Tibetan by Geshe Ngawang Dhargyey, Sharpa Tulku, Khamlung Tulku, Alexander Berzin, and Jonathan Landaw. Library of Tibetan Works and Archives, Dharamsala, India, 1981.

Ellis, Joseph J. *Founding Brothers: The Revolutionary Generation*. Vintage/Random House, Inc., New York, 2000.

Gyalwa Karmapa, H.H. the 16th. *Dzalendara and Sakarchupa*. Karma Drubgyud Darjay Ling, Eskdalemuir, Scotland, 1981.

Gilbert, Gustav. *Nuremburg Diary*. Farrar, Strauss and Co., 1947.

Kongtrul, Jamgon. *The Great Awakening*. Shambhala Books, Boston, 1987.

Kunsang, Erik Pema. *A Tibetan Buddhist Companion*. Shambhala Books, Boston, 2003.

Sachs, Robert. *Perfect Endings: A Conscious Approach to Dying and Death*. Inner Traditions, Rochester, Vermont, 1998.

Sachs, Robert. *The Passionate Buddha: Wisdom on Intimacy and Enduring Love*. Inner Traditions, Bear and Co., Rochester, Vermont, 2002.

Sachs, Robert. *The Wisdom of The Buddhist Masters: Common and Uncommon Sense.* Watkins Publishing. London, England, 2008.

Tarthang Tulku Rinpoche. *Skillful Means.* Dharma Publishing, Berkeley, California, 1978.

Zopa, Lama. *Ultimate Healing: The Power of Compassion.* Wisdom Publications, Boston, 2001.

INDEX